The mystery of human r

MW00649120

Introducing the concept of the interactive field, Nathan Schwartz-Salant shows how the states of mind that can secretly undermine our relationships, both private and public, can become positive factors in transforming a relationship when brought to consciousness.

Drawing on the insights of the ancient art of alchemy, he explains how a transformative process can be set in motion once the partners in a relationship learn how to enter the interactive field between them and discover the 'mad' states of mind that exist in every individual. This process of exploration increases mutual understanding, strengthens the relationship and releases creativity. The relating individuals are able to move beyond the apportionment of blame for 'wrongs' they perceive to be perpetrated by the other and which are often the unresolved cause of conflict between them. By acknowledging the subjectivity and states of mind that affect their reactions to one another and the existence of a 'third area' that affects both of them, they are able to transform a good enough relationship into a passionate and exhilarating experience.

Illustrated by numerous clinical examples, *The Mystery of Human Relationship* builds on the work of Jung to create a thought-provoking and inspiring text for anyone who wishes to engage the mystery of growth within themselves and within their relationships.

Nathan Schwartz-Salant was trained as a Jungian analyst in Zurich, Switzerland. He is the director of the Center for Analytical Perspectives in New York and has a psychotherapy practice in New York City and Princeton, New Jersey. He is the author of numerous clinical papers and books including *Jung on Alchemy* (Routledge).

The mystery of human relationship

Alchemy and the transformation of the self

Nathan Schwartz-Salant

Routledge
Taylor & Francis Group

LONDON AND NEW YORK

First published 1998 by Routledge
27 Church Road, Hove, East Sussex BN3 2FA

Simultaneously published in the USA and Canada
by Routledge
270 Madison Avenue, New York NY 10016

Reprinted in 1999, 2001 and 2005

Routledge is an imprint of the Taylor & Francis Group

© 1998 Nathan Schwartz-Salant

Typeset in Times by Poole Typesetting (Wessex) Ltd
Printed and bound in Great Britain by Biddles Ltd, King's Lynn, Norfolk

British Library Cataloguing in Publication Data
A catalogue record for this book is available from the British Library

Library of Congress Cataloguing in Publication Data
Schwartz-Salant, Nathan, 1938–
        The mystery of human relationship: alchemy and the transformation of self /
        Nathan Schwartz-Salant.
        p. cm.
        Includes bibliographical references and index.
        1. Psychoanalysis. 2. Interpersonal relations. 3. Unified field theories
        4. Jungian psychology. I. Title.
        BF175.S387   1998
        158.2–dc21   97–21851
                                                                         CIP

ISBN 0–415–08971–9 (hbk)
ISBN 0–415–15389–1 (pbk)

Contents

List of figures

Preface

The Mystery of Human Relationship examines transformation of the self – both individually and in interaction with others – by combining a scientific understanding of the way personality unfolds with the perspective afforded by the ancient and imaginal lenses of alchemy. Because alchemical attitudes differ so radically from the modern scientific methods which have with such apparent success superseded them, it is impossible to avoid the question of how a contemporary work about relationships could possibly benefit from, and indeed be based upon, the mysterious and seemingly irrational models of alchemical thinking.

The most heralded and perhaps even the definitive process of alchemy was the attempted transformation of a base substance such as lead or mercury into a precious material such as gold or silver. We know less about how the alchemical tradition, which endured for more than two millennia before being discredited by modern science only in the last three centuries, applied itself to subtle areas of human experience situated in the realm between mind and matter, areas which science has almost completely dismissed or discarded.

In fact, alchemical thinking is filled with strange metaphors and complex images which provide illuminating insight precisely into the way that a process between two people can develop and transform. In its recognition of the vital interplay between order and disorder and the transformative potential of chaos, alchemy can help us to accept and to appreciate areas of intense chaos within the mind, areas that I have called in earlier works 'the mad parts of sane people.'

Alchemical thinking differs from modern approaches to personality development and relationships that tend to stress causality and to base validity upon replicability of experiences and results. For example, whereas modern approaches might focus on such issues as developmental failures or the way these failures are revisited in the so-called transference and countertransference process, alchemical thinking offers an appreciation of the depth and mystery of relationship which can allow one to experience a space that is animated, that is alive with meaning, and that contains its own process. In this book I want to use alchemical thinking within the context of the scientific perspective of psychotherapy to gain an understanding of the mysterious underside of relationships, because experiencing the depth of relationship involves embracing these different orders of thinking and perception. In particular, I want to explore the alchemical notion of a subtle-body realm that exists as a 'third thing' or a 'third area' between people.

C.G. Jung found that the ancient symbolism of alchemy was admirably suited to understanding the complex interactions created by the conscious and unconscious psyches of analyst and analysand. I have used Jung's work in my attempt to understand the nature of a 'third area' which two people in relationship create and which, in turn, can have a transformative effect on each person's internal structure. The true mystery of relationship lies less in the quest for understanding who is projecting what on to whom and more in the exploration of 'third areas,' the 'in between' realm which was the main focus of ancient science in general and of alchemy in particular.

Through a study of the symbolism and practices of alchemy, I came to recognize and to appreciate the states of extreme chaos (often chaos containing a secret kind of order) that not only live within all people but which also define an important aspect of an interactive process between individuals in relationship. In coming to see that this interactive process had its own life, I also saw that the chaos at its heart was truly the life of the relationship. Rather than seeing a relationship as something two people did to one another, or as a kind of partnership, I began to see a relationship as – to use a mathematical phrase – a field that both people engaged and which, most mysteriously, moved and molded their processes, both individually and together, as if these processes were mere waves upon a larger sea.

At this point, understanding the mystery of relationship required a way of thinking that was different from modern scientific approaches. For the 'in between' world that people can (consciously or unconsciously) experience requires an approach that was the mainstay of cultures prior to the new paradigm of science and causality that began to emerge in the sixteenth and seventeenth centuries. It was precisely such 'in between' areas – for example, those between mind and matter – that drew my attention to alchemy as a way of understanding relationships. I have found no better guide to this form of 'primitive' logic than the ancient science of alchemy.

My interest in alchemy has helped me to meet the challenges in relationship posed by numerous analysands in my psychotherapy practice, by my own marriage, by my own children, and indeed by life itself. Certainly whatever this book has to offer on contemporary relationships has been profoundly informed by the work with my patients, whose clinical material – often focusing upon the complexity and vulnerability of shifts between intimacy and a madness which, like an invading god of ancient cultures, overwhelms thinking and emotional coherence – forms the substance of much of this book. I am most grateful for their integrity, for their involvement, and especially for their teaching.

I would also like to acknowledge my gratitude for the participation of the students in the 'Alchemy Seminar' at the Center for Analytical Perspectives in New York. The challenging nature of the discussions in these seminars led to a new depth of understanding and revealed important meanings of alchemical imagery and texts, some of which I have used in this book.

Furthermore, I have been deeply moved by the editorial help that I have received in writing this book. Roger Riendeau, a professional editor and writer, in addition to being an instructor and advisor in scholarly writing at the

University of Toronto, has had to become something of an alchemist himself in the process of editing this book. He has learned a great deal about the mysteries of chaos from dealing with my earliest manuscript. I have profited in numerous ways by engaging in the interactive field that his indefatigable energy and intelligence helped to constellate between us. The editorial process has also been generously and vitally enhanced by Geraldine Fogarty whose critical capacity to identify and to question the ambiguity or obscurity of ideas, assumptions, and phrasing has significantly clarified the perspective and the structure of this book. I am very grateful for her friendship and for her commitment throughout this process. And to my friend James Haba I owe a serious debt of gratitude for his careful reading, and re-reading of the manuscript. His contribution is something I deeply cherish, and his efforts have made this a far better book than it would otherwise have been. I must also express my gratitude to the Van Waveren Foundation for a grant that greatly helped in financing the editing of this book.

Ultimately, relationship has a mystery that can only be known through the challenge of intimacy and through the wisdom and sight of the person with whom one interacts, over and over again. My wife, Lydia, has contributed to this book, often by finding a way of expressing ineffable experiences and nascent ideas. But more than that, I would not today be the person I am were it not for my relationship with her. Nor would I have been able to understand the patterns put forward in this book had I not experienced the challenges and insights which came of living the pain and joy of our relationship. She has been my main guide in this our ongoing process and to her I dedicate this book.

Acknowledgements

I wish to acknowledge the Kantonsbibliotek, St Gallen, Switzerland, for permission to reproduce the pictures from their copy of the *Rosarium Philosophorum*, St Gallen, Kantonsbibliotek (Vadiana), Vadianische Sammlung, Ms. 394a.

I wish to acknowledge the British Library for permission to reproduce pictures of the *Splendor Solis* from their Ms. Harley 3469 and 1582.

I wish to acknowledge Press Gang Publishers for material from *Daughters of Copper Woman*, by Anne Cameron (Vancouver, Canada: Press Gang Publishers, 1981). Reprinted with permission of the publisher.

1 Alchemy and transformation in human relationships

EXPERIENCING THE MYSTERY WITHIN RELATIONSHIPS

All people in committed relationships inevitably experience conflict within themselves and with each other which endures despite their best efforts at resolution. Whether subtle or blatant, the nature and sources of such conflict are usually hidden within the equilibrium that can be maintained within a normal relationship, particularly in its earlier stages. One person has not necessarily 'caused' the other to feel hurt, angry, unappreciated, unloved, guilty, among countless possible negative emotions. And even when an allocation of cause or blame may have some validity, an attempt to determine who is right and who is wrong or who is conscious and who is unconscious fails to resolve the conflict, and surely fails to reveal its mystery.

A common example of the dynamics of such conflict is the situation in which a husband is snoring contentedly, sleeping the sleep of the blessed, while his exhausted wife, lying beside him, keeps hearing his snoring and is so far away from sleep that she feels as if she is being tortured. Beyond the levels of physical causes and practical solutions which such a situation immediately brings to mind lies the realm in which a kind of insane conflict lives, ready to erupt into ordinary time. The natural inclination is to assume that somehow someone is at fault. Is the husband deliberately snoring loudly to keep his suffering wife awake and in a constant state of personal disequilibrium? Is the wife merely a light sleeper who is unappreciative of her husband's vital need for rest at the end of a strenuous day? Whether the answer to these questions is, in fact, negative or positive is ultimately irrelevant.

Instead, these two people must penetrate into a deeper level of their relationship, into a domain they both share, in which neither is 'doing' anything to the other. Indeed, they would have to discover that they share not only a conscious but also an unconscious relationship. This unconscious relationship can be far larger and more encompassing than the conscious one. If they could work together to explore this deeper level of their relationship, they would find that the conflict between them was a mere fragment of a larger, more complex, and ultimately more meaningful pattern of interaction.

For most couples, it is far easier simply to avoid exploring such conflicts at a deeper level of their relationship and to tolerate ongoing emotional distractions as they try to communicate and to be intimate with one another in their customary way. But such conflicting states deeply affect relationships in ways that can easily go unseen or be dismissed. The result is a growing gulf between people, a decline in trust and intimacy, a dwindling of a passionate and exciting sexual life and, above all, an absence of any sense that their relationship holds the mystery of growth, individually and together. And without this mystery what do they have? They may play mutually defined roles, or if they are psychologically sophisticated, they may help each other deal with individual projections. But they will not feel and know the mystery of passion and change that can be explored and discovered through their relationship. Thus, their relationship diminishes in passion and becomes merely ordinary. Love, compassion, and caring may exist, but a shadow cast by the absence of passion and meaning enables both of them to know that they are choosing to live in shallow waters and to settle for an apparent security that actually diminishes them.

This book is intended for people who want to deal with such normally hidden areas in relationships, who are able to go beyond the assignment of blame or a concern with being 'right' or 'wrong,' and who wish to recognize and to engage the mystery of growth within themselves and within their relationships.

Attempts to make rational sense of chronic conflict within normal relationships invariably fail when these attempts do not probe the depths of the human psyche to discover the underlying nature and source of the conflict. Within this deeper realm, totally contradictory states of mind can exist simultaneously within each person and as a quality of the relationship itself. These contradictory states which define 'mad' (see p. 36ff) aspects of the psyche actually annihilate one another, so that attending to one state totally destroys an awareness of the preceding state. Anyone relating to a person exhibiting such contradictory states will tend to feel this process, to become confused, and to withdraw or feel an impotent rage. But to a certain degree, such an area of madness is an integral part of everyone's existence. Embracing the mad areas of our psyche and acknowledging the ways they limit us is a way to discover the mystery of the self and the other. This subtle 'madness' becomes a kind of chaotic shore that the relationship is destined to wash up against and to be bounded by.

Madness is a frightening concept, for it implies that one is out of control, distorts reality, is overwhelmed by compulsive responses and very strong emotions, and does things that are destructive to one's own best interests, all while assuming oneself to be totally in control. The mad parts of sane people are always dangerous; but if recognized and their power acknowledged, they are potentially healing. Mad areas continually confront us with the borders and limitations of ourselves and our knowledge, and they cause us to reflect and re-frame our attitudes over and over again. Without embracing our own madness, any approach to understanding relationships becomes dull and dangerously repetitive, tending to become a matter of technique and knowledge alone. Madness seems to be our best ally in restraining the dangerous and soulless tendency of knowledge used to shield ourselves from the shock of new experiences. As we accept such areas, we do not necessarily solve the problems within our relationships; instead, we transform ourselves and our relationships.

Transformation is always a very difficult process for us to contemplate and to embrace, for the psyche tends to revert to its most stable forms, typically the older ones that have been tried in the crucible of time. New forms are unstable and consequently dangerous in that they may lead us to lose a sense of identity, to become subject to strong emotions, and to become susceptible to the will of another in a way that feels threatening. So, in our established forms of relating, we tend to operate within a comfortable, chosen structure. We may be polite; we may recognize certain roles; or we may act in kind or unkind ways. For example, a couple may continually but politely poke 'fun' at each other in a public setting and deny that this behavior might point to their underlying contempt for each other and to their desire to humiliate each other since such an admission would destabilize their relationship. However, probing beneath such interactions reveals that this form of politely hostile behavior actually serves to protect against exactly those deeper and more dangerous levels of engagement. At these deeper levels, people would have to take responsibility for areas of their psyches within which they were not only harboring resentment and other negative feeling but where they were also truly out of control, that is, mad.

Transformation within a relationship can only begin with an acknowledgement that we are unconsciously projecting on to the other person, thereby distorting the other's reality and our own. Through the process of projection, we tend to diminish or enhance the identity of others by presuming that we actually know the nature and motivation of their interactions with us. The other person's own reality has little credibility in our mind, but more important, the other's unfathomable nature is not even considered. In other words, through projections, we 'know' only fragments of truth about the other and consequently deny the essence of the other's spiritual being. Therefore, the more we can withdraw projections and recognize the reality of the other person, the more each person is empowered and the relationship between the two people is enhanced.

But to sustain and deepen the process of transformation, we must move beyond the recognition and acknowledgement of the dynamics of projection. Such a possibility may be difficult largely because psychoanalytic thinking about human relationships has developed within scientific models which regard projection as a key concept. Starting with the early twentieth-century work of Sigmund Freud, the analysand was believed to project his or her inner contents on to the analyst who, through the device of an 'even hovering attention,' could perceive the nature of the projection. Within this causal structure, the interpretation of the projection is seen to unlock and resolve unsuccessful developmental transits which were part of the analysand's early life. The precise nature of this process is controversial since many competing ideas exist about how people develop in a successful or unsuccessful way given the nature of their childhood experiences.

For example, focusing on certain 'absences' in early childhood and/or on emotional or physical intrusions into the child's vulnerable psychic state is a valid and useful approach to understanding personal development. Infants can suffer specifically from the absence of a maternal presence that could calm their anxieties or generally from the absence of a parental figure who could stand against the physical and emotional intrusions which invariably leave the young child with no sense of safety or integrity. Such absences and such intrusions prevent the infant from ever experiencing a 'container' for his or her distress, and the adult may therefore suffer from neuroses such as dissociative disorders, or narcissistic, borderline, and psychoid personality disorders, or in extreme instances, psychotic disorders. Psychoanalytic treatment attempts to create a containing space so that experience of psychic states is possible. Ideally, through the transference, such early absences and insults to development can be recapitulated, understood, and most significantly, survived without regressing to primitive defenses; and the individual's development essentially can be allowed to find its natural ways of expansion. Progress on this scale requires an unusual amount of courage from the patient, and often from the therapist as well.

The personal unconscious, as defined by C.G. Jung, is a reservoir of disowned contents and processes which can be experienced as separable parts in normal space and time, and which have location. In the process of projection, the parts of the personal unconscious are experienced as existing 'in' the person, or they are projected 'out of' the person and 'into' another person. Projection has an effect, and through it one does things to another person. Approaching people and their relationships from the vantage point of someone's 'doing something' to someone else – for example, one person is unconsciously projecting on to another either expectations of abandonment, loss, and hatred, or qualities of great value, perfection, and wholeness – is a powerful lens through which to understand relationship. A great deal of modern psychological thought has gone into understanding that projections affect people, either by diminishing the ego strength of the projector and distorting his or her sense of reality, or by causing an emotional and cognitive change in the object of the projection. Projection can be employed to get rid of distressing feelings and ideas. And projection can also be a state that accompanies the emergence of consciousness: one always projects before one becomes conscious of one's ownership of unconscious contents. Projection can also be a way of disowning one's psychic structure through an imaginal process in which contents are felt to be 'put into' the other person, and subtly watched in a trance-like way in order to discern what the other does with these projected contents. This latter process is known as projective identification, and an analyst may spend many years becoming aware of its subtleties, so that he or she may recognize its existence where less trained or less sensitive souls might just act out the contents that have been projected into them.

Freud and other subsequent psychoanalysts essentially recognized that the projection-based model of recapitulating early conflict and resolving it was oversimplified, for the analyst also projected on to the analysand. From this notion of counter-projection evolved much of the current psychoanalytical thinking about transference and countertransference, the mutual projections of both people. Still, psychoanalysts believed that these projections, in the spirit of scientific inquiry, could become objectively perceived data. Some even hoped (and many still endeavor in most quarters of psychoanalytical thought) to make use of countertransference to understand objectively the inner workings of the analysand's psyche.

In an effort to overcome the difficulty of separating projections and counter-projections and to meet the standards of scientific objectivity, some analysts began to think in terms of a 'third area' or a 'field' that was comprised of a kind of mutual subjectivity. Created by mutual projections, this 'third area' could then be used to derive some objective understanding of the inner workings of analyst and analysand. Whether it was through the work of Self Psychologists or the contributions of Thomas Ogden and his notion of the 'analytic third,' the analyst becomes aware that subjectivity can never be denied in the interaction. And through the use of his or her perceptions of the nature of this 'third area,' the analyst can still craft interpretations, feel empathy, and effect interventions to help the analysand recognize his or her unconscious and maladaptations.

Jung's research sowed the seeds of an alternative model of analysis based on the exploration of an intermediate realm between analyst and analysand. Jung recognized that two people create an unconscious relationship that is comprised of psychic contents not only derived from personal experiences in early life. These psychic contents, which Jung called 'archetypes,' are the spontaneous self-organizing structures of the impersonal layers of the collective or objective unconscious. Unlike personal contents, such archetypal aspects of the collective unconscious cannot be fully perceived as stemming from inside one person and being directed outside of that person, into another. In fact, archetypal processes create a 'third area' between people that cannot be experienced or understood through the spatial notion of insides and outsides. The sense of space created within a relationship cannot be understood as an 'empty space' characterizing the area through which (largely) personal projections pass. Rather, this 'third area' has its own peculiar objectivity: a subjective–objective quality. The individual projections cannot be separated from the objective transformative trends as they interact within this 'intermediate realm,' and neither causes the other to exist. When Jung analyzed this largely unconscious third area between people, which was his way of explicating the transference–countertransference process, he also approached the archetypal aspects within the scientific paradigm of projection. Indeed, Jung's work helped us to see that more than personal psychic contents could be projected.

Moreover, archetypal levels create a 'third area' that cannot be embraced simply as things, like the projected parts that two people may encounter. Rather the archetype creates a paradoxical sense of space in which one is both inside and outside, an observer but also contained within the space itself. Furthermore, and in distinction to the emphasis on subjectivity in psychoanalytic approaches to the 'third area,' I find that a concomitant objectivity of process derived from the inclusion of archetypal dimensions must also be considered.

Indeed, we must move beyond the notion of life as consisting of outer and inner experiences and enter a kind of 'intermediate realm' that our culture has long lost sight of and in which the major portion of transformation occurs. As we perceive such a shared reality with another person, and as we actually focus on it, allowing it to have its own life, like a 'third thing' in the relationship, something new can occur. The space that we occupy seems to change, and rather than being the subjects, observing this 'third thing,' we begin to feel we are inside it and moved by it. We become the object, and the space itself and its emotional states are the subject.

In such experiences, the old forms of relationship die and transform. It is as if we have become aware of a far larger presence in our relationship, indeed a sacred dimension. We become aware of a sense of 'oneness' that permeates being alone and with our partner. It is a 'oneness' that seems to infuse the relationship with a sense of awe and mystery. When this experience is intense, respect takes over where power once ruled. Fear becomes accepted as a marker of being on the right path, because one now walks towards the unknown, on a path of expanding horizons and a willingness to be moved by the truth as it exists within the relationship. And always we look for and reflect upon our projections and our personal history as if these form the boundaries that give the interactive experience its own uniqueness and particularity, thus preventing the interactive experience from flowing into a 'New Age' haze.

Just as archetypal contents create a third area that cannot be sufficiently appre-hended through the model of projection, so too do the mad parts of sane people. Such archetypal areas are never reducible to a sum of individual projections. Consequently, the mad aspects of sane people have never been successfully embraced within rationally oriented approaches to personality development. Attempts to reduce the mad aspects of sane people to some failure in develop-ment that can be projected will amount to little more than a repressive ruse. The psychological models we have gained from studying infant development or observing development in time, that is, from infancy to adolescence and onward, do not help in grasping the strange qualities of the space that underpins the depth of relationships. We never 'know' madness as something to be 'studied' in a relationship; rather we experience it, and we must find some kind of imaginary vessel to contain it. For madness is a strange phenomenon which can be under-stood not only as existing within oneself or between people but also, like arche-typal processes, as encompassing and influencing both people in a relationship within its indefinable realm. Indeed, if relationship is to be the place of the trans-formation of individuals and culture, then we must not only expose the madness within the relationship but we must also discover the mystery of that madness.

Relationship may be viewed as the container for dealing with the archetypal and irrational forces of madness within our culture. For this reason, we must think of relationship as far more than two relatively conscious or unconscious people interacting. Relationship must be viewed as resting upon a great sea of emo-tional life, a dimension that is never understood by rational means alone. This fact was noted by Freud and also used extensively by Jung in his investigations of the depth of relationship in the transference.

Whereas modern scientific models do not help us much to think about such experiences of madness and of 'third areas' between people, traditions that pre-ceded scientific discovery and its primary emphasis upon causality can enable us to rediscover and reformulate more ancient ideas which were precisely concerned with such 'in between' areas and experiences. To understand and appreciate the transformative potential of such 'third areas,' we may profitably turn to the ancient ideas and practices of alchemy. Jung employed alchemical symbolism to grasp the nature of the largely unconscious 'third area' between people. By making fuller use of Jung's alchemical research than I believe he himself did, one can learn to experience the 'third area' and to be changed by this experience rather than depend upon analyzing it into component projections.

I am conceptualizing and analyzing the alchemical way of thinking, as presented in its myths and stories, as a central approach to psychotherapy. This alchemical approach contrasts not only with those using alchemical symbolism to amplify developmental or failed developmental processes, but also with any scientific approach to understanding the psyche's structure and changes that is based upon causality. An alchemical approach, therefore, is not primarily concerned with what people do to one another, such as through projections on to one another, but instead with their experience of a field both people occupy.

The structure and the methodology of alchemy are extremely valuable in attempts to probe the mystery of relationships. When the methodology of alchemy is applied to the psychological process, a new model of analysis emerges, a model based not on behavior modification or changes in object relations but on the recovery of soul. Coming to this new model of analysis has required, of course, a 'translation' of alchemical terms into psychological terms as well as a rethinking of the nature of the analytic session and the role of the analyst. In my experience when working with the 'third area,' including the mad parts of otherwise sane people, Cartesian thinking breaks down, and another kind of logic of opposites emerges that is strikingly similar to that embraced over the course of 2,000 years by the alchemists.

THE EMERGENCE AND DECLINE OF THE ANCIENT ART OF ALCHEMY

The ancient art of alchemy was primarily concerned with qualitative changes of substance, notably transforming a metal into another form, changing the color of a material and stabilizing that change, or creating the Elixir of Life or *Lapis Philosophorum*. Beyond such generalities, the origins, nature, and scope of alchemy are subject to conjecture and controversy. As Raphael Patai has noted in his comprehensive study *The Jewish Alchemists*, 'when it comes down to deciding what alchemy actually is (or was), scholars who have written about alchemy are far from agreement' (1994, 4). The spectrum of scholarly attitudes ranges widely from a view of alchemy as a foolish and embarrassing episode in human thought to a perspective which regards it as the most sublime, spiritual science whose true focus was the transformation of the human personality. Patai offers some insight into alchemy's ambiguous and controversial nature:

> Alchemy was everything its practitioners claimed it was, and its aims comprised everything historians attributed to it. They included the transmutation of base metals into silver and gold, the doubling or otherwise increasing the

weight of gold, the manufacturing of pearls and precious stones, the production of all kinds of tinctures and other substances, the concoction of dyes, and
the making of all kinds of remedies for healing every disease which
humankind suffered, and the creation of the quintessence, the fabulous elixir,
which healed, rejuvenated, and prolonged life for centuries . . . All this was
part of the practical aspect of alchemy.

(1994, 4)

In the process, medicines were made; vessels for chemical transformation were
developed; and remarkable theories were postulated about the process of change
in the form or inner structure of matter.

Furthermore, alchemical efforts at 'outer' material changes corresponded with
the 'inner' changes in the alchemist's psyche. This mutuality of transformation
fascinated the best minds of many centuries and many cultures. Thus, alchemical
practice is extensively documented in a cross-cultural body of literature spanning
three millennia.

Alchemy was based upon a belief in the fundamental unity of all processes in
nature. All of nature – stone, metals, wood, and minerals along with the human
mind and body – was formed out of a single substance. This essence, the *lapis*,
was the basis out of which everything grew, and if one could gain some of it, even
a minute drop, then considerable healing and transformation could be accomplished. One finds this fundamental belief in India, Europe, China, the Near East,
the Middle East (especially the Arab world), and in all other places in which
alchemy flourished (Patai 1994).

While the origins of alchemy reached well into pre-history and the wisdom of
the shaman, the alchemical tradition appears to have crystallized in Graeco-
Roman Egypt during the third and fourth centuries BCE. At this time, Greek and
Stoic thought combined to create alchemy's basic theoretical structures which
were elaborated upon and refined over the next 2,000 years. Alchemy began to
emerge as a coherent body of thought in the work of Bolos-Democritus about 200
BCE. Alchemical thinking grew out of the nexus of ideas associated with metal-
lurgy, brewing, dyeing, and perfume-making. By the third century, alchemical
ideas had spread and become linked with a large number of kindred develop-
ments in the religious and philosophic spheres (Lindsay 1970, 67). Prior to this
time, alchemical practices were often a secret affair, hidden away out of a fear of
persecution rooted in charges of counterfeiting gold and precious metals. Early
authors of alchemical texts often assumed pseudonyms adopted from mythical
figures such as Hermes or Moses or from some great master. This tendency in
alchemy was not merely an act of modesty or a desire to hide from persecution
as a forger or counterfeiter. Instead, it reflected the desire in alchemy to link
its origins and practitioners to a mythical dimension, a tendency also found in
magical practice.

The exoteric or the extroverted side of alchemical practice was largely
informed by established Greek thought which was essentially Aristotelian.
According to the scholar of the exoteric alchemical tradition, E.J. Holmyard,

Aristotle believed the world was comprised of a prime matter that only had a potential existence. To actually manifest, it had to be impressed by 'form,' which not only meant shape but also something that gave a body its specific properties. In the Aristotelian cosmology, form gives rise to the 'four elements': fire, air, water, and earth. Each of the elements is further characterized by the 'qualities' of being fluid (or moist), dry, hot, or cold. Each element has two of these qualities. Hot and cold, and fluid and dry, are pairs of contraries and cannot be coupled. The main thrust of the theory, according to Holmyard (1990), is that any substance is composed of each and every 'element.' The difference between one substance and another depends upon the proportions in which the elements are present. And since each element, as the theory goes, can be transformed into another, any substance can be transformed into any other kind by changing the proportion of the elements in it. For example, in the Aristotelian theory, the element fire is hot and dry, and the element water is cold and fluid. If one could combine them in a way that resulted in the elimination of the dry and cold qualities, one would have an element that was hot and fluid, the attributes the theory assigns to the element air. Through such processes, the form of things changes. Accordingly, by being able to alter the qualities and thus the form of things, one should be able to transform any substance into another: 'If lead and gold both consist of fire, air, water, and earth, why may not the dull and common metal have the proportions of the elements adjusted to those of the shining, precious one?' (Holmyard 1990, 23). The alchemical search for the right form of the '*prima materia*' to work on and the alchemist's relentless and often futile, but sometimes successful, laboratory efforts, informed as much as possible by divine revelation and moments of grace, make up most of the exoteric tale of alchemy.

Along with this theory of the four elements, a more introverted or esoteric basis for alchemy is found in related ideas from Greek thought which were established from the seventh to the fourth centuries BCE: (1) the idea of a unitary process in nature and of some 'ultimate substance' out of which all things are built up; (2) the idea of a 'conflict of opposites,' held together by the overriding unity, as the force driving the universe onwards; (3) the idea of a 'definite structure' in the ultimate components of matter, whether this structure is expressed by varying aggregates of atoms (*atomon*, indivisible unit) or by the combination of a set of basic geometrical forms at the atomic level (Lindsay 1970, 4). To this body of thought was added the Stoic position that the 'psyche' was material, that there was a mutual penetration of soul and body, of *physis* and the world of plants, of *hexis* and the world of inorganic matter. Stoic physics consistently saw all the more solid or specific elements as permeated and held together in the infinite network of pneumatic tensions (Lindsay 1970, 22–23).

Alchemical ideas were prevalent in Europe after the Dark Ages, and new forms were created in the culture of the imagination that graced the Renaissance of the fifteenth and sixteenth centuries. These new forms of alchemical thinking were vividly expressed in texts such as the *Rosarium Philosophorum* (1550) and the *Splendor Solis* (1582). The *Rosarium* was initially a set of images that were meditated upon, like a rosary. The *Rosarium* is believed to have originated in a

German fraternity in the sixteenth century; or possibly this group was responsible for adding the text to the pictures, so that what now exists is a series of images and commentaries on them that dates to 1550. There are several collections of the *Rosarium* in the world; some are in color, while others are in black and white, and others have been partially colored. The most beautiful collection, found in the Stadt Bibliotech of St Gallen, have a Picasso-like lyrical quality. Some of these commentaries seem to make great sense, and others seem so obscure as to make one wonder if they were added at random. But most importantly, this series of twenty woodcuts addresses one of the major problems of alchemy, the union of mind and body as it is achieved through the process of the union of two souls, or the union of two aspects of a single personality. The *Splendor Solis*, usually dated 1584, is also of unknown origin. Its copper plates have given the world the most beautiful images of alchemy. The *Splendor Solis* approaches a complementary problem of alchemy, namely the incarnation of spiritual life into material/bodily reality. Whereas the *Rosarium* is based upon a horizontal process like a face to face meeting of two people, or a joining of separated aspects of psychic life in a person, the *Splendor Solis* is concerned with the vertical dimension of incarnating spirit. It also has different variants in libraries, but the most beautiful rendition is the Harley manuscript found in the British Library.

Works such as these formed the backbone of Renaissance alchemy. The *Splendor Solis* is the most important example of a work that combines outer and inner reality, focussing both on actual substances and on the inner level of the soul (McLean 1981). The *Rosarium* is concerned with that other major issue of alchemy, the union of opposites, such as male and female, body and mind, and hot and cold. Together these two texts provide the basis for analyzing the alchemical symbolism discussed later in this book.

While its pinnacle was reached in the culture of the European Renaissance, alchemy's demise was precipitated by the emergence of science, and especially by the Reformation's attacks on the role of imagination. The demise of alchemical thinking was primarily caused by the need for a less imaginative and more rationally conceived approach to the world. Grounded in imaginal thinking and fantastic imagery, alchemy was totally unsuited to understanding nature in causal terms, as postulated in the great scientific advances of the seventeenth and eighteenth centuries. Science saw the world differently, with matter no longer alive and order in the form of the scientist's equations, to be applied to any problem. The 'mechanical philosophy' of the Age of Reason drove alchemy into a distant corner of human endeavor. Its wisdom eventually was carried on secretly, often in occult groups, and its prominence rapidly diminished as did respect for occult activity.

THE CLASH OF ALCHEMICAL AND SCIENTIFIC THINKING

Since at least the seventeenth century, alchemy has been widely scorned for its metaphor-based process that sharply conflicts both with modern scientific demands for objectivity and modern science's essential premise of causality. In contrast with modern scientific methods, the alchemical tradition is a testimony to the power of subjectivity. Rather than an 'objective' attempt to carefully situate a difference between processes in matter and the psychology of the experimenter, in alchemy the spiritual and physical transformation of the subject is an integral part of the work of transforming matter. This merger of the inner reality of the alchemist and the outer reality of the matter to be transformed exists in an area of imaginal discourse, which ancient alchemists referred to as the *imaginatio*, that was not subject to notions of insides and outsides. The merger of outer and inner occurs in a space that alchemists called the 'subtle body,' a strange area that is neither material nor spiritual, but mediating between them. Along with other 'imponderables' of ancient science that held sway for many centuries, this 'intermediary' domain of existence has long since left our conscious awareness.

Because alchemy is characterized by a peculiar identification between the alchemist and the material with which he or she works, personal and material transformation are intertwined so closely as to defy their separation. This linkage is part of the complex metaphor of alchemy which accepts the possibility that changes in the personality of the artisan somehow effect changes in the matter with which he or she is working. It was only when this intermingling between outer and inner could no longer be maintained that alchemy became subject to scorn and contempt for its failure to make actual gold from base metals. The alchemical furnaces and theory were obviously not up to the task, no matter what powers of imagination the adepts brought to it. In any event, gold-making was not the major concern of alchemy but rather was part of the alchemical metaphor of personality transformation. The intention to transform gross metals or inferior personality structures ('lead' into 'gold' in an alchemical sense) was no different from the Christian idea of the resurrection of the dead. In essence, alchemy was a system of transformation, and its genius lay in the assumption that change was part of an interaction between subject and object in which both were transformed.

Ultimately, alchemy's metaphor of change runs squarely against the notion that the essence of an individual is separate from others and is stable and unchanging amidst all the vicissitudes of life. Prior to this time, people had little concept of individualism; instead, they considered themselves to be part of a collective reality and organized their lives through myth and custom. The individual was of little import, save for the heroic changes which the 'great individual' brought to bear upon the collective. As long as people functioned through broad, mythical patterns, the individual ego held no mass appeal or value, and in fact was considered a danger. Science became the great catalyst of change in consciousness in which the ego emerged as an entity-creating order. For this reason, the Church initially viewed emerging science as the work of the Devil.

But once individual consciousness became the *summa bonum*, the ways of alchemy and the metaphor of transformation that it represents became anathema to the developing Western scientific mind. For now the scientist, as beholder of principles and governing equations, attempted to order what otherwise appeared to be disordered systems. According to the inexorable law of entropy increase, order in nature itself tends to run down and to become less ordered, but the scientist, as beholder of order, is not believed to suffer this fate. He or she may modify the conception of how to create order by changing the paradigm that science embraces. But he or she is still considered to be structurally unfazed by what the order created, save for the possible moral consequences of one's creative and technological accomplishments. Seriously engaging an experiment is not thought to change the scientist's personality, nor is the experiment thought to function to a greater or lesser degree as a consequence of the scientist's own meditative efforts and accompanying imagination. This stability and self-sameness are central qualities of an emerging ego that takes on the task of apprehending the order of the universe through a causal metaphor. Cause = effect is the motif of scientific investigation; and it is essential to understand that previous ages – those prior to the great achievements of Galileo, Kepler, and Newton, among others – did not follow this formula. If anything, the alchemical approach, rooted as it was in Greek and Stoic thought, was essentially 'uninterested' in causality (Lindsay 1970). In effect, the alchemists were not exclusively interested in the way parts of a system or stages in human development interact with one another, either within an individual or with others in the environment.

So it is not that scientific logic is superior to the so-called 'primitive' logic of alchemy, but that these systems of thinking are fundamentally different (Lévi-Strauss 1966, 1–34). In essence, alchemical and scientific thinking serve different goals and attempt to solve different problems. Alchemy is a science of the soul; science is a study of material change along an irreversible sequence of time. The extroversion of alchemy to outer, material life, was as unsuccessful as the attempts of science to understand the inner workings of the psyche by reducing them to some materialistic premise.

It should also be understood that science did not supplant alchemy. In fact, alchemy was a major concern of Isaac Newton who came to alchemy after a thorough study of 'rational' chemistry. For Newton, alchemy was no aberration; according to Richard Westfall, 'what he took to be its greater profundity' was central to his thinking:

> In the mechanical philosophy, Newton had found an approach to nature which radically separated body and spirit, eliminated spirit from the operations of nature, and explained those operations solely by the mechanical necessity of particles of matter in motion. Alchemy, in contrast, offered the quintessential embodiment of all the mechanical philosophy rejected. It looked upon nature as life instead of machine, explained phenomena by the activating agency of spirit, and claimed that all things are generated by the copulation of male and female principles . . . Where [the mechanical] philosophy insisted on the inertness of matter . . . alchemy asserted the existence of active principles in matter as the primary agents of natural phenomena.
>
> (1980, 112, 116–17)

Newton actually stood at the crossroads of two currents: that of a new science championing causality, and that of an ancient science which found causality limited and incapable of explaining how phenomena such as the affects of the human soul emerged without any experienced or observable cause. As the seventeenth century ended, and educated Europeans fully embraced the Age of Rationalism, the alchemical approach to nature all but vanished; the mechanical philosophy and the mechanism of causality dominated, as it has up to the present time.

This domination, however, was only accomplished by choosing different and indeed much simpler problems than those which alchemy addressed. For example, science knows little about the way the form of things, such as a leaf's shape, is created and changes. In science, an equation is applied to a system, and that system may change over time, but not a great deal is known about systems whose external shape or boundaries, and internal constitutive nature, also change as a consequence of processes in the system. Alchemy focused precisely upon such systems, notably the human being and ways that psychic structure changes. Why can a person have devastating responses at one period of life, but with a growing awareness and internal integration of disowned experiences begin to re-experience trauma with far less disturbance? How does internal structure change to allow such a development? What are the laws of this change, or what metaphorical properties govern it?

Science's need to separate from spiritual factors – as emphasized by Descartes' separation of earthly science from spiritual concerns, and from finality as well – and science's need for objectivity, which could be so clouded by the subjective–objective intermingling of alchemy, drove it more and more towards abstraction. The metaphorical basis of alchemy, like metaphor in general, combines different orders of reality, like matter and psyche. Science splits them and becomes the beholder of order, ordering the supposed disorder of matter.

Alchemy's insistence on the linkage between subject and object followed from its concern for the soul, the inner life that moves of its own accord, independent of cause. This quality of soul is the reason that causal concerns are of far less significance for the alchemical mind than for our own. Because the soul lives in relationship, the quality of relationship, characterized in alchemical science by a concern for the relation *per se*, and not the things related, define alchemy.

Thus, a different universe of experience is the object of the alchemical endeavor. It is an 'in between' world of 'relations,' occurring in a space that is not-Cartesian, and instead is characterized by a paradoxical relationship in which 'outer' and 'inner' are alternatingly both distinct and the same. Within the paradoxical geometry of this space, known as the subtle body, that is an 'intermediate' realm between matter and psyche, the alchemist believed that 'relations *per se*' could be transformed.

Alchemists were concerned with this intermediate realm and were hopeful that the 'things related,' such as the matter worked upon, could be transformed as well. This magnificent attempt did not simply fade away before the obvious superiority of science in dealing with causal processes in the material world. Rather, the fantasy of objectivity which is central to science, and the heroic invincibility of the ego, which developed with that fantasy, rendered the alchemical metaphor, and its quest for the imaginal perception of relations *per se*, an obscure and a dangerous domain. Yet within this domain, one builds egos that have an imaginal base and that know that their perceptions are rarely more than a flicker of the truth of a larger intertwined reality, for example, between a person's ego and his or her unconscious or between two people. The ego as developed within the scientific approach to nature surely corrects the wild misuse of subjectivity and fantasy that the alchemical approach can manifest, just as the Reformation was not only repressive but also a necessary corrective to the imaginal excesses of the magical practices of the Renaissance (Couliano 1987).

Because of their lack of interest in quantitative measurements or in conceiving material processes in terms of their purpose or final cause, the alchemists' understanding and transformation of matter was surely far inferior to what has been accomplished by modern science. Generally, alchemy is commonly misunderstood as a pseudoscience that gave way to the enlightened discoveries of chemistry. Although much of chemistry's initial development was an extension of alchemical ideas, the tale of alchemy's fate is far more complex. On the one hand, alchemy chose to address problems that are so difficult – issues of the qualitative transformations through which substance takes on new forms – that modern science has yet to truly explore them, let alone master them. On the other hand, the fifteenth- and sixteenth-century practitioners of alchemy lived in a world that was entirely animated, one in which matter was not dead or chaotic but had a living soul. This kind of consciousness sees relationship among all levels of existence, animate and inanimate, spiritual and profane, but it does not deal with distinctness and separable entities within a causal process. The alchemical approach to the world gave priority to a background sense of oneness which kept it from ever successfully separating from and adequately evaluating its most potent tool: the imagination. In a strong sense, the ideas and practices of alchemy, like the ideas underlying transformations in the Renaissance, had to retreat to allow the individual ego to develop, an ego that could believe it was separate from other people and the world and from God, and an ego that could believe in the usefulness of understanding nature as a process in historical time.

During the time of the emergence of alchemy in the Renaissance, ego-consciousness had barely developed. But without the careful discrimination of the ego, a sense of what is inner and outer, especially in union states between people, readily regresses into a hopeless muddle of fusion that blurs any subject–object differentiation. The mind in the Renaissance, and before, was characterized by an immersion in images and by a lack of critical reflection on fantasy and the use of fantasy to prove anything in an idiosyncratic way (Huizinga 1954, 225). Scientific objectivity in any experimental sense simply did not exist. Problems in relationships and disputes were resolved by reference to mythical and philosophical precedents. Everything was based upon prior models and not upon discerning the significance of events in the historical moment. This latter development came about only with Descartes' separation of mind and body as two qualitatively different entities, and with the exclusion of God and finality from theorizing about nature. These splits were radical but necessary.

This great achievement in consciousness – an objectivity about nature and the development of self-awareness – which began in the seventeenth century (Whyte 1960, 42–43) made possible the modern scientific approach. With it came the attitude, which was to become habitual, of separating processes into distinct parts and of focusing attention on the parts, broken down into smaller and smaller units. Eventually, wholeness and a unitary background to existence, mainstays of alchemical thinking, were lost sight of altogether, resulting in the fragmentation so characteristic of the lives of modern-day people. Science can thus be seen as unburdening alchemy of its need to be competent in investigating outer, material changes. But alchemical approaches and a return to alchemy's metaphor of subjectivity can be a gift to science and, in turn, unburden it of its soul-killing attempts to grasp the mystery of the psyche and its transformations.

The enduring strength of alchemy in ancient and medieval times and its innate weakness in the modern age is its tendency to relate all human activity to an awareness of the essence or Oneness of all creation. Alchemy's theoretical structure is based upon a connection to a oneness of process, in distinction to the parts that are the focal point of causal descriptions of events in space and time. Human life, organic and inorganic forms of natural process, and the vast extent of the Cosmos and whatever powers it holds – 'God' in the religious sense of the term – are all linked together. This sense of Oneness permeates all alchemical thinking. In this way, ancient alchemical thinking was in sharp contrast to modern scientific thinking which attempts to understand human organic and inorganic life without reference to their interaction and without reference to 'higher' or 'spiritual' powers. Depending upon one's point of view, humanity progressed or regressed as it distanced itself from the embrace of Oneness that pervaded alchemical science.

The alchemist's belief in a unity or Oneness of process is based on the notion of an 'essence' which pervades all creation and which connects qualities as opposites. All of alchemical thinking is concerned with opposites, states we know in our psychological being as mind and body, love and hate, good and evil, conscious and unconscious, spirit and matter, left-brain and right-brain function, imaginal perception and rational, discursive thinking (lunar and solar in alchemical terms), love and power, and empathy and scientific deduction. Somehow, the alchemist had to recognize opposites inherent in any process and then to unite them. A spiritual sense of Oneness plays a vital role, for a kind of illumination is often necessary to 'see' opposites, an act of discovering order in chaos. The 'seeing' involved may be, as William Blake said, 'through' one's eyes rather than 'with' them, but the 'seeing' is always non-ordinary, a kind of perception informed by a spiritual reality. It is as if one's being must be permeated by this 'Other,' or as if one must sense its existence in order to lift opposites out of chaos. In this it is not difficult to discern the biblical act of Creation which is often a background model for the creative process of the alchemist.

The union of opposites is a notion that contrasts strongly with modern ways of thinking. For the union process occurs in a 'medium,' a way of thinking that has long since been discarded by science. The medium is known as the subtle body in alchemy, or as the *pneuma* in its origins in Stoic thought, which also informed the early theoretical foundations of alchemy. There is no more important concept to grasp for understanding alchemical thinking. The *pneuma* is a substance that is more gross than ordinary matter and less spiritual or fine than the spirit. It is 'in between' the two and comprised of both. It permeates all of creation and links all qualities – human, organic and spiritual – together. The *pneuma* forms a vast network of pathways that carries information, and through these pathways all aspects of creation influence one another. A person's imagination can, if he or she is actively linked with another person, be transmitted to that person. In other words, a level of substantial transmission is posited, something which would be anathema to both science and psychoanalysis alike. Yet such is the nature of alchemical theory and belief: within and through the medium of the *pneuma* or subtle body, the union experience occurs. Many alchemical drawings indicate this level of a 'third area' with its own life of which two people may partake and by which they may be changed.

The alchemist's spiritual and moral involvement in his or her experiment was an essential part of the process. The alchemical approach believes in the existence of a transcendent reality as an ongoing fact, and all theorizing and practice includes this transcendent level of Oneness. In fact, the alchemist believes that, as his or her materials transform, as they are killed and reborn in a vessel, so too he or she dies and is reborn. Often imagery of dismemberment and torture are prominent along the path of reaching the goal of becoming One with the Cosmos. The alchemist carefully studied the process of attaining this state of perfection and, most significantly, while aware of the virtual impossibility of achieving this goal in a lifetime, believed that the path towards this goal was the one to follow.

Much of alchemy reflects very solid thinking which can appear muddled to our scientifically honed minds. In alchemy, the body is no lump of inert matter subject to 'natural law' alone, as Descartes and the origins of modern science would have it. Nor is the mind, let alone the brain, synonymous with spirit alone. Alchemy embraces the great mysteries of matter and spirit and sees these in the microcosm of the human being as the different experiences of our Oneness which we call mind and body.

Alchemy lasted for 2,000 years because it addressed such issues as a person's relationship to the Oneness that every soul deeply knows and easily forgets. It also retained its remarkable stability because it was particularly human, linking people and what they did and how they did it to the processes in which they engaged, to their art, to their science, and to one another. Everyone was not an alchemist, as everyone is not a scientist. But just as a spirit of science pervades our entire culture, one which believes in causes for human, economic, and social behavior, an alchemical spirit instead stressed the ways that things relate to one another. This older model is immensely appealing to the inner life, but also quite lacking in capacity to create new technologies and materials. One can imagine that the persistence of the alchemical tradition reflected the life of the soul in everyday life and in all investigations of nature, while alchemy's demise would follow from a loss of the awareness of soul or of the inner life with its own degree of autonomy. The return to the awareness of soul in modern culture seems to call once again for the values and consciousness of alchemy.

AN ALCHEMICAL APPROACH TO THE ANALYTIC PROCESS

This book is based on an appreciation of alchemical imagery as remarkably embracing of those states of mind that are often called mad or psychotic. These states of mind form an important, dangerous, but potentially creative aspect not only of mad or borderline individuals but of everyone. This madness is a central feature of the alchemical *prima materia.*

An alchemical approach further entails establishing the existence of an inter-active field between two people, experiencing the contents of the field as not belonging exclusively to either person and, most significantly, recognizing that the field has its own goal-oriented autonomy achieved through dynamic pro-cesses that link order and disorder. Objectivity of process distinguishes the field approach characterized by an alchemical attitude from other totally subjective field approaches now emerging in psychoanalytic thought.

Alchemical notions that are neither material nor mental but exist 'in between' mind and body, while also encompassing both – such as the 'subtle body,' or ideas of the imagination that can be developed into a penetrating and indispensable form of knowledge (imaginal sight), or the mysteries of union, death, and chaos – all open our eyes to a new way of seeing relationships. In particular, an alchemi-cal approach will focus upon an underlying field with its own dynamics within a relationship, or upon a field between an individual's conscious ego and the uncon-scious. This focus facilitates experiences that tend to be precluded by scientific approaches and their orientation towards separable parts of a process and towards the effect of people's projections upon one another. The conscious experience of the field with its own sense of autonomy – an experience that is similar to a vision, or a powerful dream – is the primary transformative factor. One can be changed – often gradually, but at times quite suddenly – by such 'field experiences.'

alchemical attitude

Out of alchemical symbolism and texts I believe one can define an 'alchemical attitude.' Primarily, this attitude contrasts with a scientific one in that its primary focus is not on causes. Instead, one becomes focused upon relations, on the nature of the 'third realm' between people, and not on what people are doing to one another. Consequently, a major principle of the alchemical attitude is that it is not hierarchical. No matter how much one person seems to be doing something nega-tive or objectionable to another, one still looks for the 'unconscious couple' the two people share. Another major feature of the alchemical attitude is a respect for chaos. In a sense alchemical thinking parallels the recent discoveries of Chaos Theory in science. While chaos has been ignored in science and is now, in certain limited ways, being re-discovered, chaos has always been central to alchemy. The alchemical attitude learns to embrace and suffer chaos without reaching into rea-son to dispel and dissociate from it. Moreover, the alchemical attitude recognizes a transcendent dimension of existence without which the process of transformation cannot proceed. In other words, without some degree of illumination, no transfor-mation can take place. Thus, the alchemical attitude is strongly transpersonal, without ever leaving the here-and-now reality of personal relatedness.

Generally, the alchemical and scientific attitudes have a different focus from one another and have complementary strengths and weaknesses. One can understand a great deal from a causal point of view, and it is foolish at best to underestimate the importance of the scientific way. For example, understanding a person in terms of a causal developmental process beginning in his or her infancy is a necessary focus. It acts as something like a boundary condition that keeps the imaginal approach of alchemy grounded and real. But the alchemical way offers another, complementary understanding based not on what one person 'does' to another, but rather on how people occupy an intermediate realm of relations *per se* and on how these relations are affected by the individual subjectivities of both people and also by deeper and larger currents of the archetypal level of the collective unconscious. Much can be achieved through this approach that can be superior to a scientific developmental approach, especially in the realm of dissolving rigid personality structures and dealing with mad areas of sane people.

Because it was limited to the explicit reality of 'in between' or 'third areas' that do not obey causal laws, alchemy failed as a causal endeavor to create gold from base metals in some linear, dependable and repeatable fashion. Alchemy's metaphor is not well-suited to such endeavors, as science's metaphor of cause = effect has serious drawbacks for understanding and respecting the life of the soul. We need both points of view. While this book contrasts these approaches and employs both at times, it essentially stresses the value of an alchemical approach to the 'in between' realm, the usually unseen state of relations *per se*.

Today, we must recognize the shadow side of the great development of ego consciousness, namely the creation of defenses that allow too much separation of the ego from the unconscious and from the emotions of the body. Alchemical thinking holds out a way of returning to wholeness without abandoning separation and distinctness of process. In a way alchemy's time has come. Perhaps we can now return to those mysterious realms or 'third areas' that are neither physical nor psychic, domains whose existence must be recognized if we are to reconnect split orders of reality such as mind and body. I believe that such 'third areas,' a major concern of alchemy but left behind by scientific thinking, will have to be re-introduced if we are to gain a true sense of what the soul in relationship is, especially under the eye of psychotherapy (Schwartz-Salant 1989, 1995a).

In a sense, I am returning to that juncture in history in which Newton tried to embrace both the mechanical approach to nature and the alchemical path. I do not underestimate in any sense the power of scientific and especially causal approaches to understanding, but the alchemical approach is often more useful for containing the complex states of mind usually referred to as the mad or psychotic parts of an otherwise sane person, and it offers special insight into the complexities of the usually unconscious aspects of relationships.

2 Activating the experience of the field

THE FIELD AS THE ANALYTIC OBJECT

In his 'Recommendations to Physicians Practising Psycho-analysis,' Sigmund Freud gives advice which is as pertinent today as it was in 1912, although his optimism now seems almost quaint:

> The first problem confronting an analyst who is treating more than one patient a day will seem to him the hardest. It is the task of keeping in mind all the innumerable names, dates, detailed memories and pathological products which each patient communicates in the course of months and years of treatment, and not confusing them with similar material produced by other patients . . . If one is required to analyze six, eight, or even more patients daily, the feat of memory involved in achieving this will provoke incredulity, astonishment . . . Curiosity will in any case be felt about the technique which makes it possible to master such an abundance of material . . .
>
> The technique, however, is a very simple one . . . It rejects the use of any special expedient (even that of taking notes). It consists simply in not directing one's notice to anything in particular and in maintaining the same 'evenly-suspended attention' . . . in the face of all that one hears. In this way we spare ourselves a strain on our attention which could not in any case be kept up for several hours daily, and we avoid a danger which is inseparable from the exercise of deliberate attention. For as soon as anyone deliberately concentrates his attention to a certain degree, he begins to select from the material before him . . . This, however, is precisely what must not be done . . .
>
> What is achieved in this manner will be sufficient for all requirements during the treatment. Those elements of the material which already form a connected context will be at the doctor's conscious disposal; the rest, as yet unconnected and in chaotic disorder, seems at first to be submerged, but rises readily into recollection as soon as the patient brings something new to which it can be related . . .
>
> (1958, 111–12)

Many clinicians have recognized that Freud's advice is difficult to follow, for when areas of meaninglessness, emptiness, mindlessness or blankness, overwhelming and fragmenting anxiety, intense despair, and envy are constellated, an 'evenly suspended attention' is nearly impossible to maintain. In other words, when the analysand's psychotic parts are activated, the analyst's capacity to maintain an even, free-floating attention is challenged to the utmost. An analyst might as well attempt to enter a deep, tranquil state of meditation in the New York subway system at rush hour.

Analysis has come a long way since Freud, but analysts must still travel a considerably more difficult path if they are to treat successfully patients who bring psychotic-like material into their offices. The analytical state of mind that Freud advocates typically can be achieved if analysts exclude the 'mad' parts of the psyche from their analysis. Unfortunately, such an exclusion is a sure dead end for many people in treatment. Rather than get the madness *out*, analysts must aim to get the madness *in* (Schwartz-Salant 1993), and thus open up the possibility of treating the analysand's psychotic parts. Indeed, some psychoanalysts have gone beyond Freud's proposition that awareness and consideration of the psychic states of both the analyst and the analysand are sufficient for understanding analytic interaction and thus the processes activated in the analysand. To this end, some analysts have posited the existence of a 'third area' which both analyst and analysand encounter and create and which has a powerful containing capacity.

The notion of a 'third area' which exists between the analyst and analysand has rapidly gained importance in many schools of psychoanalysis. Various analysts refer to the 'third area' in slightly different terms, reflecting their particular understanding of it: Donald Winnicott (1971) writes about 'transitional' or 'potential space'; André Green (1975) uses the concept of the 'analytic object'; various Self Psychologists, notably Robert Stolorow (Stolorow *et al.* 1987) refer to an 'intrasubjective field'; and Thomas Ogden (1994) refers to the 'analytic third.' These approaches are based upon the perception of forms and feelings created by the combined subjectivities of the analyst and analysand, and exclude any notion of the existence of an independent and impersonal objective process which itself gives rise to, and therefore is responsible for, the formation and structuring of perceptions.

For example, Ogden's position concerning a 'third area' between analyst and analysand demonstrates the parameters of such an approach. Discussing the 'analytic third' in his book *Subjects of Analysis*, Ogden writes:

> The analytic process reflects the interplay of three subjectivities: the subjectivity of the analyst, of the analysand, and of the analytic third. The analytic third is the creation of the analyst and analysand, and at the same time the analyst and analysand (*qua* analyst and analysand) are created by the analytic third. (There is no analyst, no analysand, no analysis in the absence of the third.)
>
> Because the analytic third is experienced by analyst and analysand in the context of his or her own personality system, personal history, psychosomatic makeup, and so on, the experience of the third (although jointly created) is not identical for each participant. Moreover, the analytic third is an asymmetrical construction because it is generated in the context of the analytic setting,

which is powerfully defined by the relationship roles of analyst and analysand. As a result, the unconscious experience of the analysand is privileged in a specific way, that is, it is the past and present experience of the analysand that is taken by the analytic pair as the principle (although not exclusive) subject of the analytic discourse. The analyst's experience in and of the analytic third is (primarily) utilized as a vehicle for the understanding of the conscious and unconscious experience of the analysand.

(1994, 93–94)

This understanding of the 'analytic third' allows for the analyst's reflections on experience far wider than that afforded by the principle of introjection in which the analyst internalizes the analysand's process, reflects upon the induced countertransference, then gives the analysand's process a new form, possibly through an interpretation. In Ogden's approach, the 'third' always functions in the process, affecting both analyst and analysand in a way that is not exhausted by understanding, and thus allows for greater creativity and more aggressive search for truth than do previous models of analysis.

Yet another way of viewing the role of a field in analytic practice combines such a psychoanalytic approach which deals with the subjectivities between two people and Jung's approach which deals with the intersection of an individual's subjectivity and the archetypal processes of the collective unconscious. Thus, two people can become aware of how their individual processes participate in and are affected by the objectivity of the collective unconscious. In this combined conception of field, the personal, historical acquisitions, which are the focus of object relations, mix with an objective substratum, which Jung called the collective unconscious. The objective substratum of the collective unconscious has its own dynamics which are characterized by pre-existing forms of a universal and impersonal nature and which are separate from and independent of the individuals. Yet the discovery of these dynamics is only possible by experiencing them through the individual and combined subjectivities of both people. The experience of this awareness is in and of itself deeply healing. I refer to such a notion of the field – an understanding which actively includes both subjective and objective dimensions – as the 'interactive field.' The interactive field is 'in between' the field of the collective unconscious and the realm of subjectivity, while at the same time intersecting them both.

Marie-Louise von Franz has extended Jung's approach by determining that the collective unconscious has a 'field-like' quality, 'the excited points of which are the archetypes' (1974, 61). In *Number and Time*, she states that the field is the latent source of the form of all our perceptions, behaviors, and thinking (1974, 154). In this approach, the objective nature of the collective unconscious is dominant. Jung sees an individual's subjectivity engaging this archetypal level to reveal the meaning or quality of a given moment, which means that one can experience aspects of the dynamic properties of a field which transcend one's individual consciousness.

Jung's structural analysis of the transference was based upon a quaternity of elements comprised of the conscious position of both people, and their unconscious, contrasexual components. The use of the contrasexual components, *anima* in a man and *animus* in a woman, to represent the collective unconscious is particularly significant for a field concept. For *anima* and *animus* are, in essence, 'in between' structures, mediators between conscious and unconscious. This archetypal element, along with the fact that subjectivities of two people are involved, albeit separately and individually, gives Jung's structural analysis a field quality that is 'in between' the realm of subjectivity and objectivity.

While Jung understood the nature of the archetypal dimension, and in many respects the significant role it played in shaping and transforming perceptions, he ultimately limited the use of this 'third area' to a source of information about the analysand's projections. Jung's analysis of the transference focused upon its archetypal nature, wherein the unconscious combinations of the psyches of analyst and analysand were to be uncoupled through an analysis of the analysand's projections and the analyst's counter-projections. The field's underlying dynamics are not regarded as useful or worthy of experiencing in their own right, even though Jung's frequent references to alchemical symbolism also shows that he definitely had this possibility in mind.

RENEWED INTELLECTUAL INTEREST IN ALCHEMICAL THINKING

Indeed, in his study of the transference, Jung discovered the value of alchemical imagery to understand the 'third area' of interaction between analyst and analysand. Notably in *Psychology and Alchemy* ([1944] 1968), *Psychology of the Transference* ([1946] 1954), and *Mysterium Coniunctionis* ([1955] 1963), Jung recognizes that certain alchemical imagery can represent the unconscious underside of a human relationship. As I have noted in my book, *Jung on Alchemy* (1995b), Jung found that alchemical symbolism was a remarkable mirror for the process in the human psyche that he discovered and called individuation. In this process, the form of internal structure of psyche changes. People can become more sensitive to their spiritual lives and to the wisdom and consciousness in their bodies. Archetypal, so-called transpersonal, factors become real and functional in a creative way, and the sense of meaning and purpose inheres in life. Jung was the great pioneer in recognizing that alchemical symbolism addressed just such processes. In a very real sense, his work brought alchemy back from intellectual obscurity.

When I was a student of his Analytical Psychology in Zürich nearly thirty years ago, Jung's work on alchemy was clearly presented as the heart and soul of his *opus*. Alchemy was a marvellous mirror for his own views of a process in the human psyche in which new forms were created and old ones destroyed. The goal-oriented process of individuation, crowned in that supreme form Jung called the self, was seen in the qualitative changes as well as the cycles of death and rebirth that characterize alchemy. Based upon his work, a growing body of research and creative inquiry emerged, much of which I have noted in *Jung on Alchemy*.

Jung's collaborator, Marie-Louise von Franz, has contributed many books which are especially important in not only clarifying and complementing Jung's own research but also in bringing a kind of rational coherence to alchemical studies that is difficult to match. For example, she wrote an extended commentary to the *Aurora Consurgens* (1966), a document which she and Jung attribute to Thomas Aquinas and which was published as a companion work to Jung's *Mysterium Coniunctionis* (1963). Her book *Alchemy* (1980), one of several works on the subject that derived from lectures she gave at the Jung Institute in Zürich, contains a wide-ranging historical survey of the origins of alchemy and features an analysis of Arabic, Greek, and European alchemical texts. Her *Alchemical Active Imagination* (1979) is a fine study of alchemist Gerard Dorn's attitude towards imagination and the body.

Starting in the 1980s, Adam McLean made numerous alchemical texts available in English in addition to offering illuminating commentaries from an occult point of view. Likewise, historian Johannes Fabricius, in his seminal work, *Alchemy* (1976), compiles nearly all the relevant images of alchemy in addition to contributing to an understanding of many obscure alchemical passages and offering astute criticism of the interpretations of others.

Concerning the contributions of others who were closely connected to Jung, mention should be made of an anthology and introduction to the writings of Paracelsus compiled by Jolande Jacobi (1951). And the San Francisco Jungian analyst Joseph Henderson has devoted considerable attention to the alchemical text the *Splendor Solis*. A video cassette of the interesting fruits of his research is available from the San Francisco Jung Institute. James Hillman has written extensively on alchemy, offering poetic and inspiring insights into alchemical processes in particular. His essay, 'Silver and the White Earth' (Part One, 1980, Part Two, 1981), contributes significantly to an understanding of the meaning of the alchemical Sol, Luna, and Sulphur. Another important source for a Jungian view of alchemy is Edward Edinger's *Anatomy of the Psyche* (1985), a systematic study of the meaning for psychotherapy of the various alchemical operations such as the *solutio* and the *coagulatio*. Many essays by Jungians have attempted to bring Jung's alchemical amplification of the transference into closer connection with clinical practice. In particular, Michael Fordham's 'Jung's Conception of the Transference' (1974) reflects upon the critical stage of *coniunctio* and *nigredo* in terms of projective identification; Judith Hubback (1983) has used the image of the *coniunctio* in her work dealing with depressed patients; Andrew Samuels (1985) has innovatively and usefully studied the *Rosarium* in terms of metaphorical images of analytic interactions; Mario Jacoby's *The Analytic Encounter* (1984) is a highly readable and important contribution to the transference as reflected through the alchemical imagery of the *Rosarium*.

My own intellectual journey was profoundly influenced by many of these writings on alchemy. My initial exposure to the study of alchemy came in lectures I attended in the 1960s on the mathematics of Newtonian mechanics. In those days, the history of science was a fledging enterprise; only a few people who did scientific work were aware that a long and valuable history of science existed, and those without this scientific background could do little with the older texts. But when my professor, who had an interest in this history, came upon a reference to

Newton's alchemical studies, he quickly passed it off as an aberration that one must allow to perhaps the greatest scientific genius who ever lived. Like many other scholars, this professor associated alchemy almost exclusively with the 'folly' of endeavoring to make gold from lead rather than viewing it as a spiritual science of the soul applied to transformations of matter.

My book *Narcissism and Character Transformation* (1982) shows how Jung's emphasis on the use of alchemical imagery to help form a cohesive understanding of dream and fantasy material is an invaluable approach. I demonstrated this use of alchemical symbolism for containing and understanding very chaotic and explosive material that in essence proves to be part of a creative process. In a later book, *The Borderline Personality: Vision and Healing* (1989), I employed Jung's symbolic researches differently, emphasizing how alchemical imagery could help elucidate what was happening in the here-and-now of an analytic session. In other words, rather than focus upon dream and fantasy material as reflected in alchemical symbolism, I was concerned with how alchemy elucidates the complexities of the transference/countertransference process. I argued that imaginal sight is often extremely effective in helping both the analyst and the analysand to recognize central structures of the personality hidden by the myriad of defenses the borderline personality employs. I especially underscored the necessity of learning to use one's imagination to 'see' hidden parts of the personality, as if the analyst could perceive a dream the analysand was having, amidst the characteristic emotional attacks which the analyst frequently experiences from these analysands.

I employed the alchemical series of woodcuts from the *Rosarium Philosophorum*, which Jung used to amplify the transference and countertransference process (Jung 1954, 16). I argued that the borderline personality is essentially stuck at the stage the alchemists called the *nigredo*, but that he or she occupies this distressful condition, characterized by despair and often by the mindlessness, emptiness, and the panic of psychotic process, without achieving the state of union of qualities the alchemists called the *coniunctio*. In this way, alchemical imagery is able to provide a grid for both the 'absence' from which the borderline individual suffers, and also a possible sense of meaning and even purpose for the desolate states that plague this condition. Other works furthered this approach: for example, 'Anima and Animus in Jung's Alchemical Mirror' (1992) showed the symbolism of the alchemical *coniunctio* to be extremely useful in understanding Jung's anima and animus concepts.

In *The Borderline Personality: Vision and Healing* (1989), and especially in the articles 'Jung, Madness and Sexuality: Reflections on Psychotic Transference and Countertransference' (1993) and 'The Interactive Field as the Analytic Object' (1995a), I also introduce the concept of the 'field' within which both analyst and analysand interact. Fields were first posited in science by the great nineteenth-century physicist James Clerk Maxwell, the discoverer of the electromagnetic field. This 'classical' in distinction to 'quantum' field idea posited a domain that was under the manifest world of electrically charged objects. The field moved them; one could actually observe the changes in the movements of charged objects. After his discovery, Maxwell tried to portray the field in terms of previously known ideas, such as a moving fluid, even though there were terms in his field equations that defied representation. Only with great effort and the passing of time did the field concept begin to be accepted as something that was essentially non-representable. In fact, fields were then understood to exist in empty space separate from charged particles. Now, with quantum theory, any attempts to represent a field have been totally abandoned. Thus, with the field concept we move towards the unrepresentable.

In an extremely valuable study, the notion of an interactive field has been considered by Marvin Spiegelman and Victor Mansfield (1996) from the point of view of the link between physics and psychology. They classify psychotherapy into four levels and see the fourth having to do with field phenomena analogous, in turn, to quantum-like fields in physics. A previous publication of Mansfield and Spiegelman (1989) relates quantum mechanics and Jungian Psychology, while Spiegelman (1988) focuses on the interactive field concept. Likewise, in seminal papers, Henry Reed (1996a, 1996b) has experimentally investigated interactive field phenomena, reflecting upon ways that chaos theory may be useful in understanding certain aspects of the field experience.

I find the field concept to be an excellent representation, in modern terms, for the key alchemical idea of the 'subtle body' (Schwartz-Salant 1982, 1986, 1989, 1995a, 1995b). As an intermediate realm between spirit and matter, where imaginal sight is activated in a 'oneness' of process, the 'interactive field' is meant to contain the processes two people can experience as their unconscious dyad, and the ways this dyad changes and changes them. Inherent in the field created or discovered in the analytic process is a combination of objectivity and subjectivity, as suggested by von Franz in *Number and Time* (1974), for not only do the subjectivities of both people affect the field, but it also has its own objective dynamics. Alchemy informs us of these dynamics in a way that far exceeds any other resource available to us.

Certainly, my idea of an interactive field is heavily indebted to Jung's study. His quaternity model denotes the same structure as energy diagrams in physics, which indicate a remarkable quality of information transfer between molecules that are not in contact with one another. Various energy levels in one molecule may change and induce changes in another molecule. The psychological implication of this remarkable parallel is that changes in the analyst's unconscious, for example, have an effect on not only the conscious awareness of the analysand but also the analysand's unconscious state. The same awareness is evident 400 years earlier in the alchemical text, the *Splendor Solis* (McLean 1981), in which seemingly separable states affect one another in a complex pattern of information transfer.

Thus, Jung's analysis implicitly rather than explicitly contains a model of the interactive field, comprised of mutual subjectivities and the objective level of the psyche. In a sense his study has two strands: the one an alchemical amplification reflective of the archetypal level, and the other a psychological interpretation of it. I regard my formulation as being true to Jung's amplifications and reflections upon the alchemical imagery he employed, but distinct from the manner in which he interpreted the alchemical material in terms of the analysis of projections.

ALCHEMY'S SUBJECT–OBJECT MERGER

Engaging processes of the interactive field requires that the analyst does not take refuge in a scientific model of objectivity which is ultimately limited to sorting out the mutual projections of the analysand and analyst. Instead, the analyst must allow for the existence of an area of essential 'unknowing,' an area in which one never knows if an affect of fear, anger, hate or love comes from the analysand or from the analyst. Rather, the analyst must only assume that such emotions exist as a quality of the interactive field characterized by an essential subject–object merger, a state in which the question of 'whose contents' are being experienced cannot be determined. And if the analyst does attempt to differentiate into states of individual ownership of contents, focusing upon the field itself injects a quality of Oneness into his or her experience that shows this differentiation to be of a limited nature and to be dependent upon some background developmental theory that has implicitly been brought to the encounter.

A subject–object merger was an essential part of the alchemical process. The many alchemical approaches to understanding the life of the soul and its relationship to the body and matter thus contrast with our modern approaches in significant ways. Especially significant is alchemy's insistence that the individual is an inseparable part of a larger unity. Alchemy does not conceive of an 'observing ego' considered as a separate, conscious being ordering matter. Instead, the alchemist meditates upon his experiment, sees its process through the imagination, and tests its truth or falseness, believing that this imagination is linked to a greater Oneness. And because the alchemist is part of this Oneness, the chemical changes he attempts to bring about will be influenced by, and in turn will influence his own personality development, for he is part of the transformation in his metals. If he cannot achieve a state in which he has structures which transform all varieties of chaos that would otherwise tear down and degrade his spiritual life and imagination and body awareness, then how can the alchemist create changes that he can expect to endure?

This apparent confusion between one's own processes and those which science insists are other processes, either in the material world or involving other people, can be difficult to conceive as being useful in achieving transformation of structure. But if we recognize that the alchemical universe was one in which normally unseen 'third areas' functioned, often as intermediaries between the experimenter and his or her objects, and that these areas were themselves the objects of transformation, then this confusion can be seen in a far more interesting way. The alchemical 'in between' world was a domain of subtle bodies, areas that were neither material nor mental, but partook of both. The historian of antiquity and the occult, G.R.S. Mead noted that the transformation of the subtle body, not of ordinary matter as in lead or gold, was the main point of alchemy (1919, 1–2).

The alchemical mind was immersed in subject–object mergers which are the essence of relationship and which operate at the heart of psychotherapy. When two people relate, they do so on many levels, both conscious and unconscious, and significant interactions engage those levels in which their unconscious psyches are fused together in a way in which a subject–object separation becomes obscure. So the analyst struggling with the feelings, images, affects, random thoughts and mysterious pressures which are part of his work with an analysand can benefit from the labors of those who dedicated their lives to the study of the laws governing these elusive yet pervasive and powerful phenomena. The analyst or interested individual who can engage these intermediate domains can begin to take the alchemists' words and pictures as serious attempts to describe contemporary psychic struggles and may find in these words and pictures some cogent insights and useful analyses. Moreover, such a person will find that the forces being dealt with not only transcend the delineations of his own body and mind but also pervade and organize perceptions and thoughts of the entire culture.

The connection between human and material process which was so essential to the alchemist was not necessarily a result of subject–object confusions based upon unconscious projection. Just as one can mistake a field experience in which both people partake of the same contents as a subject–object confusion, a bias stemming from an overly zealous need to have a firm ego-identity, so too alchemical attitudes can seem primitive and terribly unconscious.

The historian of alchemy, Jack Lindsay, explains the 'intentional' nature of the alchemist's intertwining himself with the matter upon which he works:

> The alchemist has to be able to identify himself with the [processes he works on]. He must realise the unity of man and nature – not as a general idea, but by the concentration of his entire mind, body, and spirit on the work he is doing, so that he truly feels himself disintegrating, torn apart and put together, reborn in a new form. This identification of the scientist-artisan with the processes he is producing is perhaps the hardest aspect of alchemy for anyone nowadays to understand or enter into. To men in whom the alienation of intellect from the world of nature has been carried very much further than among classical Greek thinkers, the whole thing seems fantastic and over stressed, unreal. But in fact it was passionately real, and in my opinion it held an element of truth which we must strive to grasp and recapture if our science is to measure up to the full demands of reality.
>
> (Lindsay 1970, 150–51)

This attitude, which is anathema to the objectivity sought by scientific approaches, is one in which the experience and imagination of the adept play a significant role in the outcome of his physical experiments.

The 'principles' of alchemy are cast as metaphors such as 'The Axiom of Ostanes' (which deals with changes in form or inner organization) or 'The Axiom of Maria' (whose evolving series of numbers, understood in a qualitative sense, underpins the entire transformation process), and as tales such as 'The Tale of Isis to her Son Horus' (an initiatory myth that instructs as to the basic attitudes necessary and the levels of illumination possible in the alchemical '*opus*'). All of these 'principles' require creativity and imaginal ability for their actualization. The great alchemical texts that have survived to this day, such as the *Rosarium Philosophorum* (1550), the *Splendor Solis* (1582), and the *Mutus Liber* ([1677]

McLean 1991), portray the transformation process in a complex series of images. The transformations depicted in these texts take place both in the material elements and in the personality of the alchemist.

The identification of the alchemist with the processes he is producing is reflected in a tale from a text attributed to the mythical Iranian alchemist, Ostanes (about the third century BCE), who describes his adventures in quest of the alchemical panacea:

> While I was examining the part I hadn't managed to decipher in this plaque, I heard a strong voice crying out to me, 'Man, get away from here before all the Gates are shut; for the moment of closure is come.'
>
> Trembling all over and afraid it was too late to leave, I went out. When I had passed through all the gates, I met an old man of unparalleled beauty. 'Approach,' he told me, 'man whose heart is thirsty for this science. I am going to make you understand many things that have seemed obscure to you, and explain what remains hidden.'
>
> I approached the old man, who then took my hand and raised his own towards the heaven . . . I praised God who has showed me all [the secrets of wisdom] and who had made all the science's secrets manifest to me.
>
> While I was in this state, the three-bodied animal, whose parts devoured one another, cried out in a strong voice, 'All the science can be perfected only by me, and it is in me that is found the key of the science . . . '
>
> Hearing these words, the old man said to me, 'Man, go and find that animal, give him an intelligence in place of yours, a vital spirit in place of yours, a life in place of yours; then he'll submit to you and give you all you need.'
>
> As I wondered how I could give anyone an intelligence in place of mine, a vital spirit in place of mine . . . the old man said, 'Take the body that is like your own, take from it what I have just told you, and hand it over to him.'
>
> I did as the old man bade me, and I acquired then the whole science, as complete as that described by Hermes.
>
> (quoted in Lindsay 1970, 150–51)

The cryptic 'three-bodied animal' referred to here is a conglomerate experience of the mind, body, and spirit and would have been imaginally 'seen' and experienced by Ostanes in his alchemical work. The guide, here an old man of unparalleled beauty, teaches that only through intense concentration of his attention on the transformations on these levels can Ostanes hope to find the key to the science he has embraced. But the transformations that Ostanes sought included, indeed could only be achieved as a result of, an intentional giving over of the old personality. This giving over is precisely the task from which most people shrink as the need for security and the terror of the chaotic levels of psyche regularly prevent true submission to the psyche's mystery.

Stand Your Ground

THE INITIATORY DIMENSION OF THE FIELD EXPERIENCE

In the cultures in which alchemy thrived, the capacity for vision and the awareness of the mystery of chaos were derived from experiences of rituals of initiation. In such initiation rites of puberty or the mystery religions of antiquity, the human being was transformed through the success of the ritual. The initiates knew and experienced another reality, different from anything they had ever previously believed to be possible, let alone exist. That other reality then guided and directed them. Their emotional life changed, and they served new-found ideals. To themselves and to those who once knew them, they were not who they had been previously: they had undergone a qualitative change.

The experience of initiation appears to be central to the formation of alchemical ideas. Lindsay suggests that the alchemists' entire approach to the transformation of substances was based on the concept of initiation:

> The concept of initiation-ordeals and death-rebirth is applied to the alchemic bodies in their changes. This analogy is not drawn on by any accident; for it was in initiation-experience that men had managed to express and develop the idea of movement from one level of life to another level qualitatively different – from childhood with its mother-world to adulthood with its totally different set of relations and responsibilities, its new lores and understandings, and so on. Alchemy above all represents the scientific application of these initiation-ideas of a leap from one qualitative level to another; and that is why the alchemists keep returning to the analogy of ordeals, tests, resurrections. And they do not do so for any simple reasons of needing an analogy drawn from human life that helps provide a schemata of stages and to make the whole mysterious process of chemical change more comprehensible. They do so because they genuinely feel a union between natural and human process; they are affirming a vital organic relationship to nature which the abstract or timeless approach, with its emphasis on the alienated intellect of men, had denied.
>
> (1970, 142)

Many alchemists underwent such initiation and, in their work, they projected the dynamic change they had experienced in themselves into their dealings with the matter with which they worked, for example, as in their efforts to transmute lead into gold. In a symbolic sense, they had experienced themselves changed from a leaden state – dominated by a depression of spirit and a compulsion of instinct – into the silver state and the beginning of illumination, a renewed passion for life, and the truth of imaginal perceptions. They believed that, perhaps, with further initiations, or through the path constellated by what they had seen and been changed by, they would be further changed into the gold of having an inner self that is stable amidst the impacts both of life's outer contingencies and the inner world of instinctual and emotional turbulence. In their art the two realms – the outer changes in substances and the inner, psychophysical changes in the mind–body self – were interwoven.

A most essential aspect of initiation is the role of the darker emotions, of the experiences of terror, dread, and deep anxieties. The alchemists used these 'death experiences' as a major metaphor in their quest for qualitative change. Thus, substances were 'tortured' and had to 'putrefy.' In alchemical texts, *putrefaction* and the *nigredo* were the secret of the art. For the alchemists knew, from their initiatory experiences, whether obtained in a secret society or through the illumination by the spirit in the *unio mystica* and its inevitable descent into chaotic, indeed mad experiences, that any true change was dependent not only upon a new vision but also upon the death of the old personality in conjunction with that vision.

While the most well-known alchemical imagery comes from the fifteenth and sixteenth centuries, the attitudes involved are as ancient as the art itself. In the Egyptian treatise, 'Isis to Her Son Horus,' dating back to the first or second century, Isis reveals the secret of alchemy to Horus, which includes the crowning injunction: 'I am You and You are Me.' This voice of initiation serves to promote the awareness of another reality that the initiate of mystery religions knew. For, 'I am You and You are Me' is a level of consciousness that does not exist within a normal space–time world in which an observing, conscious ego sees and thinks about outer or inner objects. Instead, this sameness between subject and object exists within a space or a 'dimension' which can be recognized by its unique texture and alive quality. The space is not an 'empty container,' an abstraction, or a coordinate. Rather, this space is full, a concept essential to alchemical thinking. Far from being a regressive subject–object fusion, this sense of sameness was a state of grace as well as an achievement of vision gained through the torture and trials of the initiation.

This emphasis upon initiation rites can be usefully extended through the classical scholar Walter Burkert's analysis of the initiation experience in his *Ancient Mystery Cults*. Alchemy was founded in initiation rites which were at the center of the mysteries known to have existed as far back as Neolithic times, thus allowing an overlap for the experiences of early alchemists and the experiences of those who were initiated into the ancient mystery cults (Burkert 1987, 2). Burkert further explains that the ancient mysteries:

> are not puberty rites on a tribal level; they do not constitute secret societies with strong mutual ties; admission is largely independent of either sex or age; and there is no visible change of outward status for those who undergo these initiations. From the perspective of the participant, the change of status affects his relation to a god or goddess . . . a new change of mind through experience of the sacred. Experience remains fluid; in contrast to typical initiations that bring about an irrevocable change, ancient mysteries, or at least parts of their ritual, could be repeated.
>
> (1987, 8)

Furthermore, Burkert points out that entering a mystery was a very personal choice that was anything but obligatory. Many followers of the cult were not initiated just as many followers of religions today have no immediate experience of the sacred. According to Burkert, not everyone who was initiated was changed, nor changed in the same way:

> The well-known saying that 'many are the narthex-bearers, but few are bakchoi' seems to indicate that . . . 'to be taken by the god' is an event that will happen in an unforeseeable way, and probably only to a few special individuals . . .

Proclus writes the following about the *teletai* (initiations): 'They cause sympathy of the souls with the ritual [*dromena*] in a way that is unintelligible to us, and divine, so that some of the initiands are struck with panic, being filled with divine awe; others assimilate themselves to the holy symbols, leave their own identity, become at home with the gods, and experience divine possession.' The very fact that the reactions described are not uniform but vary between perplexity and exaltation indicates that this is not free speculation based on postulates, but a description of what has been observed: *sympatheia* of souls and rituals, some form of resonance which does not come in every case but which, once it is there, will deeply move or even shatter the constructs of reality. Being ignorant of the ritual and unable to reproduce it, we cannot recreate this experience, but we may acknowledge that it was once there.

(1987, 112, 114)

Generally, mysteries were initiation rituals of a voluntary, personal, and secret character that aimed at a change of mind, body, and soul through the experience of the sacred. These mysteries were assuredly the focus of the experiences of early alchemists who then attempted to treat their 'metals' as though they too had souls that could be changed by the ordeal of initiation.

Burkert quotes Aristotle who is 'said to have used the pointed antithesis that at the final stage of mysteries there should be no more "learning" (*mathein*) but "experiencing" (*pathein*) and a change in the state of mind (*diatethenia*)' (1987, 89). Burkert also quotes Aristotle as counselling: 'be glad to have suffered the sufferings which you never suffered before' (1987, 89, note 2). This key phrase suggests the possibility that one experiences, indeed suffers, far more than a copy of some early distress, as is posited by developmental psychology, and instead finds a new creation in the adult world of experience.

The initiates who were changed speak of a fundamental change in consciousness. One who was initiated at Eleusis said: 'I came out of the mystery hall feeling like a stranger to myself' (Burkert 1987, 90). The role that fear, terror, disorganization, and madness play in the change is very striking. The alchemists, like those initiated in the mysteries, knew that extreme terror was an inevitable accompanying factor in change. At Eleusis, it was said: 'Brimo gives birth to Brimos.' The divine birth of 'Brimos,' a form of Dionysos, comes from 'Brimo,' which meant 'terror' (Kerenyi 1949, 143). The initiates at Eleusis probably saw an amazing light, as is so often described in the *unio mystica*, and as was described in Plato's *Phaedrus*: 'Resplendent beauty was to be seen, when together with the blessed chorus they . . . saw a joyous view' (Burkert 1987, 92), but there were 'exhausting and terrifying events that preceded the amazing light.' A text says that if the Eleusinian deities appear in a dream, this means 'that for the uninitiated that they bring first some kind of terror and danger . . . ' Generally, the initiates 'see' something divine, and this vision is accompanied by terror (Burkert 1987, 92–93).

Part of the Eleusinian mysteries apparently was aimed at overcoming this terror, as when an initiate touches a snake without fear. In Dionysian initiations, the initiate exclaimed: 'I escaped from evil, I found the better'; and afterwards, in the Dionysian procession some carried snakes, indicating they had learned to manage terror (Burkert 1987, 96).

The experiences of terror were often likened to a death experience, and in turn, related to myths like Demeter-Persephone or Isis and Osiris. The mysteries of Isis are to be accepted 'in the form of a voluntary death and salvation by grace . . . ' the initiate 'sets foot on the threshold of Persephone' (Burkert 1987, 99). Death and salvation by grace speak to the experience of learning that Light overcomes Darkness.

In at least some of the mysteries, the initiates were humiliated and tortured. It would seem that in these rituals the more natural experiences of terror and disso-ciated states of madness that accompany vision was imposed on the initiate. They were blindfolded, terrorized by frightening sounds, tied up, or made to stumble into a water basin – all as part of preparation for a new vision. In other myster-ies, actual physical humiliation was absent, but 'psychological terror is well attested: "all those terrible things, panic and shivering and sweat," to quote Plutarch' (Burkert 1987, 103).

The role of experiencing states of madness is most explicitly found in the Dionysian mysteries. In a series of frescoes in Pompeii that depict the Dionysian mysteries called 'the Villa of the Mysteries,' a flagellation scene depicts a girl being beaten by a sinister-looking female figure. Allusions to flogging are com-mon in the accounts of these mysteries, and 'madness is described as feeling the strokes of a whip as early as in Attic tragedy; Lyssa, as "frenzy" personified, appears with a whip in vase painting . . . ' (Burkert 1987, 104).

Thus, the role of terror and its production of chaotic states of mind is as well attested in the mystery religions as in alchemy. Such experiences of terror and chaos are part of the dark side of the *numinosum*, including one's own earliest traumatic material. If the experience of the positive *numinosum* is to have any chance of surviving and creating new structure, then one must not only survive these chaotic states of mind, but old structures must be broken up by the chaos to allow the new to incarnate. Therefore, being able to meet and to survive chaos and its terrors is essential.

The emphasis upon both a new vision and the accompanying chaotic states is as central to the mystery cults and to all initiatory experience as it was to al-chemy. It is, therefore, not surprising to find that chaos, as it links to a vision or experience of a numinous Otherness of existence, plays a central role in alchem-ical thinking. Indeed, chaos was featured as a major quality of the mysterious *prima materia* which the alchemists regarded as the vital starting point of their *opus*.

THE NATURE OF THE *PRIMA MATERIA*

In alchemical texts, the term *prima materia* refers to energies and processes which are most fundamental to the transformative process. In the *Rosarium Philosophorum* the *prima materia* is called *radix ipsius* (root of itself), because it roots in itself, is autonomous, and is dependent on nothing. The alchemists, how-ever, never clearly specified the actual nature of the *prima materia*, the mysterious starting point of their work. On the one hand, various texts speak of the *prima materia* as chaos, yet other texts just as readily define the *prima materia* as wisdom or divine illumination. As one attempts to pin the meaning of this *prima materia* down one can resonate with Jung's response when he writes:

> The prima materia [is] tantalising: it is cheap as dirt and can be had everywhere, only nobody knows it; it is as vague and evasive as the lapis that is to be produced from it; it has a 'thousand names.' And the worst thing is that without it the work cannot even begin . . . The prima materia is 'saturnine,' and the malefic Saturn is the abode of the devil, or again it is the most despised and rejected thing, 'thrown out into the street,' 'cast on the dunghill,' 'found in filth.' These epithets reflect not only the perplexity of the investigator but also his psychic background, which animates the darkness lying before him, so that he discovers in the projection the qualities of the unconscious.
>
> (1967, 13: paragraph 209)

And Jung further states:

> it is incorrect to maintain that the alchemists never said what the prima materia was: on the contrary, they gave all too many definitions and so were everlastingly contradicting themselves. For one alchemist the prima materia was quicksilver; for others it was ore, iron, gold, lead, salt, sulphur, vinegar, water, air, fire, earth, blood, water of life, lapis, poison, spirit, cloud, sky, dew, shadow, sea, mother, moon, dragon, Venus, chaos, microcosm . . . [Martin] Ruland's *A Lexicon of Alchemy*, 1612, gives no less than fifty synonyms, and a great many more could be added.
>
> (1968, 12: paragraph 425)

But consonant with the ways different authorities view alchemy, Johannes Fabricius, a scholar of alchemy, takes Jung to task for 'never specifying his general assumption of the *prima materia* as a symbol for the erupting unconscious psyche' (1976, 22). Fabricius insists that, with the aid of developmental psychology, the psychological equivalent of the *prima materia* can be clearly specified. Citing the essential feature of the *prima materia* as the awakening of love in the midst of bewildering chaos, which is experienced as a process wherein the existing elements of creation dissolve while giving birth to a new cosmos, Fabricius claims that adolescence is the psychological equivalent of the *prima materia*:

> *The psychology of adolescence corresponds with this paradoxical picture of creation.* The turmoil and upheaval of the *prima materia* express the adult ego's regressive revival of those unconscious layers which contain the imprints of the ego's tempestuous creation during adolescence where the 'dry land appears' and the sun of the conscious personality rises in full splendour from the sea of the unconscious. Two other prominent aspects of that developmental period are: (1) the awakening of adult sexuality with survival value (genital love); (2) the awakening of adult aggression with survival value.
>
> (1976, 22)

Fabricius points out that psychoanalytic descriptions of adolescence are remarkably similar to the language the alchemists use for the *prima materia*. For example, he cites Edith Jacobsen's description of adolescence in her article, 'Adolescent Moods and the Remodelling of Psychic Structures in Adolescence':

> The adolescent's instinctual development impressively demonstrates how, in climbing up the tortuous ladder to adulthood, he seems at every new step to experience anxiety, confusion, disorganisation, and a return to infantile positions, followed by propulsion and reorganisation at more advanced and more adult levels. Such processes, to be sure, can be observed at any developmental stage. But during the dramatic adolescent period we see what Helene Deutsch described as a 'clash' between progressive and regressive forces. This clash leads to a far-reaching temporary dissolution of old structures and organisations, in conjunction with new structure formation and the establishment of new hierarchic orders, in which earlier psychic formations definitely assume a subordinate role, while new ones acquire and sustain dominance.
>
> (Fabricius 1976, 19)

In a similar vein, Fabricius further cites Leo A. Spiegel who states in his article 'A Review of Contributions to a Psychoanalytic Theory of Adolescence': 'One gets the impression that in adolescence, the personality is melted down, becomes molten and fluid, and ultimately hardens again into what is to remain as the characterological core' (Fabricius 1976, 23).

Fabricius' attempt at 'specifying' the *prima materia* as adolescence goes hand in hand with his attempt to explain the entire alchemical process as a metaphor for the biologically determined development of the human personality from infancy to old age. Fabricius thus aligns himself with the attitudes of psychoanalytic writers such as Freud, Melanie Klein and Margaret Mahler, and criticizes Jung who, he says, cast aside a proper biological developmental perspective when he broke with Freud in 1912. From the biological orientation, Fabricius sees the psychology of adolescence as the *prima materia*. But since this interpretation, while theoretically logical, is far from an adequate rendering of the spirit of the alchemical material itself, it ultimately is not satisfactory as a complete or final definition of the *prima materia*. Jung offers a far more embracing, but of course less specific point of view:

> nobody has ever known what this primal matter is. The alchemists did not know, and nobody has found out what was really meant by it, because it is a substance in the unconscious . . .
>
> (1988, 2: paragraph 886)

Unlike Jung's approach, the psychoanalytic developmental view not only fails to consider the dynamics and transformative capacities of the experience of the *numinosum* but also understands personality growth to result from a reshuffling and restructuring of 'object relations' that exist from infancy and early developmental experiences. This point of view does not accept that something fundamentally new, never before experienced in any form, can emerge out of the chaos and mystery of the unconscious into the human personality. An alchemical approach to the analysis of the psyche, Jung understood, emphasizes that a previously non-existent element can appear in the personality.

When a new internal structure is emerging, it frequently does so with the phenomenology seen in adolescence; but adolescence is not the template for such experiences. Rather the complex way in which order and disorder interact in the human psyche as new forms are created governs adolescence as well as all significant changes in personality structure, including the incarnation of numinous experiences. Nevertheless, one must recognize the extreme turbulence of adolescence as a feature of the *prima materia*, which must be integrated, not merely as a developmental construct but in a way that is true to the larger spirit of alchemy, and thus to the profound ways that personality can transform.

In their experiences of initiation as well as in their respect for the merger of subject and object, the alchemists knew deep states of emotional turbulence and perceived the numinous nature of these states. These deep states of emotional turbulence were part of the depth of the *prima materia* and the alchemical transformation process. This turbulence as a feature of the *prima materia* is closely related to the alchemical chaos, the psychological manifestation of which is often found in the mad parts of a sane person.

3   Mad parts of sane people

The spirit of alchemy respects both the destructive and transformative powers of madness. In his book, *On Private Madness*, André Green insightfully analyzes madness in terms of the creative and destructive aspects of passion:

> Madness, which is a component of the human being, is linked to the vicissitudes of primordial Eros, which are in constant conflict with the destructive instincts. When Eros prevails, it is because the passions which inhabit it become bound, and psychosis is averted. But when the destructive instincts triumph over Eros, the unbinding process is stronger than binding, and psychosis wins through . . .

(1993, 242–43)

As Eros, representative of the binding power of love and sexuality, gives way to the destructive instincts, that is, to the death of structure and regression to earlier archaic and compulsive forms of behavior, unbound passion leads to psychotic processes. And, I might add, psychosis or a psychotic part can at times be bound by Eros and creatively enlivened by passion. I find madness and psychosis too intertwined to separate in practice, and I see them both as qualities of the same phenomena in which human beings are able neither to bond with nor separate from a primordial object.

This ancient dilemma is codified in the myth of the Great Mother of the Gods, Cybele, and her son-lover, Attis, a tale that probably dates to the end of the Neolithic Age. Attis's passion for Cybele is so great that he can neither remain with her nor separate from her. His individuation needs are so wholly blocked that his passion turns to total destruction and, in a psychotic act, he commits suicide through a horrible self-mutilation. The myth lives on intrapsychically and should be no more strange today than it was over 5,000 years ago.

The psychotic area of otherwise normally functioning people not only creates subtle or, at times, quite blatant distortions of reality but it can also motivate destructive acts towards self and others. On the one hand, the power of the mad area of the analysand to fragment the consciousness of the analyst can create considerable difficulties in the analyst's attempts to focus at all, let alone discover a third area. On the other hand, once the analyst overcomes his or her dissociating experience, the experience of the analysand's mad parts can then lead to discovering the nature and structure of the interactive field. Thus, when the 'waters of madness' can be contained rather than allowed to intrude into one's existence in a random manner, the psychotic areas of the psyche can become constructive rather than destructive.

As the soul in an Egyptian myth emerges out of the Primordial Waters of Chaos, a phrase the alchemists often use for the *prima materia*, so too a sense of meaning, purpose, and identity – a self – can emerge out of the chaotic areas of one's madness. The alchemists were very alert to the destructive potential of the Primordial Waters of Chaos. As Johannes Fabricius notes: 'the alchemist's initial encounter with the *prima materia* is characterized by feelings of frustration, bewilderment, dissociation, and disintegration' (1976, 20). A statement by the alchemist Alphidius in the *Rosarium* captures the threatening nature of the madness that the alchemists faced: 'This stone proceeds from a sublime and most glorious place of great terror, which has given over many sages to death' (Jung 1967, 13: paragraph 429, note 8). And the mental dangers of the alchemical art are made clear in the inscriptions to medals illustrating the beginning stage: 'This science requires a philosopher and not a madman' (quoted in Fabricius 1976, 20). Beginning the *opus* was considered a risky proposition. Referring to its mental dangers, the adepts speak of: 'The foundation of this art on account of which many have perished' (Jung 1967, 13: paragraph 429, note 1). And the alchemist Olympiodorus quotes the saying of Petasios that lead (*prima materia*) was so 'shameless and bedeviled' that it drove the adepts mad (Jung 1963, 14: paragraph 493).

By a sane person's mad or psychotic parts, I mean those aspects of psyche that are not contained by the self and in which the psyche's self-regulating function fails. The 'self' represents those aspects of the 'Self,' the larger totality of personality, that have been integrated, metaphorically speaking, into being both a center and a containing circumference for the ego. This experience of containment expands with personality integration. But the psychotic parts of a personality, like the chaotic waters of all traditional cultures, always are at the edge of this self structure, at best a boundary phenomenon, and at worst ever intruding and disrupting any felt sense of containment. These chaotic waters, the psychotic parts of a personality, are part of the Self; and they are always crucial to change and regeneration.

When the psychotic sector is enlivened in analytical work, a transference emerges that has a kinship with Harold Searles's description of the psychotic transference with schizophrenic analysands. The transference 'distorts or prevents a relatedness between analysand and therapist as two separate, alive, human and sane beings' (Searles 1965, 669). The difference between the psychotic transference with the schizophrenic person and the constellation of this transference in a non-psychotic person is one of degree and structural difference. Whereas the psychotic sector engulfs the schizophrenic, the mad part of a sane person is partially held out by splitting defenses.

Generally, mad states that have a perceptible cause are often more comprehensible than psychotic states of mind experienced when interacting with schizophrenic individuals. An analyst may discover mad states within borderline conditions in which opposites are kept separate by splitting defenses. In such cases, a flood of emotional material consisting of despair, rage, panic states, anxiety, and feelings of abandonment can engulf the person when the separation of opposites fails. But while areas of madness can then dominate, the overall picture can be made meaningful by recognizing these states to be a result of the terror of abandonment. A spectrum exists which, at one end, is bounded by mild chaotic states of a borderline nature. Then a middle ground exists in which psychotic process is less contained – notably in schizoid disorders in which a psychotic core can manifest in opposites that do not split in such a relatively stable manner, and in which a core of madness can be far more hidden. Then at the far end of the spectrum lies schizophrenia in which a separation of opposites often fails, leading to a fusion of incompatible states and a sense of bizarreness. This sense of bizarreness, strangeness, or oddness also accompanies psychotic process in non-psychotic people, and this particular aspect of the psychotic process is a key feature of the countertransference that often leads to the analyst's denial of the process at hand and to his or her manipulating the analysand towards more rational, non-psychotic discourse and behavior.

When defenses such as denial, idealization, and mind–body splitting begin to fail, the psychotic parts intrude into the conscious personality. The person then becomes dissociated to a high degree and can oscillate between phases of unreality in relationship to his or her own person and to others. Behavior and fantasy stemming from these parts can distort reality in very subtle ways. While the person may behave in ways that feel inspired, he or she may have absolutely no regard for another person, or for that matter, for his or her own soul. The analyst is commonly affected in similar ways. When an analysand's madness emerges in an analysis, the analyst will often feel disoriented and find it extremely difficult to concentrate and contain the process at hand. One's own center seems to fail, and dissociated parts predominate.

Speaking about a psychotic part is, in a sense, a contradiction. For we never experience psychotic states in another person as if they were a part of that person, as we sometimes speak of a complex. Psychotic states are, like the waters of chaos in alchemy or in myths of creation, psychic spaces in which Cartesian language fails. These states readily extend to the analyst, creating a field in which it is not possible to state who is containing 'the psychotic part.' Rather, the analyst and analysand deal with a field phenomena not reducible to separable structures. Generally, the term 'psychotic part' or a similar word construct is meant here as a shorthand term to help designate that domain of experience in which psychotic process dominates. But it is not intended to lead to an approach in which the analyst attempts to speak of an 'analysand's psychotic parts,' as if these are in any manner totally separable from the same phenomena in the analyst. In a sense, transference psychosis constellates countertransference psychosis, but to a lesser degree and in a more manageable form, if the analysis of these areas is to be successful.

An interesting parallel exists between the behavior of psychotic areas and chaos as it is understood in the field of Chaos Theory. Up to the advent of Chaos

Theory scientists learned not to focus upon chaos. In their constant preoccupation with the search for order, they seldom studied randomness or sudden changes into unpredictability. Consequently, the discovery that certain apparently random systems indeed had a kind of order within them was ground-breaking and – depending upon the enthusiasm of the writer – akin to a new scientific paradigm.

A very close parallel to this situation is the investigation of mad or psychotic areas. Such states of mind have long been thought of as essentially unanalyzable because they are so erratic in appearance that they could never find a stable containment in an analytic process. Furthermore, their affects and imagery have been considered too bizarre to decipher and without any meaning. An extreme form of this state has been thought to lie in schizophrenia.

As scientists are recognizing chaotic qualities of systems that were once thought of as supremely ordered, for example, the planetary orbits, and as they also begin to recognize the value of chaos, so too they may – as ancient science did – begin to wonder about the creative function of mad areas of the mind. Is an extreme sensitivity to small changes – the hallmark of what science regards as chaotic processes – just a regrettable weakness in the individual's creation, a bit of disorder that must somehow be managed? Or might such disorder have an unseen function or purpose? Some states of mind appear never to reveal a deeper order. They seem to remain 'black holes' in the psyche that suck away all forms of order and replace them with none. But other states of mind that appear totally fragmentary and devoid of meaning actually turn out to possess an odd kind of order that can be worked with.

The psychotic area is inherently unstable, subject to major oscillations from the emotional input of external or internal factors. It contains essentially incompatible opposites. But rather than dynamical systems known in the physical world and described by chaos theory in which a system's states oscillate radically but continuously, one would have to imagine something in which an oscillation to one state annihilated the state which had previously existed. This image would, in the language of chaos theory, be a 'strange attractor.' This oscillator would be quite unstable in terms of 'initial conditions,' which is to say that it could qualitatively change depending upon small changes in input. I believe this model offers a useful metaphor for psychotic processes. For if psychotic areas can be conceptualized in such non-linear ways, might we not better learn to live with them, both in analytical work and in life? And if such non-linearity exists, might not the chaotic forms of the transference and countertransference, in which all sense of meaning vanishes, be better embraced as, in fact, a process that can engender new meaning through a non-ordinary kind of order? Indeed, if they could find this kind of containment, might we then see psychotic areas as potentially creative forms? Achieving this new perspective would require containment not by a mind that fills and holds the analysand's process, but by a mind that focuses upon a chaotic process as it reveals its unstable form of order. This is a clinical possibility.

From this vantage point, the psyche is not seen as a stable system of objects that interact with other objects. At times, one may experience only noise and meaningless states, but then something unique appears; and if this event can be seen, one then begins to see in a new way and recognize previously hidden and creative processes. This is how viewing the psychotic area feels, and when it is contained, the creation of a self can be felt as though one were very close to the creative process itself.

Aside from the general issue of their transformative power, the analyst has a specific reason to engage these areas as a *prima materia*. During early childhood years, some people have 'seen' that one or both of their parents was 'mad.' The parent was not necessarily overtly psychotic – although that, too, occurs and can be denied by the family system – but rather the child imaginally 'saw,' behind the scenes, that the parent was run by forces out of his or her control, or was withdrawn and completely absent, even while acting as if he or she was present and sane. This madness did not necessarily intrude all the time, but either it was a terrifying background presence that the child sensed, or else it manifested at times when the parental object underwent a temporary personality shift, for example, through the use of substances such as alcohol. Parental madness could intrude in the form of physical and sexual abuse, but when mad parts of parental figures did not operate in such devastating and overt ways, they often manifested in more subtle and odd ways.

For example, a father allowed his son to drive his car but insisted that he did not use the radio. The son naturally used it and each time tried to set it back to its initial setting; nevertheless, the father, on the alert for such things, went into a rage. The tale might seem simply to represent a bit of extreme behavior. But it was far more: the young man knew that at these times his father was 'totally' out of control, indeed mad. He knew that madness was always lurking about his father, manifesting in numerous ways that could always be discounted as just being instances of his father's strictness.

In another example, a man's father insisted that his children immediately polish their shoes whenever they came into the house, even when they were 3 years old. His father's intensity and violence, lest he or his brothers be anything but perfect in their shoe shining, was terrifying to all of them. Yet his father was well adapted, loved in his community, and only showed himself overtly as frightening and out of control to others when he drank too much.

Many more such examples could be given of ways in which a parental object's madness was a background presence, always terrifying, and at times manifesting in quirky behavior that tended to be normalized, often by the other parent. As a result the child's vision of this madness had to be split off.

When such people enter into treatment, they will manifest various degrees of dissociation, often envisioned in dreams or intuitively perceived as the image of a young child dissociated from the person's normal ego state. Usually, 'the child' is extremely frightened. It is all too easy to assume that such people have been the victims of incestuous abuse, or even of cult abuse, for their traumatized behavior can be the same as that of such survivors. But this explanation can be only a hasty approach grasped at in a desire to understand why an analysand's life does not sufficiently change. An intelligent, creative, and insightful person can repeat the same destructive behavior and continue to engage in undermining object relations. My experience is that areas of madness in the analysand, formed through incorporating and splitting off from their imaginal perception of the madness in the parental object, become subject to the same kind of repetition compulsion that an analyst finds in victims of sexual and physical abuse. As a consequence of this splitting, reality is distorted, and the distortion continues throughout life, sapping away the life and vitality of the ego and the larger self. Psychotic areas also often form in people who have been physically or sexually abused, especially when the person has not been able use neurotic forms of dissociation for survival purposes.

As a result of the process of denial, the person who has been traumatized by a psychotic area of a parental object carries within himself or herself a 'foreign object,' that is, the parent's psychotic process, now mixed with the person's own splitting defenses. To deal effectively with this mixture, the person must first come to recognize his or her own area of madness and then gather up the courage to 'see' once again what he or she once saw, and now, as in an act of self-remembering, no longer split off the perception. The problem that the person then faces, however, is that owning this perception means to be alone, to have no choice other than leaving the family system. The truth that he or she 'sees' is thus in some ways cruel, but in deeper ways, this vision is the way to freedom and ownership of a self.

The key to dealing with psychotic areas is that the relationship between analyst and analysand be capable of engaging them. This engagement is rarely a matter of a constant focus; rather it is like observing a trace of a reaction in a cloud chamber in the physical sciences. For an instant, the analyst sees the peculiar structure of opposites in the psychotic area; or he or she glimpses a front–back split in which dangerous and engulfing mad contents live, split off behind the person; or he or she can imaginally perceive strange side-by-side opposites, strange because of the way they combine to produce a bizarre quality.

Karl Jaspers has noted: 'The most profound distinction in psychic life [is] that between what is meaningful and *allows empathy* and what in its particular way is *ununderstandable*, "mad" in the literal sense, schizophrenic psychic life' (quoted in Sass 1992, 16–17). Fantasies, as Louis Sass notes in *Madness and Modernism*:

> may be quite delusional without being bizarre. But in schizophrenics they are bizarre. Someone in a manic psychosis may feel like they are creating the world and this can be understood as a result of extreme inferiority feelings they are compensating for. But consider the dancer Nijinsky's description during a schizophrenic break: 'Once I went for a walk and it seemed to me that I saw some blood on the snow. I followed the traces of the blood and sensed that somebody *who was still alive* had been killed.'
>
> (Sass 1992, 17)

The sense of the bizarre, as later examples will show, occurs through the fusion of contradictory images in the psychotic area. Incompatible states fuse together but do so in a way that is not seamless. Instead of yielding a symbolic product that transcends them both, they yield a mixed state that manifests conflicting messages and a sense of oddness.

While a non-psychotic person will generally not have such blatant delusions, and while any bizarre fantasies he or she may have will usually not be stated as baldly as in Nijinsky's case, the same kind of material with its perplexing meaninglessness can at times be found in both seemingly normal discourse and also in dreams.

For example, a female analysand knew she had to leave the relationship in which she was involved, but also denied this knowledge at the same time, often saying contradictory things in the same sentence. While still desperately trying to make sense of her boyfriend's duplicitous and double-binding behavior, she dreamed:

> There is a party being given by an angry couple who are divorcing. The party is to celebrate their having been together for a year.

The contradiction is not as severe as what we find in Nijinsky's delusion, and it occurs in a dream. But the contradiction exists as an unconscious pattern that creates a bizarre sense to her communications. Often, dream images that make no sense can signify a psychotic area, as when a man dreams of a breast growing out of his calf. Obviously, if one can find meaning in such images, they cease to be bizarre and no longer are indicative of psychotic process. But to assume that such possibilities are the rule rather than the exception is naive. This type of assumption can be a countertransference resistance to squarely seeing that one's analysand can be quite mad and a stranger to us. Generally, the analyst must stay attuned to the lack of meaning an image seems to have but, at the same time, realize that this absence of meaning is a function of his or her own psyche and the analysand's interaction. Thus, in the analytic work, all the analyst has to offer is his or her own awareness and subjectivity. Yet it is exactly out of this limited condition that truth for the analysand can emerge.

Another man dreamed of a brown and white snail-like creature growing out of the side of his left foot. A woman dreamed of three breasts growing out of her back. In another example that indicates the extreme dissociation that often accompanies psychotic process, a man dreamed of being on an island and suddenly thousands of miniature bull-like creatures began to flood the island. He awoke in terror, and a regression ensued which lasted six months. Only then, were we able to return to the violent psychic images he had been encountering. A woman, in another example of a psychotically dissociative process, dreamed of thousands of indescribable, bug-like creatures crawling over her body. And a man who had been defending against his psychotic area dreamed that he was reading a book. But then his identity suddenly changed, and he was looking through another person's eyes and saw a chaotic scene in a mental hospital in which patients were all entangled and confused.

At times, psychotic areas are explicit, as when a man dreamed that he was carrying his psychotic mother on his shoulders. Or, a woman whose mother had just been admitted to a psychiatric hospital dreamed of carrying her from house to house trying to find a place to put her down. But usually psychotic areas communicate to us with more of a sense of bizarreness that can follow upon feeling bewildered or mentally blank, or they communicate through the analyst's own dissociative countertransference reactions.

Internally, a person's psychotic area is extremely stressful. Under its impact, the analysand can suffer from a chronic sense of not being able to create a life that has any continuity and stability. One woman suffered from the feeling that everything was overwhelming to her. Once, for example, she had the idea of having a dinner at her house for her friends. The idea felt so wonderful that a very rich, creative feeling surrounded her. But soon, this euphoric state turned into complete terror, for she suddenly became convinced that the dinner would be a failure. Both of these states were total, and each allowed no hint of anything from the opposite state to enter. In another instance of how the psychotic part inwardly infuses and distorts one's experience, a woman meditated and imagined seeing her teacher's beautiful cat in the room. The cat's presence left her with a sense of grace, beauty, and calm. Then she felt a radical shift, and she was totally engulfed with thoughts and feelings of the trouble that taking care of the cat would involve. As these shifting states continued, she felt deluged uncontrollably by these thoughts, and her whole body began to ache. She could not recall any of the initial experience of beauty and grace; this had been totally eclipsed. If her non-psychotic area had been involved or if she did not have such a significant psychotic sector, she might feel such beauty, and then thoughts of the reality involved in actually having the cat might have intruded, perhaps tempering any ideas of actually getting a cat. In turn, the presence of the cat could begin to internalize the development of an inner symbol, a feeling of an 'inner cat,' perhaps representing her own self-image of grace and beauty. But in her case, the opposites were so split as to preclude this symbolic process which, by definition, combines opposites together into a meaningful third.

Often, a person's mad area can be a storehouse of creativity – in alchemical terms, 'the pearl of great price' – but its extraction is no easy matter. For example, a woman who had come to know her psychotic part recognized that this madness had formed in her as a result of interactions with her father. He would appear to be wonderful and very loving, but suddenly, he would become a brute who, she felt, annihilated any sense of her identity or value. She was unable to idealize him, that is, to hold the positive father in her mind and split off the negative. Instead, the negative was always there with the positive, pressing into her mind as an ever-present possibility even when he was being his wonderful self. It was, she said, like two tracks, each with its own train, and both were ever so close, a millimeter apart. The opposites in her mad area were thus nearly fused together, and she could not get them fully apart. Each was totally true, and each annihilated the other. When she was inwardly confused and terrified, and filled with distorted idealizations of herself and others, she was also capable of being remarkably creative and productive. The problem, however, was that she was then attracted to creative men who could be quite psychotic. These relationships would turn out to be disastrous, on the one hand replicating her experience with her father and, on the other hand, representing an attempt to extract her own creativity from an area of madness. In the process, her own creativity could not emerge.

Psychotic areas, which are usually anathema to the person and to everyone in contact with them outside of the analytic relationship (and often there as well), are actually a clever hiding place for what one most cherishes, and most wants to keep away from abusive relationships. In alchemical mythology, the central symbol of a unified Self, the sought-after 'Stone of the Wise,' or the '*Lapis*,' is found in dungheaps and generally in despised places.

MANIFESTATIONS OF THE PSYCHOTIC PART

Analysts have different ways of dealing with the dynamics of the psychotic transference. When the analyst's attention begins to fragment, and states of inner deadness, emptiness, and confusion emerge, what can contain such states? An act of will, for example an intense concentrative effort, can often embrace a schizoid withdrawal or the regression that accompanies the disturbance of the equilibrium of the narcissistic character. But the dissociation from the psychotic part generally overpowers the analyst's ego. Often, but not always, a containing quality can come from the analyst's awareness that a psychotic transference is working behind the scenes. In other words, the analysand may be quite rational and also connected to affects, unlike the splitting dynamics in a schizoid state, but the person is dominated by a projection of a psychotic nature. From the point of view of this sector, the analyst is a dangerous, persecutory object; the 'as if' of a non-psychotic projection is lost. Furthermore, the way we see this state is of the essence if the psychotic part is to be contained. The analyst must know the psychotic state in the analysand not only as a psychic reality but also as an ordinary state of mind because, when the analyst sees the psychotic part, the tendency is to recoil from its reality-distorting nature. The analysand feels strange to the analyst. This strangeness is inherent in the phenomenology of madness as it erupts into one's normal day-world; the phenomenon of madness is like the Greek god Dionysos, but it is also an enactment of the analysand's fear of being seen as a psychic leper. Consequently, the analyst must be able to see the psychotic part in a matter-of-fact way. The analyst is with a wounded and limited person (as we all are), but he or she is also with someone of beauty and value, much of which is in fact a result of his or her suffering the psychotic level.

Often, if the analyst loses an embodied, down-to-earth state and talks about the reality distortions of the psychotic transference, the analysand can recognize that what is said is correct, yet dissociative states return to both of them because containment of the anxiety fails. On the other hand, if the analyst can remain embodied and actively experience and envision the psychotic sector, he or she can craft interpretations which are containing for the analysand.

The psychotic transference is a state in which some degree of analyst–analysand alliance still exists. Hence, when the analyst is able to 'see' the analysand's distrustful double, something in the analysand is relieved and a sense of containment ensues. In contrast, when the quality of analysand–analyst alliance vanishes and the transference becomes delusional, no amount of vision or empathic connection or understanding has a containing influence. Instead, analyst and analysand remain, at least for the time being, in a state where the devil has gained the upper hand.

To contain the psychotic field, the analyst must be able to recognize madness and resist translating it into some system of thought with which he or she is familiar. For the mad part, at its core, breaks up thoughts, leads to states of blankness, and especially torments the analysand with a purgatory of mental anguish in which anything he or she feels or thinks can readily be undone, leading to a state in which what was said has no meaning at all. The analysand realizes that he or she has been grasping at straws in a vacuum, with absolutely no sense at all of an inner orienting center, or background support which gives one a sense of being on the right track. Instead, no track seems meaningful. The split opposites of the psychotic part, instead of creating a state of willing suspension of knowing, become a violent shredder of thoughts and feelings and render all states meaningless.

If the analyst can contain the psychotic part by recognizing the total despair that the analysand suffers in the belief that this part and its effects never change, then a new self experience can come into existence. To facilitate this change, the analyst sacrifices omnipotence and aligns with the analysand's reality which may well be true. This is not a matter of empathy alone, but one of courage that leaves open the possibility of failure. All the analyst can really offer is a measured uncertainty in the face of the analysand's pessimism. The mystery of this measured uncertainty lies in its containing quality. Unless this uncertainty which does not abandon faith is communicated, the analyst's state of 'not-knowing' will fail to have a creative edge.

The psychotic part of a sane person manifests in myriad ways, the perception of which require the analyst to register and to use countertransference. The analyst may experience a tendency to dissociation, which can include the withdrawal and energy-loss common in encountering schizoid dynamics, but primarily he or she experiences fragmentation, making concentration on the analysand extremely difficult amidst feelings of emptiness, absence, mindlessness, and deadness. Any attempt at a fixed orientation easily falters and tends to shift to an opposite. As a consequence of these uncomfortable states of mind, the analyst can feel hatred of the analysand and a tendency to withdraw or attack.

The analyst's tendency is to avoid making affective contact with the analysand at these times, especially by splitting from negative feelings. Instead, the tendency is to allow the dissociation to pass and go on as if nothing had happened. A concomitant tendency, which is often diagnostic of the constellation of the psychotic part, is that the analyst begins to stress the analysand's strengths and address the more normal-neurotic part. Later, the analyst can often learn that, through this maneuver, he or she has been stressing one of the opposites in the psychotic part, and excluding another, in hopes of reducing his or her anxiety.

If the analyst succeeds in encountering the dissociative field that accompanies the psychotic transference in such a way that he or she maintains a cohesive presence and emotionally engages the analysand, the analyst can begin to clarify the field to the extent that it is no longer a welter of attacking, image-destroying fragments but takes the form of actual images. The analyst may then recognize a form of the psychotic transference. For example, the analysand's psychotic sector distorts the image of the analyst as an attacking animal or as a dangerous parental figure. The analyst becomes identified with parts of the parental psyche that were especially dangerous to the analysand. An example is seeing the analyst as dead, a state that can later be discovered to have been part of a parent's psychotic inner life that the analysand split off from his or her awareness. As part of the clarification of the nature of the psychotic transference, the analyst senses that the analysand sees him or her in an extremely unreal way. The analysand at these times also seems odd or strange to the analyst, for the psychotic state radically opposes the normal-neurotic part one would rather experience. If the analyst succeeds in experiencing this transference in a stable enough manner, the analysand's perception of himself or herself, and of the analyst, can often shift and change dramatically.

While the analyst is clarifying this derealized-depersonalized sequence, the analysand's resistances to experiencing the psychotic part can begin to become clear and to become subject to change. These resistances commonly show themselves to be of an erotic, compulsive, manic, or sado-masochistic nature. For example, extreme forms of sado-masochism often have been split off into the psychotic part. When this part is contained, and becomes embodied, it can become clear that much sado-masochistic behavior, such as extreme giving of oneself to others while also subtly withdrawing, is actually an unconscious defense against madness. My impression is also that the experience of sexual abuse in one's early life often resides in a psychotic sector, and recovering memories can require working with the dynamics of this sector.

To achieve a consciousness of distinct opposites within the psychotic sector often takes considerable time and effort. Generally, the opposites in this sector have the peculiar quality of being totally split and also fused: they seem to fly apart but also merge together so that their distinctness vanishes. This splitting recalls the nature of the alchemical Mercurius which is a good image of the field qualities that these opposites engender. Within this field, the analyst tends to feel identified with one or the other opposite or, conversely, to split off from experiencing the opposites. This peculiar combination of fusion and splitting places the opposites in a state at the boundary of what the alchemists referred to as prior to the second day, that is, before the separation of opposites. They emerge, separate, and then quickly fuse back into a merged, non-distinct state. But most important, fusion and separation of opposites can occur with extreme rapidity in the psychotic part, yielding an oscillation that can create panic and confusion.

The mad area, like any complex, is structured by opposite qualities, such as love and hate; but in mad areas, the opposites do not complement, compensate or balance one another. Rather, they behave as anti-worlds to each other: experiencing or being cognizant of any state of mind will often lead to an awareness of another, opposite state that entirely destroys the previous perception. In a sense, the analyst and analysand confront a process at the edge of the separation of opposites, as if one opposite, and then the other, emerges; but both do not exist unless an intentionally conscious act literally holds them together. Consequently, this imaginal process differs from a projective identification process in which one opposite is split off into the analyst; in encountering areas of madness, the perception of the opposite is annihilated as it slips back into the unconscious. At times, an analyst can think he or she has forgotten what just occurred, but on deeper reflection will see that this is not the case. Instead, some perception has been annihilated, and another perception, or a state of mindlessness has taken its place.

The process of discovery of the opposites in the psychotic part generally follows from experiencing them as extremely split within an interactive field and at times felt in projective identification. The analyst feels the opposites as split, with each vying for total attention and with the gap between opposites engendering a state of absence or void in which one's energies are dulled and consciousness is difficult to maintain. When the opposites are apprehended as a related pair together, which means the analyst becomes capable of not identifying with either one or the other of the pair, a new development is possible. A union field can emerge, a felt experience of *coniunctio*. Through this experience, the heart-center for both analyst and analysand becomes more open. This is usually a new experience for the analysand for whom the experience and vision of the heart has been closed off by strong armoring. The apprehension of opposites does not always lead to this experience, but it does lead to a new consciousness of the psychotic sector, especially its limiting nature. Analyst and analysand can learn about the power of the psychotic sector to distort reality ever so subtly, and through this awareness, they can develop a process in which aspects of the psyche hidden within the psychotic sector can emerge. Most common is a schizoid part whose essential weakness, lack of connection, and distorting nature lead to a profound sense of humiliation. Only the awareness of opposites as part of the consciousness that ensues allows this experience to be contained rather than turned into a persecutory state. As a result, what appears as schizoid and lifeless often begins to show itself as part of a highly energized field that has been split off. In such typical ways the discovery of the psychotic part and working with its energies is akin to a process of creation.

A contrast between the process of splitting in the psychotic sector with that of dissociation in dissociative disorders reveals that the parts in dissociative disorders are more whole. They are generally differentiated from each other by a memory barrier, and often lead to an induced trance-like state in the object to which the person is relating. This condition also has a dissociating effect on the person related to, but it is not fragmenting in the same way as it is when induced by a psychotic area. Dissociative disorders can form to survive abuse, or to split the opposites of frequent double-bind messages one grows up with as a child. Double-bind messages are communications composed of two contradictory messages with the implicit demand that the target of the message does not process the contradiction. In defending against the confusion of the double bind, each part of the bind forms a dissociated part. However, in a psychotic sector, splitting, abuse, and double-bind messages are not processed through trance – the capacity to do so is probably genetically based as is the capacity to be hypnotized. Instead, a psychotic area forms which is defined by opposites, which are experienced as mutually annihilating anti-worlds.

The split opposites in the psychotic sector create extreme confusion in numerous daily encounters. For example, a student in a class asked me about something I had said in a lecture which he had attended. Something about his question made me feel edgy. This feeling got worse when he went on to ask another question based upon what I had said in that lecture. At this point, I felt a surge of anger and confusion. On the one hand, he had distorted what I had said in a way that rendered it hardly recognizable. On the other hand, he was asking a relevant question, which nevertheless put me into a double-bind conflict. If I confronted his distortion, I felt that I would be attacking him by not addressing his question; and if I addressed his question, I felt that I would have been agreeing with his distortion. In this interaction, I was unable to separate the two strands of his communication, for the group situation made such an intimate communication practically unmanageable. The nature of the field manifesting through the dynamism of the psychotic part created sufficient confusion to render differentiated thinking very difficult.

Whereas different parts of a dissociative state can often be totally opposed to one another, they exist within a realm of trance logic so that such contradictions are not necessarily confusing. X and Y may be completely contradictory statements, such as a person's belief that he or she may be totally competent and totally incompetent. In the realm of trance logic, these opposite beliefs may exist simultaneously. But in the case of dealing with a psychotic complex, X and Y represent states of mind that do not exist with equanimity, and in combination they either annihilate one another or create a sense of bizarreness. Their opposition cannot be dealt with as if a hypnotic world of trance logic existed; instead, they leave one suspended in a state of confusion. The best the analyst can do, at the outset of experiencing this state, is to be confused. But it is important not to be confused about being confused. Confusion within the field created by the psychotic part is the medium in which the analyst and analysand work. If the analyst casts aside confusion, he or she will be prone to feeling an impotent rage and will tend to split the analysand away from the psychotic area, and into more competent functioning. This splitting can occur when the analyst engages with the parts of a dissociative disorder; but that is usually when he or she becomes exasperated with young dissociated parts. Or, the splitting in the analyst occurs when he or she fails to recognize the whole system of parts and tends to treat the person as if one part is the whole, only to find great resistance and regression as a result. Under the stress of such induced dissociative states, the analyst can tend to feel the same kind of impotent rage as occurs when he or she is dealing with psychotic areas. But when the analyst regains his or her bearings and finds the appropriate voice tone that can encourage a safe sense of attachment, the distress that at one time appeared catastrophic can quickly disappear. This kind of change does not occur when dealing with the psychotic area, where catastrophic feelings do not change so readily. When the nature of the split is not contained within an interactive field and the analyst's imagination and when his or her capacity to retain a self amidst confusion and attacks on the possibility of relatedness is lost, then a dangerous regression can occur. Often this regression results in the collapse of treatment and serious injury to the analysand.

Even though material from a dissociated person can seem bizarre, such communications may appear far more understandable and meaningful than they do in psychotic processes. For example, a woman dreamed that she was eating the exposed brain of a person lying on a table. It was also her own brain, and it was like strands of cheese. The image, however, made sense. It referred to how she had dissociated during abuse, how her brain was programmed, and how she was made to obliterate her own thoughts. Whether or not this construction is true or false, the point is that it was readily available as a way of thinking, while in psychotic levels this is not the case.

The role of defensive idealization in the dynamics of the psychotic part is especially important. It is employed with extreme tenacity to block experiencing hatred and rage towards an object and to maintain an ideal self-image. When an analysand was working with her psychotic part and her idealizing defenses began to diminish, she dreamed of a blinding light that quickly shifted into total blackness. These opposites rapidly oscillated creating fear and panic and causing her to attempt to restore her idealizing defenses. Another analysand began to hallucinate having the teeth of a animal, and on several occasions, I have seen dream imagery, or actual waking hallucinations in which the analysand has animal claws. When these terrifying states are lived with and contained, that is, not acted out with another person in, for example, extreme anger, then the opposites in the psychotic part can transform. Inanimate objects become animate; cold-blooded animal forms progress to warm-blooded ones; and animals transform to have partially human form or speech.

A peculiar 'neither-nor' logic in the psychotic part can be discerned once the opposites in that part begin to take on a more meaningful form, one in which their status as anti-worlds begins to change and the opposites approach a compensatory function. This logic can be discerned as well in the depths of the borderline organization and is accounted for there by the existence of the psychotic part in this personality organization. For example, a borderline woman who had successfully worked through a number of defenses hiding the psychotic part, notably idealization, spoke of not feeling dead but not feeling alive. She said she did not feel full, nor did she feel empty. Instead, any quality was felt within a bewildering state of being neither X nor not X. This state of suspension ruled.

One often encounters this state of suspension most forcefully in the attempted recollections of incest among abuse victims. The person will usually be tormented by the question: 'Did it or didn't it happen?' or 'Am I making this all up?' But the point is that whatever occurred first emerges out of a psychotic sector, where the analyst can neither experience that it happened, nor that it did not happen. Suspension rules, a state severely opposed by paranoid mechanisms which cannot tolerate ambiguity. Yet the analyst must be able to contain the question of whether it happened or not by tolerating just such a state of ambiguous suspension.

As a result of the split and incompatible opposites within the psychotic areas, people with strong psychotic areas tend to create double-bind messages in their communications. And reciprocally, psychotic areas are frequently formed as a defense against being the object of double-bind messages.

Trauma plays a major role in the formation of psychotic areas. Over time, such areas can become 'places' that the ego regresses into to avoid the pain of a young part that retains the memory of trauma. For example, a woman began to encounter her fear of expressing any needs. But this fear was of such proportions, and based upon a continual trauma with her mother, who was actually psychotic at times, that whenever she began to experience her need for my support, the field between us quickly fragmented, and I could barely concentrate on anything she said.

Out of the state of apprehended opposites, a person can learn to respect the existence of the psychotic part and can change accordingly. Psychologically a sacrifice is involved, an awareness of being limited by its existence. In analysis, the therapist must submit to the state of being limited, especially by the 'neither-nor' logic and extreme splitting in the psychotic part, states of mind which thoroughly challenge any of the analyst's feelings of omnipotence. But through this acceptance of limitation, a sense of an inner structure of self and an inner life of soul emerges for both analyst and analysand. Furthermore, both analyst and analysand can learn how living near the energies of the psychotic part has a strange capacity to open the heart, to create a heart-centered consciousness in which the imaginal realm is a powerful psychic reality and a means of 'seeing' that was previously foreclosed.

The psychotic part and the transference it creates can thus be gathered up. To achieve this relative stability, the analyst must work through repeatedly the dynamics that I have been enumerating, for the Mercurial nature of the psychotic part can induce attention and consciousness to slip away from the turmoil and depth of this area. But continual effort will often lead to a relative stability in accessing this part of the analysand, a state that depends not only upon the archetypal dynamics of the psychotic level but also upon the analyst's willingness continually to access his or her own psychotic states of mind. When the transference and countertransference are gathered up, the analysand will experience a degree of containment so that a deeper nature of the psychotic part may be faced.

In the course of this gathering procedure, analyst and analysand can experience not only being emotionally overwhelmed but also states that can neither be called mental nor physical. Rather they are both, and are most poignantly known in a sense of pain that feels boundless. Many experience this pain in the chest area, as a state in which the Other – person or god – is absent. Instead, there is nothing but an agony of dread, an experience which borders upon non-experience and leads many to believe that they are, in this awful inner hell, afflicted by unassimilated feelings and perceptions of a lifetime. These non-metabolized states occur with no images, just pain and terror at their seeming endlessness. This level recalls Jung's notion of the psyche as extending along states bounded by the 'psychoid level,' a spectrum defined and limited by a red end of instinctual and somatic process, and a violet end of mental and spiritual process. At the psychotic level, these opposites combine or were never separate.

When the psychotic level is sufficiently gathered up, it becomes evident just how an absence of bonding opens the gates to the terror of this level. To say that

this absence 'causes' this level to exist is wrong, because such domains are archetypal, prior to creation in the sense of temporally acquired structures or the
absence of what should have developed. But bonding problems are especially
evident in terms of the lack of containment that the psychotic level ushers into the
ego's awareness.

My experience has been that a quality of special importance that comes into
play as a result of bonding problems is a very deep masochism. The person
reacts to the black hole of psychosis (Grotstein 1990) with a black sponge of
masochism. To counteract the void of bonding, the person bonds with everything
that he or she feels as wrong, whatever wrong might be. Everything from the
slightest shifts of interest or attention on the part of the object, real or distorted
through paranoid process, to outright attacks of guilt by the object are absorbed
on a very deep level. This is a core phenomenon of the psychotic part, and one of
the horrors of this dynamic is that it proceeds quite autonomously. To denote this
level of masochism as dominated by the 'scapegoat' archetype is inappropriate or
is a kind of word-magic that blunts the horror of the fact that at some point, we
are all sponges for anything we perceive as dark or wrong. The person with a
strong psychotic part is ruled by this state to the utmost. He or she bonds through
this masochistic quality and does not feel contact with another person. The pain
of non-contact takes its place. To bond in a genuine way would mean to trust
another person at this level, a state that is totally alien and only becomes an image
and a possibility once the psychotic level has been exposed and contained.

Through the affects of the psychotic part, not only are object relations distorted but also ego boundaries can rapidly change so that a person may feel that he
or she is taking up all space, or no space at all. To avoid totally losing a sense of
self, the analysand may cut or abuse himself or herself or act in other self-destructive ways. Feelings of catastrophe can have a chronic, often low-level background
form, breaking through in shocking ways, such as believing that anything one says
will be totally destructive. To feel needs of any kind can be tantamount to feeling
threatened with being killed. Under the impact of the psychotic part, the transference can become psychotic. For example, the analysand can believe the analyst is
the envious or otherwise destructive parent. To the analyst, a central feature of this
transference is a sense of the analysand's bizarreness when his or her psychotic
part is activated.

EXPERIENCES OF MADNESS

The experience of psychotic transference is fleeting and easily dismissed by both
analyst and analysand. For example, a male analysand who suffered from a life-
long complaint of anxiety, fear of intimacy, and a lack of fulfillment of his innate
talents presented psychotic material in which annihilating opposites created considerable confusion for me. In a session, as I tried to concentrate on him, my mind
not only wandered but also became blank when I attempted to re-focus on his
communication. I retained very little from this exchange and found it impossible
to maintain a linear, discursive process of following his thoughts. In distinction

to dissociation that is neurotic, in which one wanders off into fantasies or thoughts that are coherent, in this psychotic level my thoughts were shredded into incoherence, and any causal sequencing was extremely difficult. If I made a supreme effort to concentrate and tried to pull my mind together, I found my thoughts becoming so dense as to render them meaningless. While in this instance I did little work with the disordered state, my own or his, and basically allowed it to oscillate in a rhythmic way, with areas of clear narrative punctuating the chaotic episodes, he benefited from seeing that I was indeed affected by him.

In another session, the same kind of fragmentation began, and this time I was able to stop my own dissociative process and noted that my analysand was also in a strong dissociative state. He likened this state to what always occurred with his mother. I then suggested that he might paint or draw this state. To this suggestion, he stiffened, and in a manner that was highly uncharacteristic for him, he became antagonistic. The field between us was suddenly hostile. I inquired about this hostility, and he said that asking him to do anything reminded him of his mother. But something more was at stake. I had suggested to him that he do some drawing, that is, actively encounter this area on his own, for it did intrude into his daily life. For a brief instant, he lost a sense of who I was, and he believed that I was his mother. When he regained his sense of who I really was, he became terrified. It was clear that his dissociative process, which literally destroyed his capacity to think, was itself a defense against this more bizarre background state in which objects lost their reality as they were assimilated by his internal maternal image. Through actively engaging these mad areas, gradually, a sense of containment emerged, and his psychotic states diminished.

Generally, such chaotic levels of experience pass in time, often in a brief time, or else they remain a kind of presence that creates a haziness in the analytic interaction, a sense of a lack of 'thereness' of both people, even though a dialogue can be carried out, dreams can be interpreted, and outer events considered. A spectrum of such states exists, extending from a strong disturbance in the analyst's mind which prevents any focus during the session to a lesser disturbance represented by a kind of haziness within which one can still often function. These states are symptomatic of an area of madness that is more successfully defended against than that in the case of psychosis, but the madness continues to dominate the interactive field and can readily be denied by the analyst and analysand alike. The analyst can appeal to the analysand's more rational side, much as a scientist tends to look for regularity rather than chaos in physical systems.

The nature of a mad area is very ephemeral and difficult to capture and keep in one's awareness. For example, Nell, a female analysand who suffered from a life-long schizoid disorder, was presenting her problem in an analytical group session. At one point, one of the group members asked her about where her anger fitted into the picture she was presenting. 'I can't deal with that now,' Nell replied, as if she could not tolerate any interuption of her presentation. In response, another person in the group remarked: 'When you say that, I feel somehow discounted, as if you have suddenly totally taken over and I don't really know what has happened.' Yet another person in the group added:

I got so outraged at you last time that I really lost it. I don't know why I was so enraged, but for a moment I was totally out of control, and I felt and feel humiliated by what I did and said. All that I have been able to figure out is that, last time, I felt totally dismissed. It reminds me in a way of my father, but not quite. And I really don't fully understand my reaction which was so extreme, like I had a mini psychotic episode.

As Nell and the other people in the group reflected upon their reactions, I began to think over my experience with her, and I could recall feeling something similar in the way she was receiving these complaints, the ways I had experienced being discounted and controlled. I remembered times when she had said, 'I can't deal with that now.' At those times, for an instant, an uncomfortable strangeness to the way she had taken control existed, but I dismissed it in the context of her simultaneous plea to 'just go on' and not to deal with some issue that had arisen. I did not focus on how odd her comment was. On the one hand, she seemed to be pleading that she was so weak that she was easily losing the thread of what she was saying; on the other hand, she was dominating and determining what would and would not be discussed. But Nell's behavior featured more than just an inconsistency between weakness and strength, her 'I-can't-handle-this' undertone versus her 'taking-control, dismissive' attitude.

In the group, as I focused on her demand that we 'just go on,' something about her and what she was saying did not compute or readily metabolize. Indeed, a sense of the bizarre prevailed. I felt that a piece of the session in question became annihilated and, instead, a blank space came into existence. Furthermore, if as a group we now just went on as she wanted us to do, I felt that something had not been digested, as if a stone had been swallowed. Yet we all seemed to feel an overwhelming desire that this uncomfortable feeling and an accompanying quality of mental blankness would just pass. While we were all trying to sort through not only the experiences the aforementioned two people in the group had of Nell's behavior but also our own feelings and states, Nell suggested that saying seemingly dismissive things made her feel very strong. She added that at these times, especially, she knew that she had two parts to her: one, a terrified little girl; and the other, a very strong adult.

When she offered this idea, the sense of disturbing oddness started to evaporate, and so did any recall of the confusion of the previous moments. Now, it seemed, she had explained what happens to her, and once again we could go on. We could all recognize that we had a tendency neither to know how nor to want to explore further. But as the sense of oddness began to slip away, I managed to catch it, as if a departing spirit were tricking us all, and at least at this moment, it had not succeeded in flying the coop. The initial reflections by the two people had set the stage for apprehending this trickster-like spirit, even though by now they were happy to be rid of their experience of it, so uncomfortable was the group's experience of Nell and so much did it defy any known form.

Barely clinging to the awareness that had existed a moment earlier, I managed to bring back my sense of bewilderment. Then I recognized that it was not merely a matter of Nell having two aspects – a small frightened child and a strong, powerful adult. Rather, the weirdness was that these two qualities were fused together into a single unit. This fusion, of power and impotence, of weakness and total control, of fragility and a steely structure, of need and total rejection of need, had dominated the moment. And that these opposites did not combine nor separate was so very odd. Instead, a bizarre quality emerged, one that was so disordering to one's normal perceptions that everyone's tendency was just to let the moment pass. Capturing the moment in the group was extremely difficult: who wants to capture physical pain and disorientation in order to glimpse a fragment of the meaning of what is going on? Instead, we could each split our disordered minds from our physical pain: a stabbing sensation in the chest for me; a twisting sense in the stomach for another; and a twinge of nausea for still another group member. And in this mind–body splitting we could lose, in a second, the awareness of the ghost-like creature that had so briefly appeared.

Focusing upon this transient episode parallels what Renaissance alchemists spoke of as 'fixing' Mercurius, the wild, wily, impish, and demonic creature that flits about from person to person, wreaking havoc yet being the source of redemption from any old, stuck consciousness. For our group situation, 'fixing' Mercurius meant gathering up both a sense of physical pain and a mental confusion and blankness. Only then could the bizarreness of the moment be captured.

And only then could we get hold of a paradox in Nell's – and also, the group's – life. To the degree that we succeeded in 'fixing' Mercurius, we could apprehend how totally incompatible qualities can combine, albeit in a very strange and meaning-annihilating manner. In alchemy, the apprehension of this destructive paradox becomes the door to its transformation into a creative paradox. Alchemists drew pictures of their hermaphrodites as negative, energy-degrading, and disorder-creating states of mind that could, however, transform into a positive hermaphrodite which represented a new and transcending order. In the negative hermaphrodite, the two opposites never fuse or merge into a symbolic third state. Instead, the opposites retain their separateness like two separate halves stuck together. In the positive hermaphrodite stage, a true transformation occurs, and the Two becomes a Third. A goal of the alchemical *opus*, not easily achieved, requires that an individual go through the very confusion, the alchemical chaos, which was the *sine qua non* for transformation, and which we glimpsed in Nell's bit of madness.

Nell, in her somewhat cavalier way, had been carrying this element of madness for all of us in the group. Now we had the chance for each person to see such states within him or her self. The person who had become so very enraged at feeling discounted, for example, had to come to grips with the fact that she got so angry that she essentially had a brief psychotic episode in her own life. For a moment during the incident, all reality as to who Nell was vanished for her. She could begin to see not only that she had been triggered by being discounted but also that the bizarre way in which it was done uncovered a somewhat mad area in herself. People facing such areas tend to get frightened, for areas of madness attack any sense of order and meaning; and often one's defensive response is to get very angry. In turn, this anger gets acted out or is masochistically turned against oneself. It is rare that someone who is the object of another's mad parts, in turn, will look at his or her own madness. However, in this group, this dynamic could now be looked at by anyone open to such exploration. But this exploration depended upon holding on to the elusive sense of madness, the sense of the strangeness that had – like the mad god Dionysos – entered the group. Entering a province unbidden, Dionysos can purify those who accept their madness but becomes dangerous for those who reject him. Thus, the group had experienced a kind of visitation by the god of madness. We could reject it by simply denying its existence or by making too simple an order of it – only recognizing that two states were present. In fact, this denial had almost happened when Nell told the group that she knew that she had two parts. Suddenly, the bizarre nature of the moment changed, as if this quality had never existed.

Capturing such moments is extremely difficult. If Nell had not been willing to participate in the endeavor of going back to the strangeness of her communication, then any attempts to do so by the group members would have been experienced as persecution. But the wily nature of her mad sector was surely still untamed. We all began to proceed with the group session when she asked the group to point out whenever we experienced her in the ways we had been exploring. Once again, a tortuous strangeness seeped into the room. We could and wished to avoid it through splitting, but the group managed to try to hold on to how Nell's new request felt strange. By now, everyone was quite weary. Asking her if she really wanted to continue this exploration seemed somewhat futile. We felt as if we were chasing our tails. Tremendous confusion was caused by the fact that her seemingly rational request was accompanied by an overwhelmingly irrational feeling (that we all shared) that she was totally unwilling to explore what she asked for. She tried to help and ended up saying: 'I know I have these two sides.' At which point, her statement even became funny. Now, she also could see that far more was going on than she could apprehend at the moment.

What can be gained by such an exploration? To use an alchemical metaphor, had the elusive Mercurius simply escaped, once again? Might we have been better off having allowed the splitting to rule? My own experience is that the psyche is, at least at times, more generous than that. Holding on to mad moments, even though they vanish, and then regaining them, over and over again, does have a transformative effect. In a sense, the containment of madness, even briefly, creates something precious – a drop of an elixir – and as long as one keeps faith and allows that the process will dissolve and, with active effort, coagulate repeatedly, this elixir can have a powerful effect upon the chaotic level that has been so persecutory.

Attention to my own hazy and dissociating state helped a male analysand to enhance his capacity to recognize the limiting power of his psychotic area. This man was suffering from a series of failures in relationships and a growing sense of alienation. He began a session with the remark that he felt he had to develop a better relationship with one of his children. I received this seemingly admirable statement with a mental haziness within which I could easily have faded out of contact while allowing him to go on to another topic, as he was about to do. Within this hazy space I also tended to forget immediately what he had just said. Prior to this session, the analysis had uncovered his psychotic sector which had been previously concealed by his considerable suffering, splitting defenses, intelligence, and psychological acumen. But it eventually became apparent that when he was overbearing and ruthless towards others, for example, by pounding his ideas into his employees, he was actually functioning through a projection in which these people actually were his mother who had been psychotic in her lifetime. As a result of this previous work, I wondered if my dissociative tendencies with him were a sign that his psychotic part was perhaps behind his new-found concern for his children. So, I asked him why he thought he should repair his relationship. He was surprised at my question, for to him it was an obvious thing to do. But remembering our previous session in which he discovered his psychotic parts, he could recognize that his overbearing behavior, which cruelly failed to see his child's own reality over many years, had been largely responsible for creating the problematic relationship which now caused him so much pain. When he gathered sufficient courage to be able to recognize that his psychotic parts were still quite enlivened and barely integrated, he had to conclude that such repair was far from easy and probably, at least for the time being, delusional. This awareness created considerable discomfort for him and anger towards me for helping this consciousness of his overbearing or narcissistic behavior to emerge. But this awareness also led him to realize how limited he was by this dark shadow quality.

He then had a remarkable dream that he had found a barely formed female infant. The child was very sad as she unsuccessfully tried to touch her ears. He picked the child up and helped her touch her ears, and when she did, she beamed with joy. The dream represented an internal repair of the capacity to hear, the very act that had been precluded by his grandiosity. This transformative act was facilitated by his ability to feel limited by his psychotic parts. Finally, through the experience of being limited by his psychotic parts, the grounds for listening to others emerged, and the sense of self that had always eluded him began to take root in his psyche.

CONTAINING DESTRUCTIVE AND DELUSIONAL QUALITIES OF MAD PARTS

Unintegrated mad areas can be very destructive. For example, a man attempting to build a career in the stock market began a session with me by speaking about his conflicts at work, and I soon found that I was in something of a daze. My mind could not follow him for more than a few seconds. I noted this state, tried as hard as I could to focus on him, and noted how I could not. I allowed this dissociation to go on for perhaps 10 minutes, grasping at areas of stability in his account, piecing together something of a narrative from these islands of clarity, and also noting how I was essentially confused about what he was saying. This confusion was characterized by my inability to remember who certain people in his narrative were, and I was not at all sure that I could say anything without betraying that I had not followed what he had just said. I could struggle with this confusion in a somewhat heroic fashion, working to subdue my own chaotic mental state, and in the process discern what he was talking about, but I seemed to fail miserably. Instead, I decided to focus upon what was happening to my mind in the moment. I realized that my mind felt as if it was being fractured. So, I asked him if he felt under an inner attack of some kind, and if his mind was being fractured into small parts creating a disorder as he talked. He readily acknowledged this inner attack, wondered how I knew, and admitted feeling ashamed of this, often chronic, experience.

So I had at least established that a very chaotic state existed between us, and surely one that often ran his own mental processes. I now took the further step of reflecting, to myself, about what opposite states of mind were present within his chaotic state. Within the fragmentation and mindlessness that dominated could I discern opposites? Asking this question directly of him helped him to become less chaotic, and he began to think about a relationship he once had.

He could now associate to opposite states with a past girlfriend in which they would have a violent argument, and then would feel sexually aroused and have sex. But it was not that simple, because the sex and the state of love he felt for a moment were quickly corrupted. It was as if the hatred he felt quickly contaminated the emerging Eros. He then could associate to similar conditions with his mother. He had never really felt a love that was just love. Instead, the love that he had felt was corrupt, vile, and not trustworthy as a positive feeling. Thus, by inquiring about opposites a kind of order emerged. I could now concentrate upon him, and he upon me. Some haziness still existed, but not nearly what had existed previously. As he became more mental in his reflections, the sense of chaos between us returned. There was this periodicity to the experience of chaos, one that was predictable in the sense of following from any mind–body splitting.

In a sense, I had gained a kind of container for his experience. Opposites existed, but while he was on one side, for example, feeling love, he could quickly and rather suddenly jump to another side in which love and hatred were merged. Then he could jump to feeling hatred alone, by recalling, for example, certain childhood experiences, and more order emerged, and even a sense of connection – Eros between us – and then a return to haziness as this faded. Were we, in the language of Chaos Theory, in a 'strange attractor?' Any slight shift in my attention caused whatever order that existed to blur or change. The entire process required a stillness. But it had a form, albeit one that must be discovered over and over again.

This analysand's mad area had a terribly undermining effect on his work as a stockbroker, and identifying and beginning to contain it led to the following awareness about his self-defeating behavior:

> If I take a profit, the market will reverse, and the next positions to enter will be bad. So, I have to hold my position even though all the indicators say I shouldn't. It's now clear that I should have gotten out earlier, but I didn't. I've lost. But I can't get out now, and I can't stay. To stay is stupid. Only a miracle could bail me out.

If the market was going down and he was 'short,' that is, speculating that it would go down further, he could function well because others, those in stocks, for example, were losing since they were going long. So, in going short, he was separating from others, in this case the losers. But if the market then shifted upwards, he could not change and go long, for this would mean joining with the others who were winning. Generally, the point is that he must be able to feel separate from others, 'to be an individual,' in his words. Only in a downturn of the market can he feel this individuality. So he might win thousands of dollars when the market was going down, but when it changed, he stayed with his short position, confident that the market would again go down even though every technical indicator that he believed in indicated otherwise. He was gripped by this stance, and always lost everything he had gained, and more. And nothing would stop him. Throughout he lost thousands of dollars. To change and go with the winners, to be one of them, for him meant to be like an employee, as did following his own system. 'Not me! I'm an individual!' he exclaimed, in a self-mockery that could not hide its bizarre truth.

This self-destructive behavior was run by his psychotic area. Within this sector of his being, he was tormented by an insatiable drive to be fused with his mother, and an equally powerful drive to separate. To stay with any representation of her meant death to him, for he was in an impossible state of yearning for what was never there, namely the love and carefulness that he needed to thrive. Instead, these were absent, and a rigid, power-hungry mother was all he knew. So he stayed fused, in his psychotic area, with an absence, and at the same time tried to flee this impossible state, always failing, always committing psychic suicide. In his trading, to go with a winning trend that included others was to join with them, which caused him to feel the terror and torment of fusion with an absence of love and with total subservience. Only separating was safe, and he separated at all costs, an act only accomplished through delusional beliefs and financially suicidal behavior. He accomplished this separation through a background sense of omnipotence and omniscience. He knew best; the rest of the investors were 'suckers.' And thousands, and thousands of lost dollars hardly made a dent in his belief system. To do anything that joined others, to devise a system that could work, and follow a trend that others were following, for him was the same as joining his mother. To separate, in any possible way, felt like an absolute necessity. While for many people, winning would be an act of separation, for him it could signify his subservience.

Psychotic parts cannot always be integrated nor will embracing them invariably lead to an integrated self. That would be a foolish, overly optimistic attitude, as the next example indicates.

A man who had many years of Jungian analysis and who suffered from years of sexual and aggressive abuse inflicted by his father often had remarkable dreams of the self. In one session, he recounted a very disturbing dream:

> I got a hold of a piece of radioactive black carbon that had an inner, red glow . . . As long as I moved with it, and did not set it down it didn't burst into flames. I wondered how long its life cycle would be. How long would it keep this heat? How should I dispose of it? I did not know the answer to any of these questions. It occurred to me that I could throw it into the sea, but I chose not to do this.

The carbon (the source of a future diamond), with its glowing, radioactive center, is an image of this man's self structure within a psychotic process, symbolized by the radioactivity. This instability is clear in the dream, for one cannot carry about radioactive material without being poisoned. This man frequently resorted to inflated identifications with a rigid, compulsive father-image for protection. The self was a reality for him only at moments and never could become embodied.

But even in less severe instances, when the analyst meets the psychotic sector in an analysand, both often wonder how anything healing can come out of experiences of overwhelming anxiety, terror, envy, confusion, and humiliation that continually reduce one to marginal functioning. This concern is always prevalent in any analytical process. But at times, dreams can tell us that we are on a positive track in spite of the presence of chaos in the analysand's experience (Schwartz-Salant 1982, 53–60).

During such a dangerous and frightening process, a woman who was filled with severe bouts of paranoid distrust dreamed:

> I must study and watch and take care of a woman who is crazy – she'll do things others wouldn't. There is a great sense of seriousness. I must see that she gets safely to the other side because she is mad and daring. In her madness is her daring.

The analysand's courage to risk exposing her paranoid madness in analysis, despite her fears of abandonment by me, was vital.

The psychotic part projecting on to another person or dominating the organization of the subject's inner world distorts reality. Usually malevolent images predominate and combine with qualities of a personal parental figure, often yielding bizarre objects that seem to defy understanding. When a person begins to integrate his or her psychotic part, that person's normal ego-consciousness expands, but in an unsettling way; for the ego knows that, in the area of its madness, it is not in control of its thoughts and behavior. The affective field of the psychotic part attempts to signal to the ego that it could act in very destructive ways within the delusion of being in control. In a sense, the psychotic part is an open wound that breeds delusion; but the ego's acceptance of the limitation both of its own consciousness and of its own capacity for control can produce a caring attitude for soul. As Lacan says, 'Not only can man's being not be understood without madness, it would not be man's being if it did not bear madness within itself as the limit of his freedom' (1977).

The next example illustrates the secret and murderous nature of a psychotic fantasy that tended to project on to the world and distort relationships. Such extreme contents are often very difficult to gather up into any kind of coherence because they do not fit the ideal image the analyst has of the analysand.

For example, after six years of psychotherapy with me, a man who was performing well beneath his capabilities in both relationships and work and who experienced panic attacks when he attempted to expand his horizons began to uncover levels of hatred towards his father that were based on extreme physical violence. These areas had been dissociated and the analysis had never previously succeeded in focusing upon them. When he was subjected to the beatings he would never cry out, attempting to defeat his father by dissociating from the pain. This process eventually became an inner splitting in which he denied the importance of the violence. It was somewhat shocking to both of us to begin to feel the terrible effects of his father's acts as they left him extremely distrustful of all authority figures. In his interactions with the world, the analysand always unconsciously changed the people with whom he interacted into his father. Forthcoming encounters with people would lead to insomnia and a nearly overwhelming anxiety that would disappear in the actual encounters, once reality prevailed and the psychotic-like projections diminished. This life-long situation was all the more painful since he was a person of unusual intelligence and creativity; but both of these qualities were only marginally realized in the world as a result of the psychotic, that is, reality-distorting nature of his father complex.

During one particular session, the analysand was referring to something his father had done to him, and I began to feel an intense anger towards his father. This anger was something I had experienced before and was able to use to help him to own his rage and uncover the violation that had occurred. But now repeating this process felt redundant, for I did not feel that finding any more anger would be fruitful. Rather, something else was involved. To describe how one gains the type of perception I had then is always very difficult. Gaining this perception requires a willingness to let go of 'knowing about' his rage towards his father or his rage towards me in the transference, and to become open to 'not knowing.' With this intention, a new perception emerged, what I would call 'seeing' processes in his psychotic area. The analysand not only hated or wanted to kill his father but under the influence of the psychotic area he actually believed that he had murdered his father. A deep secret within him was being uncovered: he was a murderer, not just a man filled with rage and a desire to annihilate his father.

I found it very difficult to see him as a murderer. But it was critically necessary for him that I see and understand that he carried this dark secret, and that he structured his life in ways to avoid seeing it or having it seen. This perception was accompanied by the feeling that, for the moment, he had become a stranger to me.

In this case, the difference between psychotic splitting and neurotic dissociation is evident. The psychotic content, that he actually had murdered his father, was not defended by neurotic dissociation. Rather, the psychotic content belonged to a deeper, more primitive level – which the alchemists depicted as the lower waters of the Mercurial Fountain, the first woodcut illustrated in the *Rosarium Philosophorum*.

Enormous difficulties are created as a result of this kind of distortion. For example, it becomes possible to believe that instances of actual physical violation only seem real to the victim because of the strength of such inner, psychotic distortions. For this analysand, 'his murder' of his father was as real a secret as an actual murder would be. Likewise, psychic incest to a victim can be as real as actual incest. Hence, both analysand and analyst can easily become confused as to what actually happened. One can then say that all that matters is the inner fantasy, since it is so powerful. Unfortunately, such a reduction is not useful, for if something actually happened and is denied, the events take up residence in a psychotic area: the person is made to feel crazy. One must thus recapture the true perception and history as much as possible in order to diminish the power of the psychotic area and the need for splitting defenses which continually weaken the person.

I always saw this man as competent, collaborative, open, and courageous. Yet during the analysis, he only seemed to develop in the smallest increments that were not commensurate with the way I – and everyone else in his life – saw him. Was this positive sense of him a seduction, a result of the way he wanted to be seen, as an opposite to the murderer? I saw him as totally honest, someone who could always be counted upon to be truthful or to try to be truthful. I held him in very high esteem. He actually did have these qualities. In retrospect, I have known these qualities in others with a strong psychotic area. But was this way of seeing him a countertransference reaction that represented a mirror of the way in which he saw himself? Had he learned to see himself this way in lieu of the opposite vision that always lurked within him? This narcissistic self-image proved to be only one opposite within a psychotic sector: the other total image being the murderer.

Prior to this session, my work with him was characterized by a quality of disintegration which made my attention wander and fragment unless I held fast to perceiving the quality of annihilation that worked upon my consciousness. Staying focused upon any perceptions that I had of him was short-lived. My perception would switch to another focus, and in the process, remembering what had previously occurred was extremely difficult. An act of will generally failed, and I regained my memory of what had happened only when my previous perception oscillated back into my awareness, as if of its own accord. Then I lost memory of the previous state. Yet when I imaginally saw his deepest secret – that he was a murderer – this oscillation vanished. Typically, whenever I lost sight of this vision of his madness, the oscillating dissociative dynamic of anti-worlds returned.

To uncover delusions within psychotic areas is often critically important. For example, having ended an affair, a female analysand had no other relationships for several years. This situation seemed strange because she was attractive and had never gone for so long without some relationship. In the course of the analysis, she revealed that she was holding on to a delusional belief that the relationship had not really ended and that the man would return. In the part of her mind associated with her psychotic area, she was still with him. Furthermore, in the same delusional way, she was still with her father. The totality of such a belief is so odd as to cause the analyst to see it as a metaphor rather than as a psychic fact, as a truth that the person does not question, yet also does not raise into consciousness.

The analyst must learn to look into areas of chaos and attempt to provide/discover the kind of container allowed by the dynamics of those areas. This act is an essential prerequisite for change, for the psychotic area is often the *prima materia* and holds the key to transformation. It is, thus, often necessary to approach chaotic areas when they are background issues, never completely dominating a session nor completely fracturing a narrative.

The problem that then presents itself is how one contains chaotic states of mind. Are these contained by another person's imagination, as in a mother's reverie upon her infant's distress? Or is another kind of vessel required? Experience shows that the 'third area' as an interactive field can be an extremely creative container through which the inner life of the analysand and the perceptions of the analyst can be greatly clarified and the relationship between analysand and analyst deepened.

4   The dynamics of the interactive field

IMAGINAL FIELD EXPERIENCES

The affects of the mad parts of the personality have so strong an inductive effect that the individual ego of the analyst often cannot attend to these affects without dissociating and fading in and out of focus. Allowing the process between analyst and analysand to exist in a 'third area' is an imaginal act, creating in fact an imaginal vessel, that contains and allows for experiencing fragmenting parts of a personality without distorting their mystery through an analysis of ownership of contents and historical origin. The notion of an objectivity of process does not minimize the mystery of subjectivity. Nor does it minimize the danger of unrelatedness and loss of particularity that can accompany attempts to set out laws or objective patterns of the psyche's behavior. But I am not assuming an objectivity of process in the sense of scientific approaches to nature, for the objectivity of the collective unconscious cannot be known except as it is experienced by an individual consciousness. Nevertheless, that experience can itself be informed and deepened by an awareness of patterns that the collective unconscious appears to manifest within the context of any subjective intersection with its processes.

According to Jung and von Franz, the key to understanding the deeper dynamics of the 'third area' as a field lies in a qualitative view of 'number.' 'Natural numbers appear to represent the typical, universally recurring, common motion patterns of both psychic and physical energy,' writes von Franz (1974, 166). Jung employed a qualitative view of number in conjunction with alchemical symbolism to illuminate the deeper complexity of transference and countertransference. In so doing, he essentially laid the groundwork for the notion of a third area as a field between people and for the use of alchemical symbolism as representative of the transformation of energy patterns within the field. Implicitly, Jung recognized that alchemical symbolism is an excellent source of information about processes of transformation in the third area. More specifically, Jung and von Franz discovered what the ancient alchemists had recognized hundreds and perhaps thousands of years before them – that processes of transformation in the third area, or subtle body as the alchemists referred to it, can be seen as energy patterns which involve the interplay of qualitative numbers one through four.

The alchemical numerical proposition which especially pertains to field dynamics is called 'The Axiom of Maria.' Jung (1954, 1963, 1968) and von Franz (1974) have dealt with it, and I have also discussed it with special reference to the clinical issue of projective identification (Schwartz-Salant 1988, 1989). The axiom, an example of the qualitative logic of pre-scientific cultures, runs as follows:

> Out of the One comes the Two, out of the Two comes the Three, and from the Three comes the Fourth as the One.

The 'One' signifies a state prior to an established order, for example the Chaos of alchemy, or the way an analytic session is experienced in its opening phase. The alchemists speak of states of mind that are 'prior to the second day,' meaning before opposites have separated. This state of Oneness is experienced as disorderly and confusing. Only through the work of imaginally perceiving currents and tensions within it can opposites be apprehended.

The 'Two' is the beginning of making 'sense' of the phenomenon, the emerging of a pair of opposites. At this stage which most forms of analysis accomplish, the analyst becomes aware of thoughts or feelings, body states, or perhaps a tendency to wander mentally and to lose focus. Such states of mind can reflect the same states in the analysand. The analyst, depending upon the extent of his or her own self-knowledge, could then become aware of the induced quality, and could employ this quality for understanding the analysand's process. Another possibility is that the analyst's states of mind or body represent an opposite, or complementary state to the analysand's (Racker 1968, 135–37; Fordham 1969). In both instances, however, the analyst follows a movement of One becoming Two. In the case of induced projective identification, the analyst has achieved an awareness of syntonic opposites: the same quality exists in the analyst's and the analysand's psyches. In the case of opposite or complementary identification, the analyst experiences his or her psyche as containing one quality while the analysand's psyche contains the opposite. For example, the analyst may experience a tendency to talk without much restraint, and the analysand may feel gripped by a silence; or the analyst may feel depressed, while a manic quality dominates the analysand; the analyst may feel disgust or hatred, and the analysand may be filled with feelings of love and attraction. Generally, any pair of opposites may register in this way.

For example, the field's dynamics in a syntonic-like countertransference reaction may focus on anxiety. Whose anxiety is it – mine or the analysand's? I can wonder whether it is an introject, part of a process of projective identification, or my own. Does the anxiety stem from my psyche or from that of the analysand? The simple positing of this set of questions leads me to wonder if I am dealing with a pair of opposites of the same quality, manifested as anxiety. This pair of opposites would be experienced as consecutive aspects of a process in which the anxiety is alternately felt as my own subjective state and then as the analysand's condition. The differentiation of opposites into successive aspects of a process, on the one hand, and as two different 'things' on the other, dates back to the pre-Socratic philosopher Heraclitus (Kirk and Raven 1969, 189–90).

The 'Three' is the creation of the third thing, the field. Normally, in the analytic tradition, an analyst who has gone through such a process of reflection will come to a conclusion about whose anxiety is essentially at issue, as in the processing of projective identification. But the analyst has the option to suspend judgment and, as Jung describes, to have 'the opposites become a vessel in which what was previously now one thing and now another floats vibratingly, so that the painful suspension between opposites gradually changes into the bilateral activity of the point in the centre' (1963, 14: paragraph 296). To enter into this kind of process, the analyst must be willing to sacrifice the power of knowing 'whose content' he or she is dealing with and to imagine that the content (in this case, anxiety) exists in the field itself and does not necessarily belong to either person. The content, therefore, can be imaginally thrust into the field which analyst and analysand occupy together so that it becomes a 'third thing.' Jung (1988, 1495–96) has discussed such a process of 'conscious projection,' and Henri Corbin (1969, 220) has described it in the Sufi notion of *himma*.

As a result of this imaginal thrust and the conscious sacrifice of interpretation, the quality of the field perceptibly and palpably changes: the analyst can become aware of the texture of the surrounding space. It is difficult to describe more exactly both the quality of the change in the field and the feeling of inspiration that is present at such moments. The senses are enlivened as colors and detail become more vivid, and even the taste in the mouth can change. Analyst and analysand sense a feeling of an adrenalin rush or, in spiritual terms, perhaps the presence of divinity. So, the 'Three comes out of the Two,' not as an interpretation, but as a field quality. At such moments, analyst and analysand are both in the analytic crucible. Entering the analytic crucible and attaining the Three comes from the analyst's sacrifice of 'knowing,' that is, sacrificing the interpretation that one has achieved and continuing, instead, to focus upon the field itself.

The 'Four' is the experience of the Third as it now links to a state of Oneness of existence. After the field has become a 'presence' for both people, then each person, paradoxically, comes to be both inside this presence and simultaneously an observer of it. Continued intensity of concentration allows for something to change in the oscillating movement of the field. If the dominant affect defining the field were anxiety, one would have been feeling inside the anxiety and, alternatively, as if the anxiety were inside of oneself. Both analyst and analysand could feel this effect. When the sense of space or atmosphere changes, that part of the oscillation in which both people feel 'inside' the anxiety – that is, the experience of feeling inside the emotion itself – becomes a container pervaded by a sense of 'Oneness.'

In the movement to the Fourth, the alchemical idea that all substances (such as sulphur, lead, and water) have two forms – one 'ordinary' and the other 'philosophical' – can be experienced. In essence, affects cease to be experienced as 'ordinary,' as 'things,' and instead become something more – states of wholeness. While the question, 'Whose anxiety?' may be sorted out in this way, the answer is never the end result, but rather the answer is the Third on the way to the Fourth in which the mystery of containment comes to be known. Within this crucible, the analysand can experience, with the analyst, his or her anxiety concerning engulfment and identity loss. The attainment of this state makes it possible to recognize and feel how this experience might be a repetition of such fusion fears with the analysand's mother. In this way, the container enables the analyst and analysand to become both objective observers and participants in the affect which is present and enlivened, to experience the dynamics of the states, thereby providing the possibility to test the ways in which one has previously experienced the affect in one's life and the behavior patterns it elicits, and to explore a host of associative material which may have been stimulated. We thus seek the 'vessel' and the paradox of process, for the vessel alone can contain the mysterious, mad aspects of our being, indeed allow us to discover their mystery, and allow for a felt experience of the relation between the world known through 'parts' and their link to a larger sphere of oneness (Jung 1963, 14: paragraph 662).

The experience of the enlivened field as it unites the participants in the Three stage and opens to the transcendent in the Four stage was called the 'sacred marriage' by the ancients in general and the *coniunctio* by alchemists in particular. Experiencing it opens one to the sense of mystery that can be transformative, much as a vision or 'Big' dream can be fateful. The resultant mutuality of shared process represents a departure somewhat from Ogden's caution: 'Analyst and analysand are not engaged in a democratic process of mutual analysis' (1994, 93–94). While the asymmetry of the analytic process must never be forgotten, important times of a shared experience – such as when experiencing the transference is more essential than interpreting it – give the analysand more courage to experience fusion desires and fears. In this 'vessel,' the analysand can begin to see that a union process exists beyond death through fusion, that this process has an archetypal dimension, and that the experience of its *numinosum* has a great deal to do with healing.

At times, the analyst and the analysand experience totally opposite states. In alchemical terms, this experience can be understood as that aspect of the process in which 'the One becomes the Two.' To begin with, either or both of the participants in this interaction must consciously separate from the fused state (the One) and recognize the pair of opposites at work (the Two). Once recognized, however, the analyst can use this dyadic level of opposites to interpret the interaction.

For example, in the case of a woman who had great difficulty respecting her own artistic creativity, the Third was an awareness that she was re-experiencing, in the transference, her father's manic usurpation of her creative ideas. Since early childhood, whenever she would share with him any insights or ideas about which she was excited, he would not receive them, acknowledge them, or react to them as one would expect in a normal interaction. Instead, he would be triggered to free associate his own creative ideas, demanding her to mirror and idealize him and his creativity. In the interactive field, I would feel an impulse to perform, to demonstrate my knowledge, while she would sit feeling withheld and reluctant to reveal anything of value to her soul. We became aware that we were re-enacting the relationship between her and her father. And she became aware of her susceptibility to register such a dynamic as an actual re-experiencing of her father's desires to rob her of her creativity and the very fabric of her sense of self. This awareness was of great value, for it brought to life a terrible interactive process that the analysand had been repressing, but which had been affecting her whole life in significant ways. She either avoided creativity, or else became gripped by a mania whenever she attempted to allow her creativity to be expressed.

At another time, the analyst may, however, choose to forego such knowledge and to sacrifice it to the state of 'unknowing,' allowing the 'unknown' to become the focus. The analyst may then wonder: what is the nature of the field between us or what is the nature of our unconscious dyad? In this manner, the analyst and analysand can both open to the field as the object of their attention. In the process, the opposites, manic speech/silence, can shift, with the analyst now feeling in the grip of silence, and the analysand having one new thought after another. The awareness of opposites can oscillate, until a new center is felt, Jung's 'bilateral point'; and from this focus the field itself begins to enliven. The opposites, in turn, may show themselves to have been only separable fragments of a far deeper and often very archaic fantasy. The analyst and analysand may discover primal scene fantasies in which the manic speech is a sublimated form of a dangerous phallus, and the opposite, the silence, is a putrefied corpse, the remains of a body killed by envy. While such images may be historical in the sense of what the analysand unconsciously experienced through her father's fantasies and her reaction to them, the field itself has archetypal processes that are different from such historical levels, as important as these may be. For example, when the analyst and analysand 'see and experience' the affects and imagery of the unconscious dyad (each person in his or her own way), archaic and destructive forms of the dyad can change into more positive forms. This new dyad could be seen as having also been present in the father–daughter relationship. Instead of being merely a historically based interpretation, the move from Two to Three can become a new experience of the field.

As in the previous example, analyst and analysand can become subject to the field in the sense that giving up the power or knowledge about another person leaves one in the position of focusing upon, and being affected by, the field itself. This focus can involve experience of less archaic forms which can lead to liberating insights. One's subjectivity enhances the field, and its objectivity interacts with the analyst and the analysand. A different kind of Three then emerges in which the opposites are transcended. In effect, Three can be a union state, the alchemical *coniunctio*. At this stage, analyst and analysand often feel a current inherent in the field in which they feel alternately pulled towards, then separated from, the other person. This dynamic is the rhythm of the *coniunctio* as a Three quality of the field becomes the Oneness of the Four. 'The number four,' von Franz suggests, 'constitutes a "field" with an internal closed rhythmic movement that proceeds to fan out from the center [and] contracts back to the center' (1974, 124). Furthermore, the move from Three to Four is one in which a sense of finiteness is felt (von Franz 1974, 122). The level of Threeness does not have the felt boundaries of the Four. In a sense, the level of the Three calls out for interpretation as an expansive act, but perhaps also as an act that defends the analyst against the kind of intimacy that can evolve into the movement to Fourness. For in the movement to Four, the observer's 'wholeness' (von Franz 1974, 122) becomes involved, leading to the paradoxical sense of a subjective objectivity, and to a felt sense of Oneness.

However, in the case of the creative young woman's experience with her intrusive father, the analysand's psyche still contains the previous image of an actual or imaginal violation. How does this psychic condition change? Surely not by overlaying a new image or by recalling remnants of some positive fantasy life that also existed, for the negative, destructive fusion state is too powerful to be affected by historical recall of other states. Does a process exist that actually extracts, dissolves, or transforms the prior image, be it an engram of an actual, abusive history or an introjected primal scene trauma? In response to this question, field dynamics play a role in ways that especially differ from field ideas based upon subjectivity alone. Experiencing the field with its own objective dynamics, and being affected by this experience, is a way of transforming internal structures. New forms that create order in otherwise overwhelming and fragmenting psychic parts can then emerge.

Field dynamics also play a central role in the process of incarnating archetypal experience into an internal, felt reality. One may take the view that every child knows levels of the *numinosum* at birth and then loses this awareness to one degree or another, depending on how the mother–child dyad is able to contain its sacred presence. The mother is the first carrier, in projection, of the child's spiritual energy; but the child may know this energy even before the projection process occurs. Or, one may take the view that spiritual levels that have never been conscious to an individual in any manner can, nevertheless, break in from the collective unconscious. In either approach, one is often left with the dilemma of an awareness of the *numinosum* that is then lost to trauma and to the demands of life in space and time and to the inertia of matter. Yet this awareness continues to live in the unconscious, either as a level of 'paradise lost,' or as a spiritual potential that the soul innately knows to exist, with the age-old problem of its incarnation into a felt center of psyche still remaining. Experiencing the interactive field constellates the capacity to facilitate this incarnating process which, as Adam McLean explains, was the focus of the *Splendor Solis* (1981, 83).

In addition, it is also possible to perceive briefly an imaginal reality which seems to be a property of the field itself, which is like experiencing the time-quality of the moment. Analyst and analysand may become conscious of an image that is felt to emerge out of the field and to reflect the state of both people. Each person may offer his or her sense of the imagery of the field as each focuses upon it, as in Jung's conception of active imagination. The result may be like a 'dialogue drawing' in which a sense of the field is constructed from the imagery each person creates. Interpretation in the classical sense of relating imagery and affect to early developmental issues blocks this awareness of the field. Rather than interpretation, one experiences the quality of the moment in the field, sometimes verbalizing the experience and sometimes remaining silent. The active, conscious experiencing of the energies and patterns that can be perceived in the field, experiencing them in the here-and-now, appears to affect the field and to enliven it as if it were a living organism. Sometimes, the affects of the field are nearly overwhelming, and at other moments, to attend to the field is nearly impossible. Extremely chaotic states of mind (in either person) can make it very difficult to allow the field to be the object, let alone to perceive the field's imagery.

If we engage the field, we can become aware of a deep, organizing process of which we were previously unconscious. Analyst and/or analysand may sense or intuit this organizing process as ongoing, but not necessarily known in the space–time realm the ego usually occupies. The field has the paradoxical nature of being created through the act of submission to it, while also being an ever-present *increatum*, a process out of time. To enter the imaginal world of the field, one must give up ego control to a high degree, but not to the extent of fusing with another person and not in the sense of splitting one's ego into an irrational, experiencing-fusing part and a rational observing part. Something more is needed, a desire to experience the field in ways that may surely reveal the limitation of any conception one had of the state of meaning of a particular interaction, be it analytic or personal. Through faith in a larger process, one can often discover that the particular form of the field is actually far more archaic and powerful than anything one had imagined. This experience of the existing form, and the creation/discovery of new forms, can have a transformative effect on internal structure and can allow new structures to incarnate.

THE DANGERS OF THE INTERACTIVE FIELD EXPERIENCE

The alchemists often said that their 'elixir' or 'stone' was both a cure and a poison. Likewise, the field as a 'third thing' with its own objectivity can be a blessing or a curse. We should be aware of four specific dangers inherent in applying this interactive field approach to relationships.

Avoidance of the *nigredo*

The interactive field creates a wide spectrum of states that can range from experiences of an intense erotic current and desire for literalization to states of emotional and mental deadness and a total lack of connection. Since these latter states are so problematic for the pain they create and the wounding they inflict – especially upon the analyst's narcissism – their opposite, in which erotic currents can appear to create intense fields of union and a deep knowing of the other, become extremely seductive. The analyst can choose to focus upon these highly charged states in avoidance of the emotionally dead ones by, for example, recalling pleasantly connected past experiences and/or unconsciously imagining such experiences. Such acts have a strong, inductive affect, and they may be used to avoid feeling the dark states of mind that generally follow the *coniunctio*.

Failing to assess the structural quality of the unconscious couple

The *coniunctio* that forms from the unconscious psyches of both people can possess either a positive or negative nature. Jung recognized that the experience of the *coniunctio* can lead to the creation of kinship libido (1954, 16: paragraph 445) which goes beyond the transference illusion. The problem is that many forms of the *coniunctio* exist, and while a field of desire may accompany a number of them, the erotics of the field cannot be properly assessed without an awareness of the structural quality of the unconscious couple comprising and defining the *coniunctio*. For example, the *Rosarium Philosophorum* depicts a couple – the 'King' and the 'Queen' – participating in the act of coitus. But an earlier alchemical text, the *Turba Philosophorum*, depicts a couple – a dragon and a woman – intertwined in a violent fusion state leading to death. The passion accompanying this image does not have the modulation and control of the passion represented in the *Rosarium*. In both cases, the erotic quality of the *coniunctio* must be seen as a field quality and not as something to own or identify with. In clinical practice, as in relationship in general, one often finds that more conscious, loving connections, while genuine, are also ways of covering up a far more dangerous fusion field. Just as sexuality can hide anxiety in the transference, sexuality can hide the monstrous nature of an unconscious couple.

In this connection, I have been consulted occasionally by analysts about cases years after their completion. The analysts reported that, although the treatment ended in a seemingly good manner, they were intermittently contacted by their previous analysand who reported feeling tormented by tenacious desires connected to the analyst for years afterwards. It became clear that these analysands were suffering the pain of not having actually lived out the erotic energies of the *coniunctio*, which would have resulted in a far worse situation. But it was crucial to these analysands that the analysts involved recognize and express that they, too, suffered the sacrifice involved in maintaining the focus on the higher good in the necessity of maintaining boundaries. The analysts had done a good job as far as boundaries were concerned, but their countertransference resistance to feeling the pain of losing the erotic connection that they also had felt left the analysands in a terrible quandary. The analysts had split off these feelings, and in reality, the analysands were left holding all the pain, rage and despair of a union that could not be consummated. These analysands were only freed from this torment when they again had analytic sessions, and the analysts could acknowledge their own suffering over the same issue.

Mistaking the *coniunctio* as the goal of the work

The greatest danger of working within a shared field arises if the analyst believes that the *coniunctio*, the state of the union of opposites such as fusion and distance into a transcendent Third, is the focal point of the analytic process. In fact, the analyst's focus must also equally be upon the *nigredo*, the dark, disordering state that follows all *coniunctio* states. Alchemical literature is a mine of information on this point. All transformation, insist the alchemists, happens through the death and putrefaction which follow a union state. If an analyst knows this sequence and is willing to seek out and work with the affects of withdrawal, absence, confusion, deadness, and emptiness after a session that has achieved the I–Thou connection of a union state, he or she will usually be on a safe path.

One cannot emphasize enough that the *nigredo*, the death of structure and terrifying affects that are usually associated with the mad parts that surface, is the prized substance of analysis, as it was for the alchemists. Although a strong negative transference or countertransference accompanies the *nigredo*, the analyst could use the previous experiences of union as a way of avoiding experiencing intense negative affects and associated painful states of mind. For he or she may either attempt to recreate a union state or else to act out an anger at its absence by passively identifying with the dissociative nature of the field quality of the *nigredo*. Instead, its affects must be sought out amidst their mildest currents, which is not an easy task when the far more pleasant and even blissful state of union has just preceded them. This respect for the dynamics of the field, in which union states and the death of structure are encountered in succession, is the best guide to employing the field concept and to respecting its archetypal dimension. Countertransference resistance is the problem in analysis in general, but it is especially heightened in a mutual field experience. If the analyst will seek out his or her negative feelings after an experience of union with the analysand, or inversely, if the analyst will register such negative feelings and reflect that some level of *coniunctio* may have unconsciously occurred, then the *nigredo* may become the focus of the work.

In the special case when one is working with people who have been victims of incest, the *coniunctio* is especially problematic because it holds out so much promise for healing. As in the adage, 'the god who wounds is the god who heals,' the *coniunctio* experience can help heal the abuse resulting from incest, but only if the resulting *nigredo* is carefully managed. For victims of incest are particularly sensitive and allergic to feelings of betrayal and abandonment which are inevitably present in the *nigredo* phase. If the analyst is unable or unwilling to deal honestly with his or her inability to relate to the *nigredo* in its denial of empathy, especially with analysands who have been violated as a result of rape or incest, the analysand will feel terribly unsafe, and the *coniunctio* will have been experienced as no more than a tantalizing object, resulting in re-traumatization.

Failure to recognize trance states

A person suffering from a dissociative disorder – which is commonly found in people who have suffered the trauma of abandonment and/or sexual or physical violations – is always, to one degree or another, in a trance state. As the field approach itself tends to constellate a mild, hypnotic state, serious errors can be committed if one is not alert. Serious errors can happen not only through what one does – that is easy enough to proscribe – but through what one says and even through what one imagines. For the analyst's unconscious tends to be acutely experienced by the dissociated analysand, as if by an enhanced capacity for ESP. Generally, the dissociated analysand tends to take the analyst's statements in a very literal way while the analyst believes he or she is speaking in metaphors. This confusion is particularly dangerous when the analyst is sidestepping negative affects and can use the binding power of processes in the 'third area,' the interactive field, to split off these affects by forcing the existence of rapport where, in fact, the main quality of the interaction is a lack of connection. Only if the analyst is alert to the process of dissociation can he or she even begin to consider dealing with processes as an interactive field. Often years of work with an analysand must first transpire in which dissociative states are dealt with, and only then can the field be experienced with any measure of safety.

Once the dangers implicit in field experiences are part of the analyst's consciousness, he or she may more confidently open to the imaginal processes necessary to apprehend field dynamics. These processes within the field lie on a spectrum existing between spiritual and material life, opposites which manifest to the ego through what Jung called the psychic and somatic unconscious (Jung 1988, 1: paragraph 441).

THE FIELD KNOWN THROUGH THE PSYCHIC AND SOMATIC UNCONSCIOUS

A person's unconscious state can express information and experiences through mental, spiritual, and bodily forms. Jung referred to the mental-spiritual forms of expression as the psychic unconscious and to the bodily forms as the somatic unconscious. The psychic and somatic unconscious are complementary in the sense that they experience the same material but through different means. Indeed, in dealing with the psychotic states of otherwise normal people, a great deal of integration of traumatic material can be apprehended through the experience of body states as they affect the nature of the interactive field in ways that cannot be so readily seen through the psychic unconscious alone. When referring to the somatic unconscious, we may temporarily lose the structure and order of our mental gains; but we can restore the sense and truth inherent in the psycho-physical totality of an event or an experience. In this way, one can revive the awareness of the interplay and constant flux between the mind/spirit and the *soma*, which is essential to the re-establishing of a living experience of the field itself.

At the mental-spiritual level, that is, the level of one's head or mind, the psychic unconscious is experienced as images, patterns, causality, meanings, and history. The psychic unconscious provides us with the imagery of our mental and spiritual processes. These images necessarily bring order and *logos* which, by nature, parcel up the unified whole in order for our consciousness to function. We cannot begin to identify or to understand anything without a thinking process and its concomitant separating and partitioning effects. Through the psychic unconscious, the analyst can perceive disordering parts of the analysand's psyche as they affect the ego, thinking, and the cohesiveness of the analytical process.

At the level of the body, the somatic unconscious is experienced as pains, discomforts, tensions, constrictions, energy, arousal, and other feelings of embodiment. Being embodied means a particular state of mind in which a person experiences his or her body in a particular way. For example, one becomes conscious of one's body in the sense of becoming aware of its size. Along with this awareness, one has a particular experience of living in it, which is to say, one feels confined in the space of the body. This state requires a free flow of breathing that is felt as a wave moving up and down the body; then, one begins to feel that one inhabits the body. In this state, the body is a container, and one feels one's age. The condition of being embodied is an experience of a medium that exists between one's material body and mind. The alchemists called this medium Mercurius; others have referred to it as the astral body, the subtle body, and the Kaballistic Yesod (Jung 1963, 14: paragraph 635); and Jung termed it the somatic unconscious (1988, 1: 441). Alchemists and magicians from ancient times to the Renaissance believed that this medium was a substance felt within the human body but also flowing throughout space and forming the pathways along which the imagination and Eros flowed.

To be embodied is to experience the subtle body, and every complex, that is, a group of associations in the unconscious designated by a common feeling-tone and resting upon an archetypal foundation, can be said to have a subtle body. When a complex constellates, its body, to one degree or another, takes over the body of the ego. For example, a male analysand having difficulty feeling his own autonomy was unusually spirited and clear at the outset of a session with me, and he stated metaphorically: 'Today I woke up in my own house.' He went on to explain that usually he awakes 'in his mother's house.' He was using this metaphor to express an experience of losing his own body-awareness; instead he felt engulfed in his mother's body image or that body image constructed by their interactions during his childhood. When he awoke 'in his own house,' in his own body, he felt certain business problems in his life as issues to attend to; when he awoke 'in his mother's house' these same problems were felt as overwhelming and persecutory. His behavior would then take on an 'as if' quality, in sharp distinction to the clarity and strength he manifested when he was 'in his own house.'

The body of the complex has to be dissolved. This idea – which on the level of the psychic unconscious would be one of dealing with negative introjects that distort authenticity – is carried in alchemical literature by the phrase 'destroy the bodies.' For example, the *Turba Philosophorum* says: 'Take the old black spirit and destroy and torture with it the bodies, until they are changed' (Jung 1963, 14: paragraph 494). The 'old black spirit' is often the person's rage, shame, and paranoia that have been split off from awareness in the first year of life, and this split drives the person out of the body. Making contact with such powerful affects, felt as catastrophic to life itself, is often the only way to 'destroy the bodies,' to cease living in body images that carry alien qualities that block life.

Psychotic material impacts upon one's consciousness as if it were attacked by sensations or pieces without meaning and order. Wilfred Bion designated such material as 'beta products,' and he developed a theory of 'embryonic thought which forms a link between sense impressions and consciousness' (1970, 49). The problem of linking these domains was the focus of much pre-scientific speculation in the theory of magic and its philosophical underpinning in Stoic thought. But the theory of magic approaches this linkage differently. Rather than a theory of thinking, the alchemists and magicians focused upon a theory of the imagination. In a grand vision of communication on all levels of reality, they envisioned a subtle body of links through fantasy, linking fibers known as vincula or sometimes referred to as *pneuma*, that connected body and mind, people, and (depending upon the author) levels reaching towards planetary realms and beyond. But in all of these approaches, the imagination is the linking agent, for the soul's language is imagery. And most important, an organ – the heart in human beings and the sun in the Cosmos – operates as a central station that orients the process of transmuting sense impressions into consciousness. The heart is a 'cardiac synthesizer,' what Aristotle called the Hegemonic Principle (Couliano 1987, 9).

From the point of view of this approach, one could work on the issues of creating links and images to deal with psychotic states through the somatic unconscious. The analyst's inner, imaginal linking of opposites, which is felt as an element of relation within the field, would interweave with the analysand's less textured and connected fabric, with sets of broken relations. As a consequence, one might be working in this 'animistic' way, which goes back to the ancient tradition of magic, on the same issues that more modern theories such as Bion's attempt to address. But in the ancient tradition, the central organ of thought was the heart rather than the mind. From the embodied connection of the somatic unconscious, one actually feels a linking current between self and other, a current that has its own heart-centered vision.

Working through the psychic unconscious has a spiritual value and generates a capacity to find order and meaning in chaotic states. But working through the somatic unconscious is more concerned with soul, with a sense of life within and between people, and especially with the experience of the energy or life of the space of relations which both people inhabit. The attitudes that evolve out of working through the psychic unconscious are concerned with knowledge and how one achieves it. The attitudes that evolve out of working with the somatic unconscious are concerned not with projections and introjections but with experiencing relations. One must remain mindful, however, that the dissociated areas of someone we may be with or that person's mind–body splitting have an inductive effect which tends to drive us out of our own embodied state.

To the alchemists the linking domain of the subtle body was known as Mercurius. His qualities, enumerated by Jung in his essay 'The Spirit Mercurius' (in Jung 1967) are all qualities of the field of relations. This field is affected by the inner relations each person carries between opposites. Domains within the individual in which opposites have neither separated nor begun to join strongly affect the nature of the field. Also, the analysand's or analyst's mind–body splitting, often existing in reaction to psychotic areas in the analyst's or analysand's own personality, will affect the field.

In the quaternity model of the transference–countertransference relationship, the analyst's conscious–unconscious connection effects the same link in the analysand. But also, the conscious–unconscious link effects the unconscious–unconscious connection. And either person's resistance to the unconscious or to the experience of linking in a subtle body or relational field has correlated effects on the other person. Thus, the series of pathways Jung describes between the four points created by the conscious and unconscious of both people represent relations that can be activated, for good or ill, by either person, and their mutual linking can have a healing or detrimental effect on the relational field within the individual.

In this way, we can speak of an 'interactive field,' although we are not implying any normal causality by this terminology, any more than Jung is when he speaks of projections as projectiles that lodge in the spinal cord! Rather it is a phenomenological way of dealing with an experience, with the advantage that this terminology allows for a kind of visualization of the relational experience.

The field and perceptions that emerge from the somatic unconscious can be illustrated by a case involving a woman who was to have minor surgery. We had explored our mutual field to a considerable degree, generally from the point of view of the psychic unconscious. I found the way she spoke about her body to be remarkable. No matter what organic condition she was describing, I had a clear sense of contact with her. I experienced no dissociation, and furthermore I had a distinct sense that her body was healthy. This 'goodness' was palpable. I felt like a physician able to talk about any body function and organ with complete openness.

But when she spoke about sexuality in any way, or if sexuality was present in her dream material, this connected body sense totally left. It was as if any reference to or association with sexuality introduced another body image. Then, the sense of the space or field between us radically altered and became diminished in energy, dark and dull in feeling, and devoid of any sense of relatedness. The only connection between this state and the previous one that I had known with her occurred when I felt dull and dead in my own emotional state under the impact of the split-opposites in her psychotic part. But I never found it fruitful to explore my inner states with her in terms of projective identification. She always insisted that these states of dullness and deadness were primarily my own responses to the interaction with her. But when we eventually dealt with her schizoid states and her terror and humiliation at feeling such ego-weakness, it became clear that the deadness she felt in me (which I no longer felt at this stage of our work) was the way she experienced her mother at numerous times in early childhood.

This state of deadness was no longer in me but had become a quality of the field between us, which she could recognize. She felt as if her body had changed and that she had two bodies – one of flesh and another that manifested in dark and disordering ways when any libidinal issues appeared. It felt as if her subtle body were possessed by some dark spirit which could dominate our interactive field.

She then had a remarkable dream that she was wearing a dark, old nightgown and that she had to get up and begin her day's work. But she could not remove the garment, and no matter how much she tried it stuck to her. She thought of taking a shower, but she knew that would only make it heavier. The only way she could stop what felt like torture was to wake herself up out of the dream.

The terrible state in the dream was gradually clarified. Rather than understanding this image of the nightgown as, for example, the analysand's shadow, an embodied focus upon the field revealed a different view: the garment was her mother's body image, and it carried madness, depression and despair in response to the fact that her mother had been an incest victim. Her mother had consistently forced the analysand to identify with her throughout her life. For example, the analysand remembered how her mother would tell her that the two of them were alike in that they did not like men. While the analysand knew this was not true, fearing her mother's unpredictable violence, she said nothing and even agreed at times. There were numerous examples of such direct and enforced projections to which the analysand was unable to say no, for these projections were the only form of contact she had with her mother, and she also deeply feared her mother's rage if she dared to separate from her. So, the analysand literally wore her mother's madness in order to feel fused with her mother's body. When her mother's body image was enlivened in her, I was unable to contact her in any affective sense.

Because we had worked with the psychic unconscious and had established her psychotic sector and a sense of mental-spiritual self, we were eventually able to access this material. But the analysand could begin to take action to separate from the ego-alien factors that her mother's madness represented only by experiencing the somatic unconscious and by becoming aware of her 'two bodies.' She could recognize how this body state changed the field between us. I could be embodied with her now and feel the death and darkness that pervaded the field we occupied. And so could she. Only the body allows for a direct experience in this way. As Jung noted, we experience the unconscious through the subtle body in more direct ways, far more tangible than through the psychic unconscious.

As a consequence of this work, the analysand eventually was able to reject her mother's projections totally, even while experiencing how frightened she was of daring to accomplish this separation. This rejection was an astonishing act for her, and it was part of her eventual successful labor of taking off her mother's garment of shame and madness. This form of the subtle body also began to diminish in the field between us.

Working with the psychic and somatic unconscious, as the information from these forms of the unconscious manifest through the interactive field, has an inductive effect on each person's psyche. Projective and introjective processes transmit through the interactive field. In this transmission – an activity not bounded by locality or temporal process, and thus not characterized by usual notions of causality – the psychic structures of an individual transform. The alchemists speak of the rhythm of the dissolution and coagulation of their 'matter' as fundamental to transformation. As unconscious processes are perceived through one form of the unconscious, for example the psychic unconscious, this perception is registered as an internal structure, a complex. In turn, this complex implicitly is used to order and understand unconscious processes as they continue to manifest. But as these processes are then apprehended through the somatic unconscious, the unconscious structures of the created complex dissolve, and form again in another structure. Thus, moving between psychic and somatic unconscious is a way of following the alchemical maxim of *solve et coagula*, and in the process help create new internal forms and structure.

THE TRANSFORMATION OF FORM IN ALCHEMY

All schools of thought in analytic practice attempt to create new forms of internal structure. This emphasis upon a change in form especially connects psychotherapy to its roots in the work of fifteenth and sixteenth-century alchemists who prefigured the discovery of the psyche (Jung 1963, 14: paragraph 150). Kleinian thought (Segal 1975, 54–81) deals with a movement from the so-called 'paranoid-schizoid position' to the 'depressive position.' For example, a person dominated by the splitting processes and affects of the paranoid-schizoid position will often react with a rage that distorts reality in a given situation, while someone who has been able to enter the depressive position will experience the same situation with much more tolerance and a capacity to see the reality of another person's complaint. A Self Psychologist will be interested in, among other changes, the transformation of a sadistic superego into a benevolent, idealized form and the development of self-objects from primitive to more adapted forms. A Freudian will be interested in changes in ego development represented by a movement from an oral to an anal and phallic-genital stage, all of which represent different forms of psychic organization. A Jungian will focus upon individuation and its myriad of changing internal forms. And an Object Relations clinician considers, for instance, the creation of psychic structures acquired by passage through stages of separation and *rapprochement*. These schools of thought all present models which are representations of change in the structural form of the psyche.

The transformation of internal structure is the main result of experiencing the field's processes. Alchemical thinking about this process is revealed in the *Splendor Solis*. Second in significance only to the *Rosarium Philosophorum* as the centerpiece of Jung's study of the transference, the *Splendor Solis* deals with issues that complement the *Rosarium*, notably the problem of the embodiment of archetypal processes. The 'Preface' of the text is comprised of several treatises. According to 'The First Treatise,' which describes the 'Origin of the Stone of the Ancients and how it is Perfected through Art,' the form of the thing to be created, the 'Stone of the Wise,' can only come from Nature:

> Nature serves Art, and then again Art serves Nature . . . It knows what kind of formation is agreeable to Nature, and how much of it should be done by Art, so that through Art this Stone may attain its form. Still, the form is from Nature: for the actual form of each and every thing that grows, animate or metallic, arises out of the inner power of the material.
>
> (McLean 1981, 10)

By 'Nature' we can understand the psyche, and by 'Art' the conscious attitudes and techniques of analysis. Then 'The First Treatise' offers an especially interesting and unusually clear example of alchemical science:

> It should however be noted that the essential form cannot arise in the material. It comes to pass through the operation of an accidental form: not through the latter's power, but by the power of another active substance such as fire, or some other warmth acting upon it. Hence we use the allegory of a hen's egg,

wherein the essential form of the putrefaction arises without the accidental form, which is a mixture of the red and the white, by the power of warmth which works on the egg from the brood hen. And although the egg is the material of the hen, nevertheless no form arises therein, either essential or accidental, except through putrefaction.

(McLean 1981, 12)

From this passage, several key ideas can be extracted. First an 'accidental form' is necessary, and this form is a 'mixture of the red and the white.' This mixture alludes to the *coniunctio* of King and Queen, Sol and Luna, or in analysis, to the unconscious marriage of aspects of each person's unconscious, where one psyche contributes the active 'red substance' and the other a more receptive 'white substance,' with these roles also interchanging. The form is said to be 'accidental,' which means it is 'acausal'; its existence is not caused by any previous operation. The passage further says that the form emerging in the material being worked with does so without the power of the 'accidental form,' and with the power of an active substance, such as fire. By implication, the 'accidental form' that arises from the union of opposites does not necessarily mediate its properties through a phenomenon of energy. A similar idea in the theory of Rupert Sheldrake (1991, 111) concerns the creation and stability of form; and his 'morphic fields' are not transmitted by energy but instead themselves carry information. But how is the 'accidental form' still essential? The text answers that it is the precondition for the creative death of structure, the putrefaction that is the secret of transformation. An active process, expending energy, is also involved, as in the allegory of the brood hen's heat. This process is akin to the energy one puts into dealing with the generally intense negative transference and countertransference reactions described above, including tendencies to withdrawal and the mental blankness that often follow the *coniunctio* and which may, unfortunately, be ignored.

Alchemical science attempted to engage imaginally in a process that would encourage the creation of an 'accidental form' – the *coniunctio*. But psychotherapy, in essence, has treated the 'accidental' union state as a 'hidden parameter.' Jung (1954, 16: paragraph 461) notes that the *coniunctio* is usually only known to have occurred in a session from dreams that follow it. But even so, experience of the union state alone will generally not forge a new internal structure. Along with the union state, one must face and integrate some of the chaos to which it leads.

Through the *nigredo*, the alchemists attempted to purify themselves from the ever-present, regressive desires to identify with archetypal processes, such as the *coniunctio*. This purification, called the *mundificatio*, achieved through numerous *coniunctio–nigredo* sequences and thus through much suffering, was symbolically imaged by the death of a dragon, itself representing the drive towards concretization. It must be understood that such drives towards the concretization of instinctual processes are not only located in the subjectivities of either person. They are also aspects of the field itself, especially as it attempts to incarnate into space and time. Thus, not only individuals are changed, but also the field they occupy takes on new forms.

With an understanding of the properties that the background field manifests, we can engage its dynamics and be changed in the process. Change in the internal structural form of a psyche is created by repeatedly experiencing the quality of a moment in time and its meaning, much as one is affected by a vision.

While two people can experience the *coniunctio*, how they process it will vary as a function of their subjectivity. For example, two people – perhaps an analyst and analysand – may experience a union state. They may experience it directly as a 'here-and-now' state. Or while they may not consciously register its existence, the following night one of them, perhaps the analysand, may dream of a wedding. Furthermore, in the next session, the relationship between analyst and analysand may have shifted from one that was filled with a sense of connection to one that is dominated by an absence of relationship and even states of schizoid withdrawal and mental deadness. One analyst may understand this condition as a need to withdraw from the closeness of the previous session, because of the analysand's attachment disorder and resultant reaction to the prior connection. Another analyst may see the reaction to a felt connection to be a significant measure of an underlying schizoid or borderline quality in the analysand.

But an analyst who is focused upon a field dynamic will also see the state of deadness and withdrawal as a natural concomittant of the previous union state. He or she may recognize, from this point of view, that these dark qualities are not only representative of developmental failures, but would exist for any individual psyche that has felt the union state. Furthermore, the analyst would see this union state and the resulting *nigredo* as being part of the essential rhythm of transformation. In turn, he or she would provide a different relationship to these states, and to their containment, than would be provided by an analyst interpreting in developmental terms.

Rather than seeing the analysand's problems with the depressive position, with *rapprochement* issues, or with fears of engulfment, the analyst would note and experience the field dynamics involved. This perception can have the same kind of containing quality that exists in many cases of extreme anxiety when the analyst knows, from experience, that these states are part of a larger, potentially positive process. Accepted in this way, the *nigredo* can begin to work towards its purpose of dissolving old structures, especially introjects which do not accord well with the analysand's essence. In a sense, this is a process in which new forms are created in the analysand, perhaps in the analyst as well, and also within the space they occupy together. In this way forms that can contain and process what had previously been severely disordering affects can come into existence through experiencing the field and its dynamics.

Thus, how we think about fields matters a great deal. As merely a metaphor for a combined subjectivity, fields are useful in reflecting the analysand's history as it unfolds in the analytic process. But the idea of an interactive field can lead to wholly different ways of conceiving the analytic process when it is archetypally conceptualized through the combined subjectivity of both people and when, at the same time, its dynamics are understood to extend beyond that subjectivity.

5 The transformative power of the interactive field

IMAGINATION AND PROJECTION WITHIN THE FIELD

In 1916 C.G. Jung began to develop the concept of active imagination. In this approach, an image of a dream or fantasy is related to in an inner, imaginal dialogue in which one lowers one's consciousness and hovers between an alert conscious stance and fusion with the image (Jung 1960, 8: paragraphs 67–91). In this way, one can re-create a dream or fantasy and dialogue with an inner figure, thereby often achieving a remarkable transformative affect. Our inner life appears to respond to being seen and related to much as a person responds to empathy and mirroring, a point Jung made most forcefully in 1952 in his 'Answer to Job' in which he stated that man's consciousness of the God-image affects God's own consciousness (Jung 1969, 11: paragraphs 564–75). Generally, inner structure, responding to conscious attention, can change from compulsive and negatively aggressive forms into helpful and loving ones. Jung believed active imagination to be essential for any thorough analysis.

This emphasis upon the power of a focused and active imagination is a keystone of alchemy. Seeing something in a person, as Jung emphasizes, causes it to come into reality for that person (Jung 1988, 1: paragraph 616). By 'seeing' is meant an act of non-ordinary sight. It may occur 'through' the eyes, in distinction to 'with' the eyes, or it may occur as a result of unconscious perceptions mediated by bodily or emotional awareness.

The imagination was always a central concept in alchemy. In the first or second century, Bolos Democritus, believed to be the founder of Graeco-Roman alchemy in Egypt, related a parable of discovering the famous alchemical 'Axiom of Ostanes' by 'apostrophizing' the dead Ostanes, that is, dialoguing with his image to gain access to the mystery (Lindsay 1970, 102). Over and over again, throughout the centuries and most explicitly during the Renaissance, alchemical literature insists on a spiritually informed vision, that is one that emerges out of a relationship to the unconscious. The Renaissance alchemist Hogheland quotes the medieval Arabic alchemist Senior as saying that the 'vision' of the Hermetic vessel 'is more to be sought than the scripture,' and they both speak of seeing with the eyes of the spirit (Jung 1968, 12: paragraph 350). The Renaissance alchemist Dorn writes:

There is in natural things a certain truth which cannot be seen with the outward eye, but is perceived by the mind alone . . . In this [truth] lies the whole art of freeing the spirit from its fetters . . .

(Jung 1968, 12: paragraph 377)

This vision perceives structures that are not ruled by a principle of locality and its differentiation between 'inside' and 'outside.'

In his *Psychology and Alchemy* (1968, originally published in 1944), Jung reflected upon the psychological meaning of the statement in the alchemical work *De Sulphure* that the soul functions in the body but has the greater part of its life outside the body (1968, 12: paragraph 396). At the time, Jung interpreted this 'outside' condition to be the result of projection. However, upon further reflection in 1955, Jung writes in *Mysterium Coniunctionis*:

It may well be a prejudice to restrict the psyche to being 'inside the body.' In so far as the psyche has a non-spatial aspect, there may be a psychic 'outside-the-body,' a region so utterly different from 'my' psychic space that one has to get outside oneself or make use of some auxiliary technique in order to get there. If this view is at all correct, the alchemical consummation of the royal marriage in the *cucurbita* could be understood as a synthetic process in the psyche 'outside' the ego.

(1963, 14: paragraph 410)

Thus, Jung traveled a considerable distance in moving from an understanding of 'outside' as being limited to a result of projection to an understanding of the psychic 'outside the body' as being a region 'utterly different' from the contents of one's interior space. In essence, the notion of the interactive field in which the *coniunctio* occurs – somewhat like the alchemical *cucurbita*, the vessel of transformation – is a space of relations that is not understandable in conventional three-dimensional terms.

Psychologically, the analyst must include this broader concept of the field in conceptualizing the space within which all interactions take place if he or she is to create a container which is safe enough for an analysand's psychotic processes to be engaged. For example, when working with a psychotic transference, if the analyst experiences a dulled-out, dissociative state of mind, communication can be very risky because the relationship to the analysand may be marginal. Using conventional psychoanalytical approaches, the analyst may attempt to overcome this dulled-out state and may begin to feel that these reactions are all 'inside' his or her own person. But beyond the conventional approach, the analyst may then wonder if the feature of non-communication is also a quality of an interactive field between analyst and analysand, a quality that is not only 'outside his ego' in the sense of a counter-projection, but existing 'inside' a space which contains both analyst and analysand. In effect, the field appears to be characterized by two parts forming into opposites which inevitably annihilate one another within the psychotic realm. And the analyst may be more open to the mystery of the 'other' if he or she reflects upon being in this field with the analysand, with the affects and structural states conceptualised as field qualities.

As a consequence, the ideas, feelings, beliefs, and identity of both analyst and analysand shift to observations and experiences of the field, and they can envision the field as a 'third thing' that exists without their personal contribution to it. Or, they can recognize that these personal contents exist as projections that create mutual, intersubjective states, these contents being a 'third thing' which are felt independently of a field quality. One way to represent these alternate ontologies is to think of an outer form that has its own life or process, one that does not require projected contents for its definition. But contents projected are also part of the picture.

For any clinical interaction to be complete, the issue of analyst and analysand as subjects in the field must be combined with the issue of analyst and analysand as objective observers of processes within the field. This combination is the essence of an alchemical paradox, the so-called 'Enigma of Bologna,' analyzed by Steven Rosen (1995, 127) as an aspect of the alchemical vessel, shines a remarkable light:

> I am a body that has no tomb.
> I am a tomb without a body.
> Body and tomb are the same.

'I am a body that has no tomb' refers to the projection of contents without the containing space of the field. 'I am a tomb without a body' refers to the activity of the field itself without reference to individual subjectivities. 'Body and tomb are the same' refers to their paradoxical combination that can only occur as a state in between opposites within a field quality of relations *per se*. The mystery that analyst and analysand must encompass is that container and contained are the same. To experience this sameness, they must experience life between opposites; they must get to know this 'middle life,' the realm that the Tibetans call a *bardo* state and which the alchemists called the subtle body.

Generally, the imagination is the key to the entire alchemical *opus* (Jung 1968, 12: paragraph 394). And in this spirit, and extending Jung's use of active imagination as an internal dialogue, we can apply this act to the field itself. The conjunction of the imagination and the field proves to have a remarkable containing power.

THE INTERACTIVE FIELD AS A CONTAINER FOR CHAOTIC STATES OF MIND

We can best approach the complexity of an analytic interaction, especially when the disordering affects of psychotic process are present, if we allow the field itself existing between analyst and analysand to be the analytic object. Then, the analyst's attention attempts to hover within the analytic space; attention is not suspended evenly over the contents of discourse, or over the analysand's or analyst's inner world, but on the field itself. This imaginal process like the mysterious alchemical vessel, has a containing effect that allows us to process material which would be otherwise too chaotic and fragmenting of consciousness.

When an analysand's psychotic area is constellated – which is to say, when it moves from a potential into an active state – it affects the structure of the field created by the analyst–analysand dyad. The countertransference will be the ful-crum upon which the possible success or failure of engaging that sector hinges. But psychotic processes, hidden within otherwise normal functioning, are extremely easy to sidestep. Generally, only through actively engaging this field can the analyst gather it up within his or her consciousness and fix it into a form stable enough to allow its existence to be pointed out to the analysand in a man-ner that can be effective. Anything less than an act of volition will generally result in the analyst's attention wandering off into a dissociated state until the affect of the constellated psychotic area diminishes, and that area returns to only a poten-tial state. The countertransference then tends to recede into a hazy form, within which the analyst can perceive a lower yet significant level of dissociation and detachment. Such recession of the countertransference readily allows for the psy-chotic area to be sidestepped and its processes no longer to be perceived.

The most typical countertransference reactions which signal the constellation of the psychotic area and which, in turn, can alert the analyst to the need for a volitional act to engage the interactive field, rather than take the more instinctive, pain-diminishing path of withdrawal or dissociation, are: a fragmentation of his or her consciousness; a sense of the analysand's strangeness; and a concomitant tendency to foreclose experiencing the states of mind induced by the analysand's process by stressing his or her health and ego strengths.

While the psychotic area can manifest an intense fragmenting quality in the consciousness of the analyst and analysand, it can also manifest as a pair of anni-hilating opposites. For example, the analyst in the process of listening to the analysand may lose focus and have no recall of anything the analysand has just said. The analyst may mistakenly rationalize that this loss of memory is merely a result of being tired or distracted. Instead, the analyst is actually experiencing the annihilating quality of the opposites in psychotic process, which in turn has a very disordering effect upon the analyst's consciousness and identity. Beyond that, the opposites may combine, but they do so not as a symbol, but in a bizarre way which, in turn, produces a sense of strangeness. The analyst commonly tries to avoid this experience of the analysand and tries to regain the person generally known outside of such moments.

The analyst's countertransference reactions to the constellation of the analysand's psychotic area bear significant resemblances, albeit of a mild variety, to the states of mind schizophrenics describe at the outset of a psychotic break. In his *Madness and Modernism*, Louis Sass has described these incipient features, noting that European psychiatrists give special diagnostic value to the 'praecox feeling,' a sense of radical alienness that accompanies the onset of a psychotic break. In this state the analysand cannot describe what he or she is experiencing; all usual meanings and coherence vanish. 'Reality seems to be unveiled as never before, and the visual world looks peculiar and eerie, weirdly beautiful, tantaliz-ingly significant, or perhaps horrifying in some insidious but ineffable way' (Sass 1992, 44). Whatever the analysand experiences seems to defy communication, and a conjoint and contradictory sense of 'meaningfulness and meaninglessness, of significance and insignificance, which could be described as "anti-epiphany" –

an experience in which the familiar has turned strange and the unfamiliar familiar' reigns (Sass 1992, 44). Countertransference reactions to an analysand's psychotic area are not dissimilar to this 'praecox feeling.' They are surely less radical and less intense, but if the analyst actively enters into his or her own state of mind and tries to perceive the analysand's process, amidst intense dissociative states, the analyst often will feel a 'radical alienness' as well as a tendency to grasp at a meaning that then dissolves into incoherence.

The process of containing one's perceptions of psychotic areas has similarities to the logical pattern the analyst tends to follow for non-psychotic areas. But the analyst experiences a qualitative difference primarily through his or her countertransference reaction. When no psychotic area is constellated, the analyst will be capable of experiencing a state of suspending anything known, and allow the free flow of ideas, images, affects, and the inductive affects of the analysand's process to mix together forming what could be called chaos. And as the session progresses, the analyst will usually be able to process the countertransference, dreams, and fantasies into pairs of opposites, for instance of states of mind split through projective identification, or related to one another as a conscious–unconscious compensation. As a result the initial chaos, what may be denoted as One, becomes Two. This 'Two state' is generally comprehensible as two sides of a larger whole, and when they are combined through the analyst's imagination, they can lead to a new state: Two becomes Three, a state that can be an interpretation or an awareness of a symbol that combines the opposites. This sequence of qualitative numbers is part of 'The Axiom of Maria,' explicitly or implicitly found in centuries of alchemical thinking. In clinical practice, the analyst often stays within the first three levels of the axiom, but there are also clinical experiences, especially those which actively engage a field between analyst and analysand, in which the Three is a union state, the alchemical *coniunctio* that leads to a smaller or larger glimpse of a transcendent state of Oneness, now the Fourth of the axiom. But even without this movement in the here-and-now of the clinical situation to the Fourth, an engagement that leads to the Three as a new state can, in turn, result in dreams that further open to the Fourth as a larger, more encompassing or archetypal level.

Dealing with psychotic areas is different. One frequently will experience a high degree of fragmentation. But this initial, chaotic state – which often recurs throughout a session – can reveal a kind of order as a pair of opposites, even as these states of mind have the unsettling quality of totally destroying one another: the awareness of one tends to oscillate to the other and, in the process, to annihilate any memory or meaning of what had just transpired. The Twoness that the analyst can perceive in this instance is thus very different from what it is in normal processes, for each state does not fill out the other to create a larger whole, a third state. Rather, when the opposites combine, they create a bizarre object, a state that yields a feeling of being strange to oneself as well as a sense of the analysand being odd or strange as well. This mixed state tends also to be experienced as an inner deadness of thought, a state that is devoid of meaning and that does not produce a symbolic state. In psychotic process, this form of the Three can allow us to see more deeply, behind it, and to glimpse another state, the Fourth, which now is a terrifying Background Object. Rather than the One becoming the Fourth as a positive numinous level, in psychotic process, the One becomes something rather more demonic. There, we see the dark side of God. For example, we see images of abuse and abandonment so intolerable that they have become merged with deeply negative archetypal images which imprison the person in despair and hopelessness.

The interactive field can be remarkably containing of such chaotic states of mind. For example, another stockbroker consulted me about his difficulty with becoming disciplined in the market. Although he had the ability and intelligence to be a successful commodity trader, he barely survived economically in this endeavor. For him, the stock market was a 'self-object,' that is, the stability of his identity was tied to the upward or downward fluctuations in the marketplace. In analytical terms, he had a narcissistic character disorder. When I saw him, he was usually disillusioned, anxious, withdrawn, and despairing because he had failed to gauge the performance of the market accurately. In such states, he would tell me about his difficulties, but it would be difficult for me to listen carefully for more than a minute at a time, for my attention invariably wandered because he was so internally dissociated. Yet when I regained my focus and recalled what he had said, I realized that, had I read what he had told me instead of having listened to it, my attention would not have wandered. In effect, the affective field he communicated shrouded his narrative in fragmentation and boredom for me, and indeed, for both of us.

At the beginning of one particular session, I allowed my attention to hover within the space between us, and after a few moments, I began to imagine that we were in a violent storm. I focused on this image throughout the session, with the result that everything he said was easy to listen to and to empathize with. The storminess was clearly related to his envy and intense anxieties; yet to interpret them would not have been helpful. Seeing that the storm had a containing influence not only for me but also for him, at times during this session, I reflected aloud upon his life as a terrible struggle to survive storm after storm. He ended the session by telling me about a commodity trade that he had successfully completed in the stock market and about his hopes for the effectiveness of a new trading system he was planning to implement. He seemed to be unconsciously communicating to me that he felt more emotionally contained and more hopeful about embarking on a new beginning.

Another example of how the field was useful in containing psychotic processes concerns a woman with whom I had already established the existence of a strong psychotic part. At times, I had managed to perceive her psychotic part as violently attacking her, or I had helped her to see her inner distress as a result of her own pent-up fury and paranoid process. But this psychotic part still lacked any container. Then, I attempted to focus upon the field between us, even though my attention tended to fragment under the impact of the psychotic material. She began speaking about her boyfriend and aspects of his behavior that caused her concern. After she finished, she characteristically asked if her worries were 'crazy.' Even though the allusion to the transference was clear, I did not focus on it, for that would have foreclosed the field experience. Instead, I explained that I found her thinking to be clear yet did not know why she felt so much anxiety and fragmentation. Throughout this experience, maintaining attention on the field between us was like being lost in a fog. Still, I could attend to her process with some consistency. The sense of a fog between us remained until she told me about her dream involving a man who, to her surprise, was able to control her mother. In reality, the mother could be psychotic. Again, noting but not interpreting the transference, I began to realize that perhaps the field between us was dominated by her mother's psychosis. The analysand had incorporated this psychotic process which, in turn, lived within her as an alien factor and dominated the field between us. If I tried to listen to her, this madness fragmented both my thinking and hers. Attending to the field as the object seemed to help, as she ended the session in a way unusual for her: speaking about strengths she knew she had.

These brief examples illustrate what I mean by attending to the field as an object. Usually, the field between two people, at the outset, will be felt as empty, like a modern scientific notion of space. If the analyst attends to the interactive field as the object, which means that he or she has the courage to carry out this seemingly absurd act – imagining into empty space and assuming something may be there – the analyst may find that the analysand's form of communication becomes more cohesive. The space may then cease to feel empty. A clear image of the field process does not necessarily appear, but often the analyst and analysand can imagine a sense of texture and fullness, or a sense of fragmentation and torn fabric. Clearly, these are but two of the endless possible metaphors for the experience of the interactive space.

When psychotic processes are constellated, the field is extremely difficult to focus upon as the analytic object. The field is present but like the psychotic or mad area itself, it is not contained and has no working or workable structures or images. The experience of this kind of field is dominated by broken links and by extreme affects, notably deadness, and meaninglessness. At times, the analyst can process such material through projective identification, and this activity can have a containing effect which, in turn, allows the field to become the analytic object.

For example, an analysand entered my consultation room, threw down her purse and briefcase, quickly walked to a corner of the room, and sat on the floor. As I looked at her, I sensed that I had better say something or she would explode, as she had done in the past. Feeling unnerved by this possibility, I tried to hold my ground and wait until I could perceive something more spontaneous and pertinent to the moment. But I lost containment for a moment and began to combat her intense despair and self-pity over losing her job with an exhortation that she should not act out her hysteria. Yet I too, for the moment, had become hysterical. The air was tense, and a feeling of containment was absent. Then, I began to reflect upon my feelings. I wanted to get rid of her. I wanted her to stop asking me to fix her life. I wanted her to get well and become more optimistic. It was clear that I had become her mother. At that instant, she said: 'You're just like my mother.' And I replied: 'That is what is being created here, a situation in which you are not contained and are treated as a terrible problem.' By virtue of having processed the projective identification (of her mother image), I could make this assertion and thus radically change the environment. She was no longer over-whelmed, nor was I. She sat down on the couch and the session progressed with-out her acting out or my acting in behavior.

In this case, this session initiated us into work upon her psychotic part. Having never engaged it before, the interpretation through projective identification was necessary to establish some way of approaching the disturbed field. By focusing upon the field as the analytic object, we could gain both a sense of containment and the imagination or perception that made it possible to perceive imaginally a 'front–back' split in the analysand, with a strong background component of a split-off exhibitionism. As part of an imaginal act to contain her psychotic parts, I encouraged her to portray her exhibitionistic fantasies through painting and to share these drawings with me. Engaging her unconscious material in this imagi-nal way helped to diminish her level of psychotic fragmentation.

By focusing on the interactive field as the analytic object, the nature of the psychotic transference and countertransference, which is ever so subtly acting behind the scenes, can fall into view, as can the 'front–back' split that often tends to hide the psychotic process. In the same fashion, the analyst can become sensi-tized to the existence of the other major splits that generally exist: the vertical splits that characterize dissociation and the horizontal splits that characterize repression, notably mind–body splitting. The awareness of these splits and their mutual interaction is made possible by focusing upon the field, and the paradox-ical experience that this focus implies is a significant advance in analytic work. An analyst who does not focus upon the interactive field can still discover some of these splits through, for example, projective identification; but this mode of discovery will be unlikely to gather up all of the dimensions of splitting within the analysand. However, the field, experienced as the analytic object, is in a way the Fourth that contains these three major dimensions of splitting. Unless the split opposites are combined along these various 'fault lines,' no fundamental change in internal structure can occur.

The usefulness of the field as analytic object was also evident in the case of a female analysand who was attempting to deal with severe early abandonment trauma. Through projective identification, we focused on deeply disturbing states of deadness and meaninglessness which covered paranoid levels of envy and rage. This psychotic material created an intensely disturbed field that was char-acterized by broken connections. While the projective identification approach revealed how her psychic defenses attacked any connection between us, focusing on the field itself allowed for a far more comprehensive understanding of the psychotic process.

For example, in a state of anxiety, my analysand felt the need to talk to me, but she resisted calling me at home on a weekend, even though we had arranged for this possibility. When I finally did meet with her, she offered the following explanation for her failure to telephone me at such a critical moment:

Maybe I feel I only take what I get and have no right to anything else. It's like I live with the various pieces and nothing in between. I live going from piece to piece and never ask about what's in between. To do so is too threatening. I may lose what I already have. I have no sense of what links one state to another, I just hold on to each state as if each were an island in a sea, entirely isolated until the next appears, but I have no way of getting from one to the other. It's frightening to think of how they connect for if I want to know anything I might lose what I have. Each state is a potential catastrophe.

My internal response to her explanation was to feel attacked and distanced from her. I had dealt with this kind of interaction for many months during which time she became more conscious of her desire to attack the connection between us as a way to avoid feeling needs which she found terrifying. When she touched this level in herself, psychotic anxieties emerged that led to numerous acting-out behaviors to quell the pain. But I felt that she would experience my attempts to point out her tendency to attack our connection as a direct attack on her; in any event, I would only be going over ground she knew so very well. Instead, I focused upon the extremely fragmented field between us, and I was surprised to discover that what I perceived as an attack could be seen as an exteriorization of the chaotic inner fabric of the analysand's subtle body.

Severe trauma causes loss of an inner sense of a connective fabric, which the analysand may feel as an absence that is evil or dangerous to his or her soul. To repair the connective fabric of the soul, the person may desperately cling to something that was or was not said. He or she does not dare to check out its validity; to do so implies trust in the process of getting from one thought or memory to another. But such trust does not exist. Also, to ask anything about what the analysand thinks is real is to risk losing it. The analysand is threatened with being told he or she is crazy or has somehow got it wrong. The analysand believes that the analyst knows the 'rules of the game,' while the analysand does not.

By focusing upon the field and recognizing how persecuted the analysand felt by its fragmented state, I was able to maintain a connection to her amidst such fragmentation. She was then able to reach out when she was in need, a situation that she had been unable to dare to risk since re-experiencing severely traumatic events of her infancy. My interpreting the interaction between us solely in terms of projective identification would have blocked the possibility of a stable and conscious field experience.

While we had previously worked on her areas of madness that were dominated by extremely attacking energies, we had not been able to connect them to split-off attacking feelings towards her mother. Her early history and family structure did not allow for such a thought. But using the field as the object gradually allowed this crucial historical link to be made. Furthermore, a sense of containment emerged through the field that allowed for extremely negative affects to emerge in the transference and to be readily linked to her maternal experience. Thus, the field as an object not only has a containing influence on psychotic processes but also allows for the historical reconstruction of trauma.

CHANGING STRUCTURES OF PERSONALITY THROUGH FIELD EXPERIENCES

In addition to its capacity to contain the dissociative and psychotic features of the analytic interaction, the interactive field can transform the internal structure of the analyst and the analysand; and in the process, the field structure itself changes. To experience the interactive field in an imaginal sense is the key to its transformative power. This transformative process can be illustrated by the case of a female analysand who consulted me about a life-long narcissistic disorder with strong dissociative features. She wanted to tell me of an important event in her life, but she was concerned with being coherent enough in telling me about it. She had become aware of her chronic state of being dissociated as a result of many sessions with me during which I felt blank and dissociated as a result of her splitting. During this session, she was especially worried that she would typically be 'in two places at the same time' and that this split would have a disorienting effect on me. I could imaginally visualize her as being simultaneously embodied and withdrawing, as if she were escaping out of her body. Being with her was physically and psychically painful for me: my body felt tight and inwardly tormented.

Given the clarity we had achieved up to this point, for reasons I did not understand myself at the time, but which included a trust and belief that we could 'use' each other, I chose to ask a question aloud: 'What do we constellate together. Not just you or me but both of us?' She replied, after reflecting: 'You're like my mother. I reach forward, and for a moment, she is there, but then she is gone.' She felt that she was in a state of extreme deprivation; I also felt very deprived by her, deprived of connection and any feeling that would take away the pain and confusion I felt. My admission surprised her, as she had little idea she could have this effect on me. The field between us seemed to be manifesting in a tendency towards connection and then to a quick withdrawal and a sense of loss and deprivation.

We agreed that these opposites were present to both of us. I took special care to insist that these opposites were not hers any more than they were mine. I especially did not suggest that she essentially was responsible for creating the opposites in the field and that I was inductively experiencing them. I did note to myself the extent to which these opposite states were part of my own psychic life. The success of any attempts to define the interactive field and to experience its dynamics depends upon the analyst's willingness to avoid dealing with field contents only as projections.

The nature of such interactions is somewhat difficult to describe because it is subtle. By recognizing the nature of the field as having an intense attraction-avoidance/deprivation quality, and the pain associated with these opposites, we were closer, more intimate than we had been previously. Such intimacy often gives way to a sense of fear. Who is this person I now experience in ways that I never have? What have I gotten into? In this case, such concerns were mild; instead, we were both able to hold to the quality of the field and to our individual relationship to the opposites.

All forms of analysis will generally differentiate opposites in the analytic process. Whether it be through noting the difference between the analysand's conscious and unconscious attitudes, or between projected contents and defenses, or as opposing attributes of internal structure or transference dynamics, opposites will play a central role in all psychoanalytic thinking. The manner in which these opposites are dealt with will distinguish an approach that recognizes the field to have its own, objective process from one that considers the field to be comprised only of the combined subjectivities of analyst and analysand, from which the analyst can extract information about the analysand's personal history.

In the case being cited, the analysand and I were thus able to grasp the unconscious couple in the field between us, a couple with a grotesque quality of union and desire followed by a quick retreat into deprivation of any affective contact. The act of each of us owning these states of mind and associated pain had a very freeing effect upon her needs for a narcissistic defense. In her case, this defense took the form of what I call a narcissistic-bubble; that is, the analysand acts as speaker and listener simultaneously. In effect, the object world is then all but shut out. In listening to her, I typically felt mindless and deadened, like an observer with no real contact with her. I found myself nearly uncontrollably asking questions about topics that had absolutely nothing to do with the subject at hand. In one instance I was jolted out of the trance-like state induced by the analysand's narcissistic-bubble transference by her startled response: 'What in the world are you talking about?' Having finally made contact with me in this way, she emerged from her narcissistic-bubble, but I was left to deal with the mess that I inadvertently had created. It was then possible to reconstruct the previous interaction and the narcissistic bubble structure.

From this experience, I have learned to control my nearly compulsive effort to talk through the 'bubble', with the result that I have been able to understand my inner state of mind. Such process-disturbing and, at times, bizarre utterances have had the purpose of enabling me to escape from a state of inner pain and mental blankness. Such reflections on my nearly compulsive effort to talk often afforded a good way to begin sorting out the nature of the psychic opposites involved, opposites such as attraction-avoidance which had previously been impossible for me to register.

Entering the field, with its opposites experienced and mutually perceived, had a dissolving effect upon the rigid, narcissistic-bubble-like transference, and upon this character structure in the analysand. The issue of opposites is especially significant in understanding the dynamic qualities of the narcissistic-bubble transference. If the analyst manages to focus enough so that he or she arrives at some meaning in the person's communication (which I would emphasize is no mean task given the nearly insular fashion in which the analysand communicates and the concomitant dissociative process), and if the analyst holds on to this meaning, another possible meaning will soon arise which, typical of psychotic processes, annihilates the former one.

On another occasion with this analysand, I could glimpse the delusional nature of the process that lived within this narcissistic-bubble-like structure. She began her session with what she termed a dilemma about which she felt confused and overwhelmed. Recently, she had met a woman on the street, someone she does not really like very much but who has been very helpful to her professionally. At the moment, she felt she wanted to do some reciprocal deed for this woman, and she suggested that the woman might be able to get consulting work at the place she herself was employed. But soon after, she realized that she had a good friend, someone who had really helped her in many personal ways, who also needed work and would also like the job. So, the analysand wondered to whom should she 'give' it?

As she told me this conflict, I soon began to develop a splitting sensation in my head, a feeling of real pain and a general sense of confusion. It was clear that she was very dissociated, as she often was, but this instance was different. For, instead of a tendency to dissociate with her and become vague until I recovered my focus, I now experienced actual pain. After a brief attempt to figure out to whom she might 'give' the job, thinking to myself in terms, for example, of loyalty issues versus the woman's economic welfare, I just felt more and more confused and pained. As I thought about favoring one friend, reasons to favor the other arose and totally annihilated in my mind any of the previous thoughts about the other friend. At that point, I began to wonder if something 'mad' was going on, and I thought that perhaps there was no real job at all for her to be 'giving.'

I asked her about the nature of the job, if it really existed now, and she recognized that in fact it did not. All that existed was her fantasy of someone whom she could talk to, so that one of these people might then call and ask for work. But she had no factual basis at all to go on. For example, she had no reason to believe they might really need help. It was then clear that she was dealing with her own fantasy, which she was treating as real, and with it came an inflation, a grandiose state in which she was the endower of this potential job. Until this point, I had believed that an actual job existed and that my analysand had the capacity to secure it for one or other of the women.

She could now see that she had created this near-delusional state. I wondered aloud with her if this creation came from a need to be powerful with them. She answered quite quickly and clearly: 'No, it's that I feel so insignificant.' And then she continued, saying that she felt that she did not matter to them, nor to anyone. She further reflected that they actually said nice things to her and, in fact, did helpful, loving things for her. She wondered why their behavior did not matter and why she continued to feel so insignificant. People for her are often not real in the sense of being of relatively equal size and power. Instead, they are bigger than life, capable of lifting her sense of self-esteem or causing it to crash. Her only option was to become her own mirror and to live in a narcissistic bubble in which she was both speaker and listener.

In a narcissistic bubble, other people are 'self-objects' not real objects, and her life experience has been with self-objects that tormented her, rarely seeing her value. But if people are not real objects, nothing positive can be introjected. Attacks can jar her and reinforce paranoid belief systems, but little by way of a process of introjection of positive qualities can fill out her ego into a relatively stable structure that carries a sense of meaning to the question: 'Who am I?' Thus, she is left prey to the kind of mirroring she receives, and this state is generally too dangerous to present to the world.

The question that arises is how to dissolve this narcissistic container and allow a more life-creating form to emerge. I have found that the discovery of the imagery of the interactive field, apprehended from opposites manifesting often as psychotic splitting into anti-worlds, can lead to the emergence of a new form of the transference, one that is more related and far less psychotic. Heinz Kohut calls this development a mirror transference in 'the narrower sense,' in which the analyst becomes an object for the analysand, but it is important for the analysand only 'within the framework of the needs generated by the therapeutically reactivated grandiose self' (1971, 116). The analysand becomes capable of incorporating the analyst's image while making use of it as a source of identity in a wide-ranging manner. But when this state of felt-incorporation is too dangerous to allow, the analysand feels wholly unwanted, his or her insides feeling filled with hate, and is thus incapable of having anything good inside without destroying it or being destroyed by the object's rejection. Instead, the narcissistic-bubble transference takes its place, and the analysand becomes both subject and object. Transforming this bubble state then becomes the analytic task.

This narcissistic structure is common, to some degree, in everyone. Who, at times, is not both speaker and audience? We have all been created to an extent by our early object relations. Anyone dealing with child development can well appreciate that the manner in which a young child is responded to and mirrored as to his or her actual qualities is essential to later development of a spontaneous self and a sense of essence. But who is ever totally mirrored? Secret areas of the self that cannot be communicated always exist. And when the analyst gets near these areas, forms of communication readily move towards the narcissistic-bubble-like quality. With some people, this narcissistic structure can substitute for relating in any genuine sense where the 'other' has a felt significance and process that are registered; but I have rarely found that this structure is omnipresent. Rather, the person is, at times, capable of a keen empathy and emotional contact. At other times, this capacity is totally absent, and the bubble transference dominates. Years of work can pass where both states are part of the same analytical hour. However, prior to work with the bubble structure of defense, entire sessions are dominated by it. Then, as the bubble transference dissolves, only segments of the hour are dominated by it until, at times of distress in the analysand's life, it again emerges. But generally, the narcissistic bubble can diminish more and more, and the person's capabilities for emotional contact, consciousness, and empathy can come forth. In a sense, these people do not fit a simple diagnostic scheme. They surely exhibit narcissistic as well as schizoid features; but they also possess a competent and empathic quality.

A main feature that occurs as a countertransference resistance when facing these areas is non-communication. The analyst tends not to communicate his or her experience of the analysand, even though later experience may prove that this kind of communication and 'mutual exploration' are frequently central to transforming the narcissistic structure. This non-communication is a frozen state, and communication can feel like the last act in which the analyst wants to engage. While defending against the sense of the bizarre and the pain associated with psychotic process may be one explanation for this countertransference resistance, another explanation is that extremely sensitive levels of trauma are involved in which the analyst's identity is shaky; and exploration with the analysand at this point can feel like a risk that is too much to take. But the analyst asks the analysand to take such risks, and both can learn that taking risks in communicating and exploring the field experiences can be healing.

CHANGING STRUCTURES OF RELATIONSHIP THROUGH FIELD EXPERIENCES

The experience of field dynamics is effective in the transformation of structures of not only personality but also relationship. The latter is illustrated by the following case of a 50-year-old man whose intimate relationship with an older, married woman was a source of both intense passion and feelings of devastating loss. Days and often weeks passed between their meetings. In his sessions with me, I began to notice that whenever he mentioned the woman's name or began to speak about her, my attention would fragment. Although he appeared to be speaking words of concern about the issue he was bringing to the session, his real essence or vital attention was elsewhere, pulled away from the present moment. I did not feel as if I were with someone recalling another time or place but rather I felt that he had been stolen away from himself and that he was struggling with not being really present, having had a blankness replace the feeling underlying his words. I would exert extra force to glue myself to his words, but my attention continued to dissociate, and I would often lose much of the content of what he would be reporting. At other times, when he spoke of matters other than this woman, he was 'present' and my attention did not wander or fragment.

We could both notice an atmosphere of fear and paranoid elements that seemed to drive us out of an embodied level. During a session I pointed out this tendency, and he asked: 'Where is this fear? And I replied: 'In both of us,' for I had no true way of seeing it as a projective identification phenomenon. I could have constructed an interpretation from feelings of abandonment that I experienced when he fragmented. We had done considerable work interpreting his psychotic areas, and we had understood them as related both to how he experienced his father and to ways that his father probably experienced him. But to stress this interpretation based on abandonment now seemed too limited and repressive of the field between us.

He asked me what could contain these feelings. Jung's assertion that the archetype is the container came to mind. Certainly we could together reflect on a son–lover myth as structuring the space between us, and we could choose numerous other images, for example, the alchemical myth of the son swallowed by the dragon which then cuts him up into thousands of parts. I noted that such a powerful image might be organizing our interaction. Focusing on this image changed the field: we both felt more in control and far less fragmented. We could then gain some sense of understanding and relatedness, but the experience between us was soulless, and embodiment in any depth was not possible. Archetypal amplifications, like developmental understanding, could create a mental-spiritual kind of order, a discovery of order but not of soul. Such interpretations would not allow for a field of attachment that alone could perhaps create the bridges necessary for helping him leave the magnetic sphere of the son–lover field without heroically repressing it, and, by necessity, losing his body awareness.

His dream and fantasy material presented a pattern dominated by a mythical type of son–lover/mother–goddess interaction. Like the son in these dramas, he was caught in a web of passion – quite deadly to his own psychological integrity – from which he could not separate. His growth demanded emergence from this web, yet his passion – elements of which included commitment, honor, faithfulness, a sense of noble purpose, but especially of feeling intensely alive – demanded that he embrace it ever more strongly. Either option led to torment and an overwhelming sense of despair. The relationship could not and did not have any firm basis in reality. The woman he loved was heavily committed to her duties as wife and mother. Younger and unmarried, he was highly ambivalent about his relationship with her. They would meet erratically, with long intermittent periods of absence. In fact, no really stable, space–time matrix could contain this mythical pattern. He and the woman met in a state of psychic transport, and they never entered into a world of a real relationship, namely one that lived in normal space and time.

Considerable gain was made in our work through analysis of the actual object relation, and on the level of his own interior object relations as well. The son–lover pattern was very enlivened by his own maternal and paternal issues. He sensed his underlying incest desires for his mother and her threats of abandonment, aggravated by his father's emotional absence during his childhood. Inevitably, this absence created an intensely critical internal father-image which prevented him from challenging himself in the real world. He could function well enough, but his abilities far outreached his achievements in both his professional and personal life. As he became increasingly aware of the son–lover pattern and began integrating it into his consciousness, he became somewhat less enchanted by the woman he idolized and recognized that his passion was not under his control but was highly dependent upon her incestuous resonances with both his mother and father. His ability to enter the world more fully then began to expand and develop. For example, some of his renegade or negative 'outsider' status dissolved.

In the process of this work, I dealt with my subjective, countertransference reactions, which were both a tendency to be critical of him and an opposite tendency to idealize his thoughts and attitudes towards the importance of passion. Making use of these countertransference reactions, I could be a guide to help him to integrate his unconscious material. Was it enough for me to process his material in this way? If I acted impeccably in this regard, consistently inquiring about my own countertransference, using the information acquired in this way, attempting to listen to the unconscious references in his discourse as they pertained to my role in our relationship, and methodically inquiring as to how his dream material responded to our work together, I would be acting as any analyst might. Such attitudes would be necessary, but not sufficient to meet his therapeutic requirements for containing his psychotic elements. That required an alchemical approach, the activation of alchemical vision inquiring into the nature of the field we both constellated.

The presence of a field only gradually began to become conscious to both of us. In the course of our work, it slowly became clear that he was overwhelmed by anger towards this woman. At times, his rage took on psychotic proportions, having little containment, leading to considerable fragmentation, and continually, albeit subtly, distorting reality. Much of our work was focused upon this reality distortion, especially as it split his relationship with his partner into states in which he perceived her as alternately a deceiving witch and a beautiful lover. We often explored how unwittingly he continued to deny his perceptions of the woman's actual negative character traits, aspects of her behavior that were unethical and untrustworthy. At times, this denial kept him in a state dangerously fused with her and cut off from other people and things. He feared that he would lose his passion if he saw any of her dark side: his passion would turn into overwhelming hatred and sadism. This loss would throw him into the part of his psyche that created this reality distortion, that is, into the psychotic area within his psyche. Furthermore, his psychotic areas typically were structured by 'anti-worlds' in which anything that was said about the woman would lead to a totally opposite view that annihilated (his and my own) awareness of the previous opposite. The fusion of these opposites can lead to the bizarreness that characterizes psychotic process. I would often have the impression of a subtle bizarreness in listening to his comments about their relationship. I felt as if something was always being withheld, and if it were to be revealed, his discourse would become less understandable.

This process continued for several years. I repeatedly wondered about the way in which my attention fragmented. Was this a result of his fear of my judgment? Did I dissociate because I could not stand losing him to this woman? Did he want me to feel his loss because his father abandoned him to his mother, and was I to be the father who finally claimed him? Or, was this my own process fusing with his? Individually and together we explored these permutations, to his benefit, both in regard to his relationship to the woman and to the world. But his rage did not seem to diminish, a source of consternation for both of us. In the mythical drama, the son's rage frequently results in his death, often by his own hand in a mutilating suicide. Sometimes, the goddess's animal kills him, sent by the enraged, betrayed goddess. Was his rage present between us? Was it 'attacking the links' in our field of relations, rendering aspects of our work futile?

One day, during a session in which he was speaking about his relationship with the woman, I began noticing my now familiar tendency to split off from focusing on him. I asked him if anger was attacking the connection between us. He replied: 'Whose anger?' The only truthful response I could give was that there was no way to know. We were both in a kind of energy field in which anger was present.

By replying in this way, I consciously began to engage a 'third area' between us, one signified by the affect of anger. We both experienced this shift to an imaginal presence, in this case identifiable by a quality of anger. We were experiencing a change in the quality of awareness of the texture and space around us, that is, the 'field' or the 'third thing.' We felt as if an 'other' was present with us. The nature of the field was such that we could both experience being inside of and contained by it. At other times, we felt as if we were observing the field, its nature and qualities in the space between us. Sometimes, we felt as if our need or will determined whether we would be the subject or object of the field. And sometimes, we could observe that the field had its own rhythm which caused this oscillation in subject–object. So, sitting there together, we could imaginally begin to perceive the anger to be a quality of the field itself, as an object we could sense, or imaginally 'see' between us. The field exerted an affect which our bodies registered. We could perceive that the feeling of this affect had the potential to move us to behave in certain ways. For example, with this process came a degree of fear which pushed us to the edge of feeling contained. Would anger or a boundary-less fusion take over in some undefined sense? A high level of anxiety was also present at this critical moment.

I could easily have sidestepped this encounter, and perhaps I had been doing that for some time in our work prior to this session. I could have diminished the anxiety by reflecting upon 'his' anger, but in so doing, I would have become the active one, or as Jacques Lacan says, 'the one who knows' (1977, 230). As a result, I would have denied the field between us with its expressive, but basically unknowable quality. Essentially, I would have deconstructed and depotentiated the field between us in a particularly seductive way. I would have unconsciously transmitted the experience of the supremacy of power in dealing with relationships over the experience of relatedness and suffering, all under the guise that it was for his own good.

But having allowed the truth, namely that I did not know whose anger it was, the discourse moved on to another level. Now an imaginal presence of a strong anger, even rage, could be tolerated, and with it came a respectful awareness of the mystery of imagination. Had I dealt with 'his rage' at this point, I would have been projecting on to him my own rage as it connects to this archetypal pattern. He would have been made to carry my rage as well as his own. Instead, the imaginal presence was tolerated without our knowing whose it was. And with this move to the imaginal, a sense of body was activated. In this case, we could both feel an energized sense of that body and its aliveness; and we became conscious of our bodies as energy fields. Perhaps it is only this kind of experience of body – the alchemists would think of this as a subtle body experience – that can create a feeling of containment for dangerous passions.

Then, the field experience between us changed. He felt that his body wanted to embrace mine, and I could also feel this sense of embrace, indeed, of a longing for him. But even with this new experience, the rage did not go away. It oscillated with the sense of longing in the energized field between us. And so, we now had a pair of opposites defining our interactional space: rage and longing. Rage annihilates, longing joins. In alchemical terms, the annihilating hot substance was known as 'Sulphur,' whereas the joining-longing-melding substance was known as 'Salt.' In the process of experiencing these, we were really creating a kind of vessel for the relationship that was both so precious and so destructive to his life.

The act of containing and objectifying his conflicting affects made it possible for him to begin to see his partner in a far more real way.

Like other analysts he had worked with before me, I had analyzed his relationship with the woman, related it to the transference and transference resistance, interpreted his oedipal and pre-oedipal desires, and reflected upon his separation fears. But it was only when we were able to engage the field between us – and this continued to happen over a period of time – that the magnetic quality of that relationship began to lose its compulsive, magical nature. The relationship's beauty was not destroyed, but the quality of longing, which was so much a part of it, could be moved out of the incestuous pattern of destructive passion. The transference to this woman could be transferred to me, back to her, then to others, and then to his longing for an internal self. His relationship with her was no less real because it had earlier roots in parental relations than was his relationship with me. Both relationships had a reality; neither were functions of illusion which dissipated with consciousness. Slowly but effectively, he began to be able to engage the world around him in more individual and significant ways. He was able to risk more vulnerability and to test his creativity.

From the various states of mind encountered in the preceding examples – envy, anxiety, fear, chaos, paranoia, rage, hysteria, splitting (front–back, mind–body, or side-by-side), dissociation, abandonment, trauma, passion, incestuous desire, despair, among others – we might recognize any number of starting points for discovering the transformative potential of the field.

But is one starting point better than another? The containment of chaos, or what I have called the mad parts of sane people, seems to have a special significance in alchemy. Chaos, or the *prima materia*, was a vital starting point for the *opus*, the process of material and personal transformation. Indeed, the emphasis on chaos and its containment within the alchemical approach can inform modern approaches to the analytical process, particularly if and when the *prima materia* is experienced as an aspect of an interactive field.

6   The alchemical view of madness

'CHAOS' AND THE ALCHEMICAL WAY

From the point of view of psychoanalysis, the states of mind we have been considering – such as extreme fragmentation, blankness, deadness, and the bewildering annihilation of opposites – are all part of psychotic process. While some analysts (Eigen 1986) and Jung (Schwartz-Salant 1982, 1989) appreciate the transformative value of such states of mind, generally those states are regarded as dangerous and regrettable instances of failures in development. This negative point of view is born out of a scientific frame of reference. Just as a scientist doing an experiment or solving a problem attempts to create order in disorder, the analyst traditionally confronts a heap of scattered communications which at first do not make sense, and then attempts to discover an order and possibly even meaning in them. From such an ego-oriented reference point, the phenomenon known as madness cannot be ordered but remains bizarre and, by definition, devoid of meaning.

Jung and others insisted that if an analyst could understand the products of a schizophrenic, then the analysand was no longer mad. The countering point of view was that if the analyst could understand a schizophrenic then the diagnosis was wrong. The problem with understanding products of madness, however, is that one has to ask: Who is doing the understanding? Can meaning ever be found in bizarre states, such as annihilating opposites by the consciousness of an ego observing these states? Or, does one have to 'see' in a completely different way?

Alchemical thinking offers a different, imaginal way of seeing that can be born out of actively encountering mad areas. But the meaning or vision the analyst gains is not, like some developmental sequence of personality growth, steady and repeatable. Rather, this vision is brief and easily overlooked. The often instantaneous vision in which the analyst succeeds in gathering up split opposites by living 'in between' them seems strongly dependent upon the quality of the moment in which the analyst and analysand interact. Even if relatively infrequent during an analytical process, such moments are extremely valuable. The analyst must see beyond the opposites as well as seeing them together, and this seeing is like the alchemical elixir, a drop of which was remarkably transformative.

In a sense, 'the alchemical way' is one in which the analyst sees with the larger vision of the self; the scientific way is one in which he or she sees through the vision of the ego. The alchemical way sees 'through' the eyes, whereas the scientific way sees 'with' the eyes. Whereas the scientific way cannot encompass both opposites at the same time, the alchemical way can encompass both opposites simultaneously by situating in a middle realm, the subtle body or the interactive field, the very existence of which scientific thinking denies. The scientific way is repeatable and is accessible to anyone who has had sufficient training and who has capacity for processing projective identification or an awareness of the structures of empathy. On the other hand, the alchemical way is not repeatable at will and depends upon the *kairos* – the quality of the moment – which is largely determined by the ontology of the analyst as he or she embraces the moment and situates himself or herself in the interactive field.

Thus, the realm of mad parts of sane people will be encountered and valued largely as a function of how one views this level of psychic life. The alchemical view greatly enhances our approach to these commonly encountered, and generally avoided, areas. While anathema to one person, mad areas are a *prima materia*, a vital starting point, for another. Finding this vital beginning point may take many hours or even years; it is rarely found in the first analytic hour or the first encounter. In the alchemical way of thinking, this beginning is a highly sought-after state, which might be found quickly or which might require a lifetime of work. But the self or inner world and the nature of relations that can be created through engaging mad areas make the quest an incomparable source of meaning in relationships and individual growth.

The alchemical way of the transformation of personality does not seek out social and economic adaptation, ego-strength, capacity for relationship, sexual maturity, and spiritual ideals. These hallmarks of all cultures, past and present, are not the primary goals of the alchemical way. They are either assumed at the start, or they are a secondary result of a more central search which is the core of the process: the search for the *lapis* or 'Stone of the Wise,' which is the self. The self is the center of one's being and is felt as neither personal nor impersonal, neither 'mine' nor 'not mine.' The alchemical way is characterized by a quest for a self that has kinship to a larger Self, one that is never known as an internal object but only known, in religious terms, in the soul's ascent to God or in the soul's ecstatic mingling with another soul in the subtle-body space wherein one may know the sacred union, the *coniunctio*. The self will never be a collective value because it is too unique, never capable of description in anything other than terms that seem to be mystical to those for whom the experience is unknown. The terms 'Oneness,' 'Other,' 'Light,' 'Infinite,' and 'Awe' are ready metaphors among many to describe the experience of the ineffable. But such experience is only a beginning, from which a sense of innerness of the sacred and an embodied sense of its numinous quality is achieved. Religions have always been the gatekeepers of such realms, and doctrine and images have carried the experience of the *numinosum*. In the alchemical way, the self is a unique experience for each individual, and this experience can be, and has been, known by many.

Yet the 'many' are part of a once larger number, for in the work, according to the commonly encountered alchemical phrase, 'many men have perished'

(McLean 1980, 45). Anyone who embarks upon a thorough restructuring of his or her being, as in the alchemical way, and not simply upon a path of symptom relief or greater relatedness and adaptation to others and society, begins with an experience that is always filled with fear. This beginning requires a willingness to give up what one knows – one's objects as they form security and one's beliefs as they create illusions that work well enough. In numerous alchemical works, the beginning of the *opus* features a flood which symbolizes the total dissolution of personality. The alchemists were part of a tradition that knew that a total change was in store for those with courage enough to begin and strength enough to survive this chaotic state.

This chaotic beginning is illustrated in the first of twenty-two paintings that comprise the *Splendor Solis* (Figure 1). Two alchemists look with great trepidation at the waters they must enter, a turbulent stream that goes from their right to their left, implying a descent into the unconscious in an undetermined way. Fabricius associates these waters to the famous 'Waters of Styx' (1976, 17), which in the ancient Greek tradition are terrifying to humans and gods alike. These waters can only be contained by a mysterious vessel, as in the myth of Eros and Psyche with a crystal horse's hoof being symbolic of the vessel creativity (von Franz 1970, Chapter 7). In general, the *Splendor Solis*'s first image points to a dangerous entrance into the unconscious, and one whose container will demand the best of one's creative being and the best of one's companions.

The first painting of the *Splendor Solis* depicts the sun above and the same sun below, embedded in a shield, symbolic of matter (Figure 1). The goal of this alchemical work was the incarnation of spiritual forces into matter or into an embodied existence (McLean 1981, 83). This process is always associated with chaotic experiences. Generally, one experiences considerable disturbance when a consciousness emerges that conflicts with one's established personality. The stronger this awareness, the stronger the conflict. On the one hand, the realization or embodiment of this consciousness requires that old structures, which once defended against the new awareness, dissolve. On the other hand, the affirmation of the new awareness requires that one be willing to be led further in ways that are not necessarily predictable. Change is always frightening, and the image from antiquity that most resists change is Narcissus. Our narcissistic investments in appearance and prestige always oppose change, and the loss of our narcissistic structures always opens us to very disorienting areas of the unconscious. However, when the incarnating spiritual experience is of the order of the *numinosum*, the chaos one experiences can be overwhelming.

In the alchemical way of thinking, the soul experiences a level of numinosity which it then endeavors to incarnate into space and time, a transition which creates considerable disorder. Disorder always accompanies the change from a lower to a higher form of consciousness, meaning a change from a structure or form that is old and stable to one that is new and unstable (Schwartz-Salant 1969). As in the sun's descent into the shield of matter in the first painting of the *Splendor Solis*, the soul's descent into space–time existence seems to require that it travel through one's earliest experiences, as if the soul knows something of eternity and

Figure 1 First painting from the *Splendor Solis*

traces its steps back into birth in space and time. But as the soul, the organ of psychic experience, re-travels this path, it also encounters early trauma, where madness often lurks, perhaps a hidden parental madness or an experience of abuse. And as the soul touches these areas of the mind, considerable anxiety and panic can emerge, as reflected in the distorted appearance of the sun's face on the shield of the first painting of the *Splendor Solis*.

Figure 2 First engraving from the *Mutus Liber*

The descent into matter and embodied life can bring on a flood of unconscious material characterized by dangerous and dissolving states, as seen in numerous other alchemical works (Fabricius 1976, 16–23). For example, the first engraving from the *Mutus Liber* features a sleeping alchemist where angels, symbolic of a link to the numinous realm, are trying to awaken him and urge him to ascend to a higher consciousness (Figure 2). And in the background, the sea represents the flood that will assuredly occur, that is, the chaotic state of mind that the alchemist will experience. But alchemists believed that within chaos one could find order

Figure 3 Michel de Morolles' engraving of the alchemical chaos

by apprehending conflicting opposites, as illustrated in an engraving by the alchemist Michel de Morolles (Figure 3). This engraving captures the life of psychic opposites within chaos – for example, a bull and a scorpion, a water carrier and a lion, and a goat and a crab, respectively representing the astrological opposites of Taurus/Scorpio, Aquarius/Leo, and Capricorn/Cancer. The chaotic nature of psychic opposites is further indicated by human heads, some spitting fire and others spitting water. Beyond these conflicting opposites, more extreme states are depicted such as a dragon opposing a dog and a bear devouring the sun, both indicative of the death and putrefaction that will surely follow any states of union of opposites. The death that will inevitably follow union is depicted in the embracing couple about to be struck by the arrow of a centaur. And at the top of the engraving is the figure of a woman, herself standing on two fish swimming in opposite directions, signifying the wisdom of alchemy in uniting opposites. Thus, the chaos apprehended by the alchemical way contains forms of order and the vicissitudes of union that will occur over and over again as the *opus* unfolds.

The most complete and significant portrayal of the alchemical process, the *Rosarium Philosophorum*, describes in its series of twenty woodcuts the transformation of chaotic states understood psychologically as the mad parts of sane people. Chaos and states of mind akin to madness are essential to engaging the mystery of the creation of the alchemical conception of the self, the *lapis philosophorum*. The *Rosarium*'s series of woodcuts forms a core of wisdom unmatched in any alchemical treatise, and I regard it as the core of what in pathological terms can be thought of as the alchemical way. Essentially, the engagement of an interactive field not only is a container for mad states but also becomes a container for unconscious aspects of the psyche out of which a self is created.

THE 'MERCURIAL FOUNTAIN' AND THE DYNAMICS OF THE DOUBLE-HEADED SERPENT

The first woodcut of the *Rosarium Philosophorum*, the 'Mercurial Fountain' (Figure 4), is a portrayal of the mysterious basis of the *opus* (Jung 1954, 16: paragraph 402). The 'Mercurial Fountain' is an awkward image: the top, containing the double-headed serpent, known in alchemy as the Binarius and often signifying the devil, is split from the bottom, containing the Mercurial Fountain which is filled by the three pipes spouting three streams of water. At first, the link between above and below is only made through the fumes which stem from the mouths of the serpent.

In alchemical tradition, the square that encloses the picture is an image of the hostile engagement of the opposites, leading to a state of chaos, an initial Oneness. When the analyst experiences this level of chaos he or she suffers a very disordering state. For it is common that the field induction from psychotic areas intrudes into the analyst's awareness and has a fracturing effect upon his or her attention. The qualitative logic of the woodcut continues, following 'The Axiom of Maria.' Out of the Twoness of the Dyad comes the Three, depicted as the Mercurial Fountain fed by three streams. These are the 'lower waters' that Jung likens to the Lower Anthropos or to Dionysos. The waters in the fountain circulate, and the fountain itself is fed both by the Dionysian element and by the fumes descending from the mouths of the serpent. These fumes connect above and below, and they also fill the vessel. The link shown in the 'Mercurial Fountain' partakes of the dynamics of projective identification. States of mind that can be described as mad areas of sane people fill the analytical vessel from above, as do those states of mind associated with the mad god, Dionysos. The two 'waters,'

Figure 4 'Mercurial Fountain': first woodcut of the *Rosarium Philosophorum*

from above and below, are identical, as the inscription on the rim of the vessel states. The fountain thus represents two aspects of the same process, one engaged from the viewpoint of the psychic unconscious, the realm of Apollo in Greek myth, and the other from the somatic unconscious, the domain of Dionysos.

These two forms of mad states of mind are experienced differently, but the point of this first woodcut of the *Rosarium* is that together they create a field that is itself the mysterious vessel in which the *opus* develops. And again in accord with 'The Axiom of Maria,' out of the processes in this vessel, the Threeness is felt, for example, as unconscious dyads between two people which are encountered, and their autonomous dynamics experienced, leading to a new sense of Oneness. Hence, out of the Three comes the Fourth as the One.

Out of the initial disordered state of Oneness, represented by the square bounding the first woodcut, emerges the quality of opposites, symbolized in the *Rosarium* by the double-headed serpent. The image of the double-headed serpent is also found in many diverse cultures outside the alchemical tradition. For example, in ancient Egyptian imagery, the cosmic serpent is double-headed (Lindsay 1970, 339). The Ancient Greek god-hero of medicine, Aesculapius, carried a staff upward along which two serpents entwined ending at the top with their two heads facing each other. Even to this day, this symbol is used by the medical profession to symbolize healing though it is often confused, perhaps through some mysterious wisdom, with Mercury's staff, the *caduceus*. Moreover, images of the Greek god, Hermes, feature him with two heads facing opposite directions. Among the Aztecs, the double-headed serpent was a symbol of the god Tlaloc, a powerful and beneficent god of rain (Burland 1980, 30, 110). The image of the double-headed serpent can also symbolize the self containing opposites that the ego cannot embrace, especially opposites that have the annihilating quality found in mad sectors of the personality.

This particular feature of the self can be found explicitly described in Chapter 74 of Herman Melville's (1962) novel *Moby Dick*, which deals with the nature of the whale's vision:

> A curious and most puzzling question might be started concerning this visual matter as touching Leviathan. But I must be content with a hint. So long as a man's eyes are open in the light, the act of seeing is involuntary; that is, he cannot then help mechanically seeing whatever objects are before him. Nevertheless, any one's experience will teach him, that though he can take in an undiscriminating sweep of things at one glance, it is impossible for him, attentively, and completely, to examine any two things – however large or however small – at one and the same instant of time; never mind if they lie side by side and touch each other. But if you now come to separate these two objects, and surround each by a circle of profound darkness; then in order to see one of them, in such a manner as to bring your mind to bear on it, the other will be utterly excluded from your contemporary consciousness. How is it, then, with the whale? True, both his eyes, in themselves must simultaneously act; but is his brain so much more comprehensive, combining, and subtle than man's, that he can at the same moment of time attentively examine two distinct prospects, one on one side of him, and the other in an exactly opposite direction?

Perhaps the most complete and vivid representation of this configuration of opposites is found in a myth from the Kwakiutl Indians of the Pacific Northwest which deals specifically with Sisiutl, a god who is a double-headed serpent (Figure 5). Sisiutl is regarded as a dangerous, fearsome sea monster who is an important participant in Kwakiutl war ceremonies. Sisiutl invariably appears in

Figure 5 Sisiutl, the Kwakiutl Indian god

the form of a serpent with an elongated head at each end and with a human face forming the central body. Sisiutl has a large mouth and teeth, a long, sharp tongue, large flared nostrils, and two curled horns on his head. He is believed to be able to bring harm to anyone; his baleful gaze can cause a victim's joints to turn backward, whereupon the person dies, having been turned to stone. Any warrior who bathes in his blood will become invulnerable, for the scales, spines, and blood of Sisiutl give tremendous power.

His power is so great that the image of Sisiutl is often painted over the entry doors of houses in tribute to his role as a protector of 'the Above Ones.' If properly assuaged in ritual, Sisiutl will come to the warrior when summoned. Yet many dangers are connected with any contact with the sea monster: if one stumbles on to the trail of Sisiutl and rubs one's hands or feet in the slime, the limbs will turn to stone; or, if the serpent's clotted blood is rubbed on to one's skin, the skin will likewise turn to stone. However, it is thought that killing Sisiutl may be made possible by biting one's tongue, covering a war staff with the blood, and striking the monster. The Kwakiutl Indian myth specifies how to face the mighty Sisiutl:

> When you see Sisiutl you must stand and face him. Face the horror. Face the fear. If you break faith with what you know, if you try to flee, Sisiutl will blow with both mouths at once and you will begin to spin. Not rooted in the earth as are the trees and rocks, not eternal as are the tides and currents, your corkscrew spinning will cause you to leave the earth, to wander forever, a lost soul, and your voice will be heard in the screaming winds of the first autumn, sobbing, pleading, begging for release . . . When you see Sisiutl the terrifying, though you be frightened, stand firm. There is no shame in being frightened, only a fool would not be afraid of Sisiutl the horror. Stand firm, and if you know protective words, say them. First one head, then the other, will rise from the water. Closer. Closer. Coming for your face, the ugly heads, closer, and the stench from the devouring mouths, and the cold, and the terror. Stand firm. Before the twin mouths of Sisiutl can fasten on your face and steal your soul, each head must turn towards you. When this happens, Sisiutl will see his own face.
>
> Who sees the other half of Self, sees Truth.
>
> Sisiutl spends eternity in search of Truth. In search of those who know Truth. When he sees his own face, his own other face, when he has looked into his own eyes, he has found Truth.
>
> He will bless you with magic, he will go, and your Truth will be yours forever. Though at times it may be tested, even weakened, the magic of Sisiutl, his blessing, is that your truth will endure. And the sweet Stalacum will visit you often, reminding you your Truth will be found behind your own eyes. And you will not be alone again.

(Cameron 1981, 45–46)

The contagion from Sisiutl that can contaminate hand or foot represents ways that madness undermines ego-functions and reality standpoint. Madness is contagious, and this contagion also spreads through the field that madness creates. Being turned to stone corresponds to the common experience of feeling dead or inert when faced with the psychotic part. Facing opposites as represented by the opposing heads of Sisiutl, one often feels overcome by a mindless, empty, despairing state. Identifying this condition, rather than passively enduring it, may lead to biting the tongue that would lie by speaking quickly and thereby making the condition go away before it is known. If instead one suffers the state of impotence that one feels, a new-found capacity to feel empowered against the confusion engendered by the psychotic area can grow. Only through the strength of recognizing limitation and the impotence of one's rage can a new strength appear, one that can see the Sisiutl force without spinning out of control in a frantic effort to find some kind of order.

The experience of the two heads and their two conflicting messages is terrifying. While we do commonly experience such things as a daily occurrence in life, we can often fade out of experiencing them or find some other defense, notably anger. For example, when confronted by a person's mad sector in which conflicting opposites simultaneously broadcast their message, one's common tendency is to be right, to get the person to see that they are distorting things, to see their dark side. We tend to do anything to avoid being driven crazy. For example, I once received a carefully crafted letter from an extremely intelligent person saying he could not pay a debt he owed me. The letter brimmed with intelligence and fine prose, yet it contained glaring inaccuracies – both about the amount, and the spirit in which the loan was made – that I knew the person would deny. I struggled with two states: one admired the beauty and clarity of the letter, the other was repulsed by the lies and deception. Both wanted to be the entire story, and this conflict tended to create a sense of impotence and rage in me. Or, another person asked me to quickly explain something which was particularly difficult to put into concise language. This request was especially maddening because I wanted to communicate with the person, but I was only being allotted a short time to do so. If I refused to give a quick answer, I frustrated both of us; and if I tried to answer I would undoubtedly be inaccurate. Yet the request, amidst the incessant demands of life, seemed reasonable. I wondered if, perhaps, it was just my narcissistic need to be careful and to take time. Why could I not simply meet the request? It was difficult simply to be honest and to refuse. Within such dynamics of madness pulling me in opposite directions, I could feel a deep conflict in my soul. I could feel how my soul was severely depleted by a lifetime of such 'hurry up' messages and by a need to split off from their destructive impact.

When one faces such madness, one's soul is in danger. For madness, like Sisiutl, is contagious. One's soul can get lost, and it may then be found. But even if it has been conserved, its luminosity, its link with one's essence, can be sharply diminished.

While such experiences are all too common in life and can, more or less, usually be dismissed, they ring deeply in our interior life and recall to us the terror we once knew when, as children, we glimpsed bits of madness in our mothers and fathers. Often, sensitive souls who as children were all too aware of this hidden dimension grow up withdrawn from the world. Sometimes entire facets of individuals – otherwise quite sociable and well-adapted – are withdrawn. They have been made too keenly aware of the world's madness and the madness hidden in any encounter. They dare not experience their panic, and thus they can no longer see the madness within themselves or others. They cannot feel how unrooted they are, how unallied they are with their own bodies, and how their minds, once citadels of brilliance, pale under the impact of the unbearable confusion they experience. To 'spin' nearly out of control, as in the myth, is to feel impotent, to lose direction, to not know what to believe. Which head is true? Look left and one hand claps; look right and the other hand claps. They never clap together, and life feels ungrounded and faithless. Nightmares can come from such encounters, nightmares in which the core of one's being falters, in which panic reigns, and in which one wanders helplessly, like a lost soul pleading for the terror to stop.

But one can learn to stand firm and fight one's terror while still holding on to one's humility at being overwhelmed – not by another person, but by a phenomenon, by two talking heads and by the terror they engender. One learns to stand firm by accepting one's fear. One learns that faith – even a bit of it – is crucial. Everything one knows about the psyche can help, as long as one does not allow such 'protective words' to mean too much. For that lack of judgment will assuredly take one away from one's body and again cause one to 'spin.' As one stands firm, one will gradually begin to see the opposites separately, 'first one, then the other will rise from the water.' This experience will be frightening because each face can distort reality to the extent that one sees the person with whom one is experiencing such a drama in radically different ways. Through 'each head' one sees differently, and with this sudden change comes the threat of loss of reality, of becoming attacked, verbally if not physically. But if one stands firm, and stays conscious, a change can occur. For, as the myth says, each face can then see the other, and the opposites can begin to come together and cease to exist as all-or-nothing states, with each vying for complete supremacy. The myth asks that one keep faith, that one refuse to flee in the face of a single opposite, and that one believe, even in this condition, that a larger, compensatory world – a world of unity – will prevail and will show the other face before one is devoured. A partial truth then becomes possible; a capacity to work together gradually to know the truth becomes possible. For when the two faces see each other, the Truth appears. The truth may be awful, an awareness of what really happened or perhaps what did not happen in one's childhood, or in a current life situation. But a paranoid rigidity has finally passed. One feels that one has barely survived an ordeal which could have lasted for many years.

The quest for truth becomes one's leverage, even in one's most psychotic levels. In fact, one's soul hides in these psychotic levels, for madness is the best hiding place. Madness can completely confuse everybody, causing them to leave you alone. Only the person who accepts entrance into one's world of madness is worthy enough to see one's soul. Only then may he or she be trusted enough to be given the chance to prove that he or she will not be another violator.

And through this experience, one is able to gain a certain stability based upon a belief in one's own Truth. And this Truth is to be found behind one's own eyes, according to the myth of Sisiutl, meaning the imagination that sees 'through' one's eyes, not 'with' them. Then, one is never alone, which is to say one is forever in touch with the Self.

The mythological images of the double-headed serpent act like a map that can guide the experience of opposites from being destructive of consciousness and psychic structure into a creative act of structure-enhancing vision. The myths inform us of how the ego cannot contain the opposites, how a containing presence stems from the self, and how actively and courageously interacting with the field that the split opposites engender must be an intentional act that struggles for vision amidst strongly dissociating fields.

For example, a man whom I was treating for a mid-life crisis that was adversely affecting his work situation and marriage with episodes of anxiety and abandonment fears, was speaking with great praise about his wife's business achievement. He also noted how she was being opposed by negative forces at her workplace. The night before, she had asked him to mail an important letter for her. He left the house to do an errand and never mailed the letter. As he told this story, of which he was very ashamed, and while he expressed that he really wanted to know why he had acted so badly, I felt hazy. In the past, I had avoided this state and instead held my attention together with great effort while I listened to him. But now, recognizing that this avoidance was not fruitful, I chose to focus upon the hazy condition I had been resisting. So, I asked him if he felt somewhat fragmented, and he acknowledged that he did.

As we further explored what was at stake in her business, I suggested that he may have been angry at a loss of income, for his wife's letter had to do with a previous business which she had started and which had failed. This suggestion struck home and, after a pause, he said, 'So my noble feelings about how great she was doing are a sham.' 'Why do you think so?' I asked. 'Perhaps both attitudes are there.' This awareness easily evaporated between us, and he said, 'Sure, that makes sense.' But then I began to focus upon the existence of both attitudes more fully, for I was beginning to see that he was exhibiting two opposite states which were actually incompatible. In response to his 'Sure that makes sense,' it was tempting just to go on, and it took a volitional act not to be swept away. Instead, I stayed with the odd way these two states were structured, for when I focused on his hostile feelings towards his wife, those feelings were all that existed. It was not at all easy to remember any good feelings. Conversely, when his good feelings were attended to, any and all negative ones were completely annihilated. The opposites in this field were not split, as they are in projective identification. I did not feel one opposite while the analysand identified with another. Rather, one part of the pair of opposites was present for both of us and dominated completely, and then the other dominated completely.

He said that he always uses his goodness to annihilate the dark side of his psyche, but I pointed out how the reverse had just occurred. In this way, we managed to establish a pair of opposites within his chaotic life. During this process, the fogginess vanished; a clarity of contact existed between us as would not be present by simply waiting for clarity through periods of haziness or fragmentation. He began to notice a deep rage within himself, at his wife for losing money, and then at his mother for her control and use of him as a child. He noted, with some fear, that he had been identifying his wife with his mother, and, at this time, he also noted that he was holding his breath, frightened to breathe. He could recognize that his overwhelming rage at his mother lived in a front–back split felt to be behind him, and that he engaged in dissociative processes to obliterate awareness of this rage. But he also engaged in a general restriction of his life, of his capacities and his rewards. Like all people with a mad area, he was limited by it. But he did not consciously accept this limitation. Instead, a kind of self-imposed masochism prevailed, a very non-creative state.

He asked me: 'Why are you exploring this now, today, and not before?' I was somewhat surprised by his question. I felt reluctant to tell him that it was because I had been writing a paper on chaos theory and psychotic states, but I did. I then told him about the value of such states of mind, that they were the alchemical *prima materia*, and he felt relieved. He could split again, the haziness returned. My manic behavior – the speaking of thoughts in which I was interested – opened the door to a mind–body split; but I was able to catch this splitting, and we could return to the opposites within his mad sector. I suggested that he write down the session and take the time to reconstruct it. With this suggestion, his anxiety returned. He knew he had to tackle this area, and he remarked that his life was run by the avoidance of this area. He saw that his background fear was of being psychotic, for example, that his wife was actually his mother. I also sensed that he was protecting me from such a delusional transference and the rage it entailed. But acting out the dissociative processes within mad states was no longer a viable option for him. He had to encounter his own chaos creatively.

The analyst can often be guided in such processes by reflecting upon ways that previous civilizations have dealt with madness, especially those ways which they regarded as a necessary and functional component of the transformation of personality. As such, alchemy's penetration and understanding of the *prima materia*, particularly as it is outlined in the *Rosarium Philosophorum* is an indispensable guide in reckoning with the ambiguities and transforming potential of mad aspects of sane people.

DIONYSOS AND THE LOWER WATERS OF THE 'MERCURIAL FOUNTAIN'

In the *Rosarium*, the 'Mercurial Fountain' fills from below, indicative of the 'lower' or chthonic dimension of existence. With this realm of passion, of eruptions of emotions, and of spontaneity often comes madness. For as boundaries are broken, and structure is dissolved, the waters of chaos have a ready access; only through them is any thorough transformation accomplished.

Dionysos (see Detienne 1989; Otto 1965; Hillman 1972; Kerenyi 1976; Paglia 1990) is an excellent mythological example of the nature of passion in the mad part of a normal personality. This part can be dismissed as hysteria if one lives only from a mental-spiritual vantage point as represented by the Olympian gods such as Apollo. The psychotic part, like Dionysos, creates a sense of strangeness. One does not know the person when this part is constellated, and he or she only marginally knows us. Dionysos corresponds to this experience that contains both mystery and danger. The psychotic part, with its split opposites, gives forth a sense of emptiness, of being emptied out and deadened. Yet when these opposites are brought together the experience shifts to one of fullness.

Dionysos combines such states of absence and presence. The person one sees, when the psychotic part is enlivened, always wears a mask. One sees a stranger, someone one truly does not know. The strangeness is unsettling. But like the experience of Dionysos, there are two masks, two strangers, one seeming to pull toward life and the other toward death, to fullness and to deadness. One cannot see this duality unless one sees through one's own psychotic part, that is, through the experience of felt limitation by our own madness. This experience of limitation in the face of madness is a sacrifice to the god – as the Greeks said an *epidemic* – in which one participates when the god appears through the analysand. For those who are aware of their own defilement through madness, Dionysus becomes a purifying god, an essential issue when it comes to relating to mad parts. The analyst must know ways in which he or she has defiled another soul through acts that were either blatantly destructive at the time or, more to the point, through acts that were driven secretly by a hidden madness. Such behaviors often take the form of intrusion or withdrawal, based upon a belief in one's sane, courageous behavior that dares to break with conventional wisdom. Yet, later, one learns that the actions in question were mad and destructive to a high degree. All instances of sexual acting out in psychotherapy fall under this category of madness. At the time, the analyst really believes he or she is sane and is serving special energies; the god Dionysos takes a toll from those who deny him.

This toll may play a role in acting out, for many who have succumbed in this way will speak of feeling that a higher power was being served and to have done otherwise would have been an act of cowardice and failure. But Dionysos, in fact, does not demand that one become mad; he only demands that one acknowledge that madness is present. When Dionysos asks to be worshiped he asks that one acknowledge the presence of his power in the moment, within oneself. He becomes purifying to those who know they are up against energies so powerful that they do not have the capacity to know whether or not they are mad. Respecting the power of such unknowing respects the god, whereas, as so many in Greek myth discovered when they became mad after rejecting his rites, acting in mad ways does not. In the myths, those who reject Dionysos commit horrendous acts such as the murder of their own children. They then are themselves dismembered, literally torn apart by madness.

The awareness of our serious failures, defilements of soul, and a capacity to carry this history and speak and be with it as alive, within us, creates the proper voice tone and feeling for the analyst through which an analysand's psychotic part can be known and accepted. The analyst may, through rational understandings that appeal to the analysand's normal neurotic side, deny Dionysos, and as a consequence madness will take its toll as severe dissociation and a brutal attack upon one's inner life, states of mind usually felt by the analysand as the analyst subtly withdraws and gives the message that he or she does not want the analysand's madness in the room. Dionysos is not one to forgive slights even when attempts are quickly made to change one's attitude. Manic defenses emerge, and the analysand will often turn to drugs or food to soothe the inner rage that is so unbearable and destructive.

Dionysos is a god who leads to large-scale invasion that spreads among people. He is contagious just as is the psychotic part. He causes us to stumble which, in turn, creates a new view of life. We are called upon to rebuild anew our images of psyche, and not over too long a period of time. When one knows the opposites in their split form, one knows Dionysos in his most death-like nature, as Camille Paglia says, 'in the slow, ooze and muck of the chthonian' (1990, 6). When the analyst encounters him in the interactive field with the analysand, heart-connection and spontaneity are non-existent. Both feel a sense of alienation, deadness, emptiness, and if they look further, of an ever-present sense of strangeness. One may approach this development from an Apollonian vantage point and speak of a 'derealized-depersonalized sequence.' Although this Apollonian talk is clear, one is left with an uncomfortable feeling: the analysand is strange to the analyst and the analyst is strange to himself or herself.

A murderer lurks in Dionysos and in the psychotic part. For a person's psychopathy resides in the psychotic part in the form of a ruthlessness that knows little compassion for others. Yet does the analyst ever meet this part by interpreting it to the analysand? No matter what the analyst does along the way, no matter how he or she may inwardly experience the contagion of the 'god,' and no matter how he or she may frame this experience in an interpretation, the analyst still has shifted levels, having gone from the Dionysian to the Apollonian. Interpretation often yields a knowledge that represses, not a living knowledge of the way one is forever limited by madness.

The analysand is to know this part only by being 'seen' through it by the analyst, only by being seen in his or her strangeness and in the felt moment of an interactive field. Moreover, the analysand will see the analyst's psychopathy, will know such parts in him or her, and when the analyst can acknowledge the analysand's perceptions, then the analysand can dare to accept more readily these parts within himself or herself. At this level of interaction, one does not deal with a conscious–unconscious split alone, but rather with a split that also includes a radical separation of opposites within the complex itself. The analyst encounters this split within the interactive field, while conscious–unconscious repression can be employed to deny its pain and sense of strangeness. This split can also be employed to deny the powers involved. Dionysos has been depicted as a bull and a panther. Such wild energies inhabit the psychotic part and can be known when seen as such, when the defenses of idealization and dissociation are successfully gathered up and dissolved.

Dionysos is a god not only of death and emptiness but also of life and fullness. Sometimes in his stories, he comes in forms that appear sane, for instance, as a young man or beautiful woman. So, too, we can often appear sane and be unaware that we are acting in mad ways. Yet, when Dionysos's opposites are finally held together, distance gives way to closeness, emptiness to fullness, and a containing heart forms where the felt-experience of the heart had previously been absent.

The Greek word *psychosis* really means 'soul-animation.' At root, we are seeking the animation of a soul that has been frozen in early terrifying experiences of chthonian life. Camille Paglia offers a succinct and vivid account of the Dionysian level in her book *Sexual Personae*:

> What the west represses in its view of nature is the chthonian, which means 'of the earth' – but earth's bowels, not its surface . . . I adopt it as a substitute for Dionysian, which has become contaminated with vulgar pleasantries. The Dionysian is no picnic. It is the chthonian realities which Apollo evades, the blind grinding of subterranean force, the long slow, suck, the murk and ooze. It is the dehumanizing brutality of biology and geology, the Darwinian waste and bloodshed, the squalor and rot we must block from consciousness to retain our Apollonian integrity as persons . . . The daemonism of chthonian nature is the west's dirty little secret.
>
> (1990, 5–6)

This chthonian nature can be transformative. The chaos can become order, but it always remains dangerous and bloody.

In their fullness, Dionysian energies have always been felt to be dangerous in their flooding capacity. To partake of these energies in a positive way, one must learn of the power and danger of the chthonic realm and of its fundamental Otherness to the ego. Today, the chthonic life of the body is essentially taken for granted, and sexuality is not generally understood to have a numinous (that is, religious) component. Spirituality is reserved for the disembodied world. But sexuality is an archetypal power the numinosity of which is only thinly veiled in modern culture. While representing a one-sided point of view, Freud's insistence upon the sexual basis of our internal fantasy life accounts in large measure for his work continuously being taken seriously.

Sometimes, it is possible to feel how chthonic life lurks at the edge of our consciousness as we become aware of our bodies, aware of being part of and inside the flesh. As we approach chthonic life, it threatens the light of our solar-rational nature, and this light does, in fact, go out as we enter our bodily depths. Actually, only lunar consciousness, imaginal light, will suffice to see in the dark; and usually this form of vision means a consciousness that comes from the heart.

The analyst may feel the dangerous aspects of chthonic life lurking within the psychotic sector of analysands, especially in a hazy way before the psychotic transference has coagulated. Prior to this experience, the analyst may experience the analysand's splitting and an induced dissociation. But in the intervals during which the analyst is able to remain focused upon the analysand, the analyst can often gain a glimpse of the nature of the chthonic level.

The chthonic level, which was characterized by a strong erotic field, appeared in the beginning of my work with a woman suffering from a schizoid disorder. She ignored it by splitting from her body. When I interpreted the splitting, she could then, albeit momentarily, recognize her sexual feelings and her fears of them. I wondered if she was an incest victim, but while she was quite certain that nothing like actual incest had ever occurred, her fears of the erotic level were intense and her spontaneity with men was nearly absent, which caused her great suffering. When for a moment during one session, I could help her focus upon these feelings, she imagined her mother violently attacking her. In fact, she had been her father's favorite child, but always intellectually so, and as far as she knew nothing physically inappropriate occurred between them. She appeared to suffer from a strong oedipal complex, perhaps antagonized by her father's unconscious sexuality and by her mother's competitiveness with other women, of which the analysand was acutely aware from a very early age. Nevertheless, an intense erotic life appeared to have existed between her and her father, and this energy pattern quickly emerged in the transference to me, along with her need to split from being attacked. I was both the attacking parent, the mother, and the object of her incestuous desires, her father. Clearly, the two were not separable, which would have been indicative of a capacity for repression. Instead, in the transference, I was a double-sided object, both stimulating and attacking, seductive and sadistically punishing her for her erotic feelings.

We usually felt this aggressive-erotic or sado-masochistic quality of the field amidst an intensely dissociated process. These qualities did not present features of the engulfing and eruptive sexuality that an analyst often finds with schizophrenics, nor was it controlled through repression and the structural gains of having developed into the beginnings of an oedipal period.

At one point, when I attempted to hold my own attention together for a span of several minutes, I asked her to associate to, or to imagine, what she expected to happen. She looked inside of herself and was startled to discover her response: 'I expect you to slam me against the wall and fuck me!' The brutality in this was shocking and was completely out of character for the erotic field between us, the nature of which had been rather warm and caring. At another time, several months later, I again held the opposites in the field together long enough to ask her to go into herself – this holding was necessary because without it she was so fragmented as to make any act of will impossible – and she discovered another shocking image. She saw me as an animal – something like a bull – attacking her head.

Usually, analysts think of such archetypal layers as manifesting in a florid way in the schizophrenic, or else as working behind the scenes in so-called primary process, but not overtly intruding. Freud had said that the psychotic sees too much. Yet these levels of chthonian nature exist in the psychotic part and form the basis for the psychotic transference. Clearly, these chthonic levels are terrifying to the analysand, and the art of the analytic process is to be able to gather them up into a stable, cohesive psychotic transference that does not become delusional.

The double-sided transference and intense dissociative process was an example of the constellation of her psychotic sector. The opposites in this sector can stem from the analysand's experience of both parents, or they may stem either from a mind–body split in a single parent or from sources that cannot be totally understood in terms of developmental issues. Within the psychotic area, the opposites either have not separated or, when they do separate, they can take on the form of the opposites that I have described as anti-worlds. At both stages, the energies of which the analysand is terrified belong to the chthonic realm of total dissolution – the lower waters of the Mercurial Fountain. But opposites can combine in the psychotic area in a particularly confusing and controlling manner, which can influence the structure and dynamics of the interactive field.

THE PSYCHOTIC AREA AND THE NEGATIVE FUSION OF OPPOSITES

Beyond fragmentation and strangeness, and an array of intense affects such as rage and hatred, and mental states of absence and deadness, something else lurks within the psychotic process. The analyst senses something which is so terrifying as to feel world-destroying to the analysand. Most usually this intense anxiety exists as a background process that is felt to be split off from the front of the analysand, yielding a front–back split. The 'background object' (Grotstein 1981, 77) of this split constellates feelings of catastrophe. In the background object of psychotic process, destructive forces rule – a situation which is a characteristic feature of psychosis. The analyst will usually experience a strong tendency to avoid feeling any of these features of the psychotic area, and this foreclosure can be acted out in the countertransference in numerous ways. Perhaps the most dominant form of avoidance is a tendency for the analyst to wait out any experiences of dissociation, blankness, and the state of strangeness that prevails until such features pass, or for the analyst to shake himself or herself out of this kind of reaction by stressing the analysand's strengths.

This background object exists in a split-off state related to other axes of splitting: vertical splitting, in which one finds incompatible opposites that combine into bizarre objects; and horizontal splitting, characteristic of mind–body splitting. Vertical splitting has the inductive effect of further splitting off the background object and of enhancing mind–body splitting. Conversely, gathering up the opposites in a vertical split has the inductive effect of making the background object more present to consciousness, and bridging mind–body splitting has a similar inductive effect. This inductive interplay of axes of splitting was well-known to ancient science, especially to Renaissance alchemy, and a similar interaction of dimensions is found in modes of energy and information transfer in certain quantum mechanical processes.

The analyst at times can engage the background object through an imaginal act. This imaginal act is a kind of sight that is non-ordinary such as that found in Ludwig Wittgenstein's concept of 'seeing-as' (Monk 1990, 508), or in Carlos Casteñeda's (1971) notion of 'seeing,' or in William Blake's (Damrosch 1980, 16) conception of 'seeing through one's eyes rather than with them,' and in Sufi and alchemical notions of the imagination. The analyst's act of imaginally perceiving the background object often uncovers a sense of terror that resides in the analysand, making him or her aware of a deep-seated feeling of humiliation. This humiliation is born of living with such states of mind, and especially with a consciousness of having been hated. While the act of seeing these background conditions temporarily diminishes the splitting along the other axes, such splitting tends to return when the analyst's vision recedes. Within this dissolving and coagulating rhythm, the negative, overpowering nature of the background object can, at times, be gradually contained and transformed.

The background process is of a Dionysian nature, and the splitting that blocks its full impact generally leads to mental disruptions, such as the creation of 'anti-worlds' and bizarre objects. Louis Sass has made a strong point of criticizing the use of the Dionysian analogies, usually derived from Friedrich Nietzsche's view of the god, as a way of comprehending schizophrenia. Sass believes that schizophrenia is also, if not primarily, an Apollonian illness. He suggests that although Dionysian states – such as boundary dissolution and 'self-dissolution in intense physical sensation' – may exist, he insists that such states are actually a defense against the more characteristic features of schizophrenia. For Sass, these features include core issues of a 'sense of division, deadness, and de-realization or of avoiding the terror of solipsistic responsibility for the world' (Sass 1992, 312). He supports his position by noting that Nietzsche's view that the Dionysian flood of passion and boundary dissolution may be a momentary release from Apollonianism itself: 'The propensity for drawing boundary-lines, and . . . enjoining again and again the practice of self-knowledge' (quoted in Sass 1992, 312). Generally, Sass's view is that schizophrenia is actually far more an Apollonian or Socratic illness 'whose central features are hypertrophy of consciousness and a concomitant detachment from instinctual sources of vitality' (1992, 74), along with a 'fragmenting hyperawareness and a kind of cerebral self-interrogation' (1992, 37).

Sass's critique is unusual and useful, but his argument could easily be turned on its head through an insistence that his 'Apollonian' features are actually defenses against the 'Dionysianism' that lurks in the background. For example, I experienced the 'fragmenting hyperawareness' and mindlessness that Sass focuses upon with a certain female analysand whose narcissistic structure was extremely insulating. While sexual fantasy had never been a part of our sessions together, in one particular session, I had the unusual experience of feeling an inner injunction to allow no sexual fantasy. The material she was talking about on that day had to do with beginning to date men, but she had made no allusion to either sex or fantasy. As I looked at her, I found myself averting my eyes and stifling my imagination, as if a taboo were present. It was as though an Eleventh Commandment had been proclaimed from on high and now hung in the consultation room: 'Thou Shalt Not Imagine.'

I suddenly recognized that this taboo had always existed in my work with her and that it was so total that, in the years of working with her, I had never even imagined having a sexual thought in her direction even though she was a very attractive woman. We had previously discussed the fact that our work together seemed limited by a lack of intimacy that felt restrictive and infertile. Now, I realized that the absence of the erotic in our work could possibly have something to do with the arid feeling we experienced in her analysis. Several facets emerged as we explored this quality of our interaction. Sitting and experiencing the injunction to have absolutely no sexual interest in her, I became aware that I felt totally undesirable. But when I told her this feeling, she reflected upon her interactions with men, and she was certain that she did communicate this 'anti-erotic' injunction to me. Then, she confessed that she felt totally undesirable and believed no man could have any sexual or intimate interest in her. After nursing the feelings involved with this belief for a while, it became clear that her anti-erotic injunction was her denial of her father's sexual intrusiveness during her childhood years.

Her father's intrusion had not been literally enacted but had existed within the domestic atmosphere of her childhood as a powerfully dangerous presence. She had internalized the dynamics of her childhood home, as everyone does, and through her unconscious denial, she could keep this traumatically intrusive state in check. She succeeded in protecting herself through a horizontal, mind–body split in which her mind did not allow recognition of erotic energies that her body might perceive in her environment. Through projective identification, this split was transmitted to others, largely through the device of cutting off her breathing below her diaphragm. Her breath only marginally came up from her lower body, and it barely ever returned to these depths. This mind–body split became a major way that the interactive field in our work was affected and through which mind–body splitting was communicated.

This discovery of the nature of her mind–body splitting – and her front–back split, with the background object dominated by intrusive sexual fantasies that terrified her – had also been defended against by a vertical splitting and associated mental characteristics, notably the deadness and mindlessness Sass describes. The vertical split in this analysand was characterized by completely opposite and mutually annihilating states. In its vertical splitting aspect, the field with her was signified by, on the one hand, a fullness of desire for connection and, on the other hand, a concomitant state of deadness and mental emptiness. These splits successfully blocked the Dionysian element and her terror of fusion which that state triggered (Green 1993, 243). So while Sass has keyed upon extremely important features which he calls Apollonian (an unfortunate choice since Dionysos is a mad god, while Apollo is not), it might be more exact to keep in mind that not only do both 'Dionysianism' and 'Apollonianism' exist, but indeed they coexist. While at times, one can be a defense against the other, they are both necessary points of view. Dionysian may better characterize the background split, while Apollonian seems more to describe the vertical splitting that is also very common and which is often more obvious than the background life of psychotic process. Mind–body splitting appears to combine both Dionysian and Apollonian elements.

The analyst can at times feel the dangerous aspects of Dionysian, chthonic life lurking within the psychotic sector, especially in a hazy way before the psychotic transference has coagulated. Prior to this coagulation, the analyst may experience the analysand's splitting and an induced dissociation. But in the intervals during which he or she is able to remain focused upon the analysand, the analyst can often gain a glimpse of the background nature of the chthonic level.

AREAS OF MADNESS AND THE DOUBLE-BIND MESSAGE

When the anti-worlds fuse in the Apollonian aspect of madness, the field that is created has a particularly confusing and controlling nature. This control and confusion is known as the double bind. Gregory Bateson has developed the concept of the double bind as part of understanding family systems, and he also believed it to be a major aetiological factor in schizophrenia. While this latter idea has not proved to be fruitful, Bateson's concept of the double bind is often a strong factor in forming the psychotic part of an otherwise normally functioning person. In Bateson's double bind, two messages are given simultaneously, and they contradict one another. But beyond this contradiction, and critical to its disastrously powerful effect, the double bind exerts a field that has the unspoken injunction that the object must not leave the field of the double bind; the object must not betray the influence of the double bind by consciously reflecting on it. The analyst is caught in the dilemma of being fused with the object while at the same time trying to separate and finding that neither option is possible. The unconscious demand to 'not notice' the double bind leads the object of the double bind to dissociate its contradictory injunction into two parts; and if this object does not have the facility for hypnotizabilty that dissociation requires, then he or she tends to form psychotic areas of incompatible opposites. Generally, these processes intertwine and multiply.

Bateson *et al.* give the following example which occurred when a schizophrenic boy was visited by his mother in a hospital:

> He is glad to see her and impulsively put his arm around her shoulders, whereupon she stiffened. He withdrew his arm and she asked: 'Don't you love me anymore?' He then blushed, and she said, 'Dear, you must not be so easily embarrassed and afraid of your feelings.'
>
> (1972, 18–19)

Her body gives one message and her mind another, and together they lead to a state of confusion and madness. One does not have to become schizophrenic under the impact of such messages, but one's soul certainly tends to get lost, and inwardly one's reaction is to keep the two messages distinct. As is usually the case with such defenses, this separation then becomes a radical split in which the two messages become totally separate, and each tries to be the whole story. When the dissociative mechanism is psychotic, leading to the opposites existing as anti-worlds, this mechanism produces great distress for the person and for anyone trying to communicate with them.

The injunction to 'not notice' the double bind, to deny its existence, is illustrated by an analysand who was telling me about his visits with his elderly father. During the evening, his father was 'holding court' as usual and creating an atmosphere very difficult to tolerate. For example, his father had been insisting that he never worried about anything, which left his son flabbergasted and confused. Something did not feel right; he felt irritated, but he did not know what to say. He knew his father was not being truthful, but he also felt inhibited to speak. Back and forth he went between these polarities, as if there were a secret injunction to say nothing. His father had set up an atmosphere in which 'everything was okay,' and in which no conflicts existed. Yet there were plainly many conflicts. Both messages were prominent. Listening to his father, he suddenly began to smile, not knowingly but very obviously, so that his father asked him what was amusing. This question broke a spell, and he said, 'because what you're saying is patently not true. There are many nights when you awake at 4:00 a.m. and cannot go back to sleep because you're anxious.' His father looked shocked and dumbfounded. That night the son had the following dream:

> I am looking at two parallel columns of information and I am matching them, comparing items between them. As I succeed my father announces that there is to be a large meeting, and in it he will announce to everyone that I am crazy.

The unconscious has picked up the significant ordeal the man went through during the previous day. It replays the events – the father's double messages and the way the son struggles with receiving them – in a new metaphorical context. Then, the 'father's announcement' unveils an aspect of the difficulty – which apparently eluded the son's awareness – which was that something was really maddening in the father's message. In a way, the struggle between the two of them was over which of them was crazy. For by the rules of the double-bind game, one of them had to be crazy. Whatever the father was trying to work out through his own psychotic message, the mutually annihilating states made the son feel he was going crazy.

Generally, double-bind messages will actually stem from a mad area of the projector, which makes dealing with that person very difficult, for facing one's impotence in relation to another's madness is often an unacceptable option. Instead, fear and feelings of impotence turn to impotent rage. Perhaps the most difficult lesson to learn when facing a double bind is that one cannot win. One must learn to leave the field of battle by knowing that one's own soul is in danger. All one can really do is not win and, instead, care for one's own inner life. At times, this act will allow one to have some imaginal experience that moves the double bind to another level in which the injunction to 'not notice' the opposite messages vanishes. At other times, one is left with the necessity of recognizing and stating something to the effect that 'this is not good for me.' The potentially infantile sounding quality of such a response is often felt as humiliating for a person wilting under the impact of the double bind and believing that he or she must be a hero and overcome it. Generally this heroism takes the form of trying to get the projector of the double-bind message to understand how he or she is being contradictory. Little could be more futile.

In this case, an analyst would, of course, not know what the analysand's father is really like. The analyst must learn to support the analysand's experience and not identify with induced, irritating and confusing effects of the double bind. To do this, analysts must learn to respect their own limits which are imposed by their own psychotic area. For example, within this specific experience, one may begin to learn these limits if one can process one's own states of mind and perhaps one's experience with one's own father. Someone else may be able to see objectively, but the analyst must not automatically believe that he or she is doing so. Supporting this subjectivity is the most difficult thing for an analyst who has been traumatized, for one's reaction to being re-traumatized is either to fight, to withdraw, or to become compliant. The analyst's supporting of himself or herself in an honest 'just so' way, in which his or her felt limitations are taken as genuine and important, is a necessary but extremely difficult step to take. The analyst may feel as if he or she is opening up himself or herself to being even more traumatized, and often the only ally seems to be power. But the lesson the analyst can learn in such a process is just how foolish and eventually how impotent such power responses are.

The impact of the double bind is seen in more detail in the following case of a man who had a chronic history of losing his temper and frightening his family. He could never really understand these eruptions, and he felt powerless when they occurred. He began a session talking about how he had hurt himself playing soccer. He asked me if I believed in accidents just occurring, just happening, or if I felt they always had some deeper meaning. I inwardly felt annoyed at the question. I did not answer as I tried to sort out my own feelings. His question had a leaden quality that made me feel somewhat deadened. If I answered factually – for example, by saying, 'Yes, accidents happen,' or perhaps, 'Yes, I do think that such events often have meaning' – I would feel hollow and punitive. I wondered:

> Does he really want to ask me this? He has been in analysis for years, and he surely knows that such events often have a symbolic meaning. Is he being hostile? Is that why I am angry? He seems to be caricaturing analysis.

But none of these thoughts captured the sense of the moment. My sense of his oddness or my feeling of his weirdness came closer to the point. Eventually, I was able to find some ground within the minor storm his question created, and when I shifted to a different level and asked a question in return – 'What might it mean?' – he answered: 'Maybe, it means I won't have to try out for the new position on the team.' With this exchange, the atmosphere in the room altered, and a more normal state of reflection and separation of states that were not violently incompatible prevailed.

This introductory statement he had made led to a very mild experience, but far deeper states ensued in the session revealing how areas of madness are created and can hide beneath seeming neurotic behavior of ambivalence and anxiety. Specifically, having gotten through this initial phase of the session, he posed the next dilemma:

> I have a conflict. A soccer coach is coming to teach, but it is also my birthday and my wife has made theater plans and also plans to have dinner at home first. I feel very conflicted. When I first trained a lot for my position and got it, upon returning home my son said: 'Hooray, Daddy is finally back with us.' I felt terrible. I just did my thing and totally neglected them. Am I doing the same thing now?

As the analysand spoke, I found myself inwardly switching back and forth between two feelings. On the one hand I tended to think: 'Why not take your remarkable accomplishment for yourself and enjoy it?' But then I felt myself switching to an opposite thought: 'Your family, and your son are important, so maybe you might have been too fanatical.' I felt a pressure to tell him something, especially when he said: 'What do I do with this conflict? It seems that I am being selfish, as they say, yet I have to train three nights a week.'

I could have dealt with different states such as love and hate, thus shifting the session on to this kind of level. For example, thoughts of telling him to 'be a man' came into my head, and it was almost hard to control a desire to inspire him to 'take for himself' and not to be bound by the expectations of others. But these impulses were actually calculated to stop the discomfort I felt. Something was strange about his presentation and the situation in which it put me, as if anything I said to him would only be a way of escaping something more fundamental.

At this point, the session could have degenerated into problem-solving or reflecting on how his conflict was related to early issues in his childhood. I wandered again into thoughts about his great difficulties with separation from his mother and his equally traumatic experiences with *rapprochement*. To see his conflict as a repetition of old wounds dating back to a critical 2 to 3-year-old time of life was tempting. We had dealt with these issues many times in our sessions, and turning to them now was a way of escaping something very uncomfortable, for the deeper I allowed myself to feel what I was presently feeling, the less comfortable I felt. A strange sense of a chasm existed between the state of mind signified by his desire to train and his guilt about not being with his family. At first, this chasm felt like a subtle state, and I was tempted to ignore the quality of the split and to side with one or the other state, or to try to link them together. But the more I accepted the discomfort of truly not knowing what to do or say, it became clearer that these states actually represented different worlds: states of mind totally in opposition with each other, each completely self-enclosed and dominating the other. Thus, if I tended to think about one state, such as training, and to urge him to take hold of a heroic spark and to meet his individuation needs, an opposite state would surely take over with just as much or just as little validity. Because I understood that these switches would be stressful and confusing, I chose, instead, to deal only with the state of opposing worlds. I then asked him if he experienced these states in the way that I have just described, and he was relieved to know that I was aware of his internal process. Such awareness is important because people are generally ashamed of having splits of this kind which, at times, can be pushed away but which return with a paralyzing effect. However, having achieved such awareness, what then does one do with these two worlds?

His conscious mind could not deal with the conflict. He did not have the strength to carry the opposites, and for years, when confronted by such dilemmas, he had fallen into a gulf of impotent rage, after which he would then feel terribly guilty. He seemed to be confronted by two impossible choices, and he could not get them together. I wondered about his wife's role in the creation of his state of mind, and I again inquired how she related to his training-versus-family conflict. He said:

She always says she supports me one hundred percent, but then she goes and makes a dinner and theater plans on the night before the day of my important game. If I ask her about this she'll say I'm just being rigid, and if I don't have my position down by now I never will. This sounds right. Why do I have to train up to the last minute? Why am I so compulsive? But, I feel it's the right thing to do. Yet she makes perfect sense and she explains it to me with a lot of psychological understanding. So I feel I should relax, be less uptight, yet I also feel upset with this and can't think clearly. I get confused and angry and I know that's not right. I'm a mess!

I then asked him how it would be if he told his wife the process he goes through. For example, I asked, why not point out to her that, while she says that she totally supports training, she also makes a huge dinner and other plans for the evening when the soccer coach arrives. I further asked how the analysand's wife would respond to his explanation that he felt in a double bind, and specifically, if she recognized that she was part of this process. He laughed, explaining that there was no chance that she would recognize her role. She would only tell him that he was being crazy and that in no way was she giving double messages. No, she truly cared about his training, but surely his birthday dinner was also important, and it was only his rigidity that was making trouble.

He felt truly stuck. What could he do with the murderous rage he felt? I refocused his attention on the opposites that he was feeling, the anti-worlds, and decided to try a different approach. Clearly, since he could not process the double bind with his wife, it was necessary to get beyond it by moving the analysis to a different level. In this case, this movement was facilitated by reflecting upon the mythological parallel of Sisiutl from the Kwakiutl Indians which amplified the conflict he was experiencing.

I am not sure if telling the myth helped him or me, but it surely broke the spell of the double bind, and a solution did appear. He could not find it himself, so I thought of it for him, and I suggested that he could tell his wife that he had decided what he wanted for his birthday. He could say:

> What I want is to go to the training, and for you and the family to eat alone. Then, when I arrive at home I'd like you to welcome me, to thoroughly like what I have done and support it. Then we can all go out somewhere.

This approach was obvious once it had been formulated. He could not deconstruct the double bind, for his wife was not available for this kind of honest exploration, but he could gain some of the strength of his inner Sisiutl, the strength he never felt when he became enraged and impotent and would spin out of control, and he could now simply state what he wanted in terms totally different from hers. He was able to incorporate the suggestion, and it worked well enough for him to feel unconflicted about what he would do. Then, that night he had the following dream:

> Two primitive tribes are at war. One chieftain is talking to a shaman. He tells the shaman that his tribe does not have the technological supremacy of his opponent, and they are not a match for them and will lose. But the shaman says that he has the right spells to employ, and with them he will succeed in his battle.

I think his unconscious represented my use of myth in this instance as a shamanic device, but one that worked to deal with his wife's superior armament of psycho-babble that would ordinarily overwhelm him. The 'spell' that we found was the simple statement of what he wanted; yet so often in the face of madness, his own and that of others, such simple statements were nearly impossible to reach.

In the myth of Sisiutl, the apprehending of his two heads results in the Truth, and in gaining a sense of power that can only be likened to ownership of the self. One owns the self by not owning it. One sees chaos and a miracle of order within the chaos; then that order fades away and reconstitutes anew. The analyst does not hold on to thoughts in a solid way. A kind of humility in this process appears to favor the appearance of the self, and the chaotic or mad process that precedes this appearance can then be transformative rather than further constricting growth. As Sisiutl brought about such changes, and as the Greek god Dionysos did the same for those who respected his power of inducing madness by respecting and being limited by their own, so the mad parts of our psyches can also turn out to be the most significant organizers of a new attitude towards life.

Thus, madness, especially as the mad part of sane people, is part of the alchemical *prima materia*. Without these parts, and especially without knowing how one is limited by one's madness, the central mystery of the alchemical process, the *coniunctio*, becomes dangerous rather than life-enhancing. For this central union experience must live in a subtle body of relations *per se*. One's madness rejects this condition and insists on either a literalization – an acting out of the image of *coniunctio* – or an outright rejection and avoidance of this condition's power. But our mad parts are far more than a boundary condition; they are also a source of life that has been deeply repressed by cultural and personal forces and a source of the dissolution of structures that would never allow an experience of the *numinosum* to become an inner reality.

Always threatening the dissolution of what must be preserved, the dangerously continuing chaos of madness was always a central feature of the alchemical art and, often, a factor for its ignition. The fumes of the Mercurial Fountain fill the *vas hermeticum*, the mysterious vessel, from above, and the Dionysian-like energies fill it from below. Together, they are the same: the one is an experience of the *numinosum* from the vantage point of the psychic unconscious, and the other, from the vantage point of the somatic unconscious. Hence, the upper and lower forces are identical, and together, they form the *prima materia*.

7 The central mystery of the alchemical process

THE DARK SIDE OF THE *CONIUNCTIO*

Alchemists recorded their theories about the *prima materia* not as developmental constructs but as depictions of myth. The core dynamics of the *prima materia* are embodied in the ancient and enduring myth of Attis and Cybele. The tormenting fusion depicted in the Attis–Cybele myth leads to the *nigredo* that follows the *coniunctio*, and this *nigredo* can be extremely dangerous. The Attis–Cybele myth is always a shadow side of the *coniunctio*, and dealing with this fused and frightening form of the union state is the *sine qua non* for the eventual acceptance of and confrontation with passion in the *rubedo* stage of the alchemical *opus*. The myth of Attis and Cybele is part of a thread running throughout Western culture, and the myth represents a state of mind and body that has never been adequately addressed. The alchemical approach is the most detailed and serious attempt in the last 2,000 years to integrate the forces this myth presents.

Cybele is the Great Mother of the gods and of men, and Attis is both her son and her lover. Their intensely fused and passionate relationship is characterized not only by deep love and jealousy but also by revenge, betrayal, and madness. Cybele and Attis are bound together by a fierce and passionate love for each other. An equally strong force, however, also pulls them apart, a force that expresses itself in the various ways by which Attis attempts to break free of his bond with his mother/lover. In the many variations of this story, Attis usually dies – needlessly, it seems, unlike other dying gods such as Dionysos – and no resolution of the elemental struggle enacted by Cybele and Attis ever emerges. Attis is sometimes killed in a hunt, sometimes hanged from a tree, and sometimes driven mad. And Attis, or someone associated with him, is usually castrated. Castration sacrifices, in fact, were once the mark of the ecstatic festivities dedicated to Cybele in ancient times.

The dynamics of the mother–son myth in its various awesome enactments have been particularly identified by Jung as portraying the qualities of the *prima materia* in alchemy. While the myth can be seen as addressing the vicissitudes of adolescence, like the *prima materia* itself, it is more fundamentally a portrayal of the most compelling and distressing interpersonal problems we deal with throughout our lives. Most specifically, the Attis–Cybele myth explores the qualities of the *prima materia*, and the myth involves the nature of relationships in their vital and turbulent aspects when energies are on the move (Attis) in the midst of strong, binding counter-forces (Cybele). The myth addresses the issues we all face individually in our interactions with others while, at the same time, it essentially documents the developmental level of consciousness which humanity has struggled with to date.

In this myth, the son represents the expansive, explorative, and separating nature of the psyche that is held tight in the magnetic sphere of unconscious forces represented by the mother. The myth is a statement of an impossible passion – a love that can neither exist nor not exist. The myth presents a picture of tragic and failed separations and equally tragic states of fusion or bonding. Whether in a man or a woman, these dynamics are a central feature of the alchemical *prima materia*.

A man or a woman never separates from the Great Goddess without integration of his or her 'shadow side.' But this shadow, especially when it is imbedded within narcissistic character issues of rage and sadism – automatically emerging at any affront – can be used to suppress rather than to integrate her wisdom and chthonic life. Alchemy addressed the mystery and importance of chthonic life, not by heroically overcoming it but by relating to the central mystery of union. Accordingly, an understanding of the Attis–Cybele myth plays a vital role in addressing this central mystery of union. For as the alchemists knew, any union state is followed by a death, the *nigredo*. The great wisdom that alchemy embodies is that the sequences of union and death are the process by which the *prima materia* is refined into an embodied self, the *lapis*.

In one Attis story, Attis is born in a miraculous way. In a passion of love, Jupiter approaches Mount Agdus which appears in the likeness of Rhea (Cybele). But she rejects him, and in the ensuing struggle Jupiter spills some of his sperm on the mountain. The mountain conceives from the divine semen, and a terribly wild and androgynous creature called Agdistis is born. This hermaphrodite constitutes a danger to both gods and humans because it can multiply without the aid of others; so the gods must take action. They reject an openly murderous assault and instead invoke the cooperation of Dionysos. They know where Agdistis bathes, so they ask Dionysos to mix the spring-water with wine.

> While the brute is sleeping himself sober Dionysos steals up to him and with a stout cord ties Agdistis' genitals to a tree. On awaking, Agdistis 'deprives himself of that which made him a man.'
>
> (Vermaseren 1977, 91)

From his blood, a tree shoots up. When the king's daughter Nana walks past, she is astonished by the beauty of the tree's fruit. She picks some and puts them in her lap. Suddenly, one of the fruits appears to have vanished, and Nana finds herself pregnant. Her father, Sangarios (which also happens to be the name of a Phrygian river), wants to kill his daughter to avoid disgrace. But the goddess intervenes and arranges the premature birth of Attis. The child is abandoned, kept alive by a goat, and raised by shepherds. He grows up to become a highly attractive shepherd whom even the mighty Mother of the Gods finds herself unable to resist.

In this story, unbridled passion in the form of Jupiter leads to a destructive self-structure, the hermaphrodite Agdistis who is actually a form of Cybele. In other words, passion leads right to the destructive aspect of the goddess, total fusion, and the impossibility of any object relations. A positive hermaphrodite is a representation of a union of opposites, a conjunction, or 'third thing.' But in the story of Jupiter's unbridled passion, the hermaphrodite is the result of a forced union, rape, or incest, and thus is a monstrosity. In the negative hermaphrodite, the opposites do not conjoin into a third, but remain in a bizarre condition, a fusion state that denies meaning and furthers concretization of affects. Passion in the form of Agdistis leads to withdrawal and the denial of Eros. In the story, spiritual gods intervene. In the same way, psychologically, anyone encountering the intense energies of passion must mount a mental-spiritual effort of restraint to avoid the destructive reactions that assuredly emerge when passion is enacted in a driven, compulsive way. This restraint includes recognizing and submitting to the power and value of one's own madness, and it requires knowing the extent to which one is limited by this sector, as did the ancient Greeks when they celebra-ted the god Dionysos. And from this restraint, a new cycle emerges: Attis is born.

Psychologically, it is possible to use this myth as a guide to one's experiences in relating to others. A person can recognize the Agdistis aspects in his or her unrelatedness and insensitivity to others. Jupiter's passion can be recognized in undisciplined or undiscriminated feelings that clamor for fulfillment, and the Attis aspect of a person is that part that strives to find a self-identity within his or her love for others. Internally, one suffers the dynamics portrayed in the Attis–Cybele myth, and in the process, consciousness and a spiritual attitude towards the *prima materia* can emerge. As a result, the alchemical way teaches that one can acquire an internal sense and structure which can lead to experienc-ing both creative restraint and the creativity of passion with full awareness of its potentially destructive nature.

Attis's death always follows upon a marriage: the goddess either kills his loved one, and he dies through his own self-mutilation, or else he is killed while hunting a boar, symbolic of the very dark side of the goddess. In alchemical lan-guage, this death is the *nigredo*, the dark suffering that always follows the expe-rience of the *coniunctio*.

Another version of the myth presented by Ovid in his *Fasti* shows Cybele in love with the handsome shepherd boy who must pledge eternal fidelity to her. When he falls under the irresistible spell of a nymph, the avenging hand of the goddess strikes: the nymph Sangaritis (daughter of the river Sangarios) is killed and Attis goes insane. Obsessed with delusions and believing that he is persecu-ted by the Erinyes, he deprives himself of those parts of his body which were the cause of his infidelity. Flowers spring from his blood, and he himself is changed into a pine tree (Vermaseren 1977, 91–92).

The connection between the myth and madness proves central to any devel-opment that achieves a separation and respect for the goddess. Symbolically speaking, one has to die to develop in a way that can deal with the passion of union and the potentially devastating reactions that follow. Just as Narcissus – the arch-opponent of suffering and change – dies and becomes a flower, which in turn leads to the redemption mysteries of Eleusis, so Attis's death leads to a ritual of transformation. This mystery of the *nigredo* is very far from our patriarchal consciousness that values solidity, stability, constancy, and strength. For most people, it is a long and arduous path even to begin to appreciate the wisdom of this 'other' way, the way of union and death.

Cybele's vengeance when Attis betrays her by relating to another woman is a recurring theme in the myth. The festivities created in his honor consist of Tristia, the commemoration of the sorrows, and of Hillaria, the feasts of joy for his – often partial – resurrection. Following his example, the priests of Attis dedicated themselves entirely to the goddess, submitting to her power and majesty. When one entered her cult, one was initiated into being a sacred slave without any hope of freedom. In exchange, the goddess was believed to stretch out her hands protectively over her slaves (Vermaseren 1977, 92).

This incredibly regressive way of dealing with the power of Cybele represents a strong psychological drive. Men and women still psychologically castrate themselves, albeit in seemingly small ways, in order to avoid the attack they fear is inevitable should they take their power and authority. Generally speaking, the notion of being wounded by the complex interplay of union states, or attempts at union, and the resulting attacks of disorder and despair plays a central role in alchemy. The healing that the alchemists discovered for one's castrated being is brought about through a substance called 'balsam' (Jung 1963, 14: paragraph 663). This healing medication, which purifies fusion drives of incest and acting out tendencies, is created through the conscious suffering of numerous *coniunctio–nigredo* cycles. But always, the Attis–Cybele myth represents a dark, shadow side of the union experience, and the myth forms the archetypal structure which molds the many facets of the *nigredo* following the *coniunctio* experience.

Ovid's telling of the Attis–Cybele myth explains the rite of castration of the priests of Cybele. But the myth contains the main issue of the 'impossible passion' that is never resolved. In Ovid's *Fasti*, Attis breaks his vow, and Cybele takes vengeance, killing the nymph Sangarios. And in the midst of his self-mutilation, he cries out as one whose guilt is overbearing: 'I have deserved it! With my blood I pay the penalty that is my due' (Frazer 1989, 205–06).

The guilt and madness depicted in the Attis–Cybele myth are states of mind deeply hidden within the psychic life of most people. But these states and the associated pattern that excludes possibilities of creatively experiencing states of fusion and separation can also be a quality of an interactive field. Two people experiencing the field can lead to each person's awareness of an impossible fusion state and to its transformation into less destructive and more creative forms of union.

THE DYNAMICS OF FUSION AND SEPARATION WITHIN THE INTERACTIVE FIELD

Especially since it portrays the son–lover of the great goddess, the Attis–Cybele myth can at first appear only to represent the trials of separation from the mother world, and especially the separation of males from their mothers. From this limited perspective, both the mother goddess and a real woman are seen as dangerous to a man who must develop the capacity to separate. When the energies of the myth are interpreted this way by a man, he tends to relegate women to limited functioning: they should be anything but Cybele. That is, they should be understanding, loving, giving, but not people with their own needs and patterns of existence. This kind of concrete understanding of the myth reduces its meaning at great cost to both sexes.

More productively, this myth can be understood to represent both an intrasubjective drama and the vicissitudes of union states between two people. Gender does not limit the applicability of the myth to any relationship; either the male or the female can experience the dynamics which the Attis–Cybele myth puts forth as an intrasubjective drama. A man will experience his consciousness and his capacity to enter and discover new psychic territory as if his consciousness were in the grip of another force that prevented such discoveries. He may project this force on to the woman, or he may experience it as an inner conflict, which is of course preferable. Aggressive inquiry and new or independent acts incur anxiety because they imply leaving the world of fantasy and eternal possibilities. Also, on an intersubjective level, he will experience separation as fear of becoming abandoned in a relationship. A woman in the grip of this kind of Attis–Cybele complex will experience a similar intrasubjective field. An inner force, which is experienced as 'other,' compels her into involvement and fusion with others. Her own desire for separation and autonomy and her active, separating capacity are terribly hindered because these individuation drives are Attis-like. The male-dominated culture wants the Cybele aspect of woman to be controlled. But the Cybele factor can also lie in men, and especially in their feminine sides and irrational moods which they can project on to women. And a woman can project her undeveloped and terrified Attis-like side on to a man. Both will hold each other in secret contempt. Then, the woman, in a sense, has become like Cybele to the man, and he like Attis to her. The myth has thus projected outward and turned especially destructive.

Another possibility, and more in the alchemical way of thinking, is to envision the Attis–Cybele dyad as dominating, like a force-field, the way in which a couple interacts, as if another – unseen couple – were dominating the conscious interaction. This unseen and unconscious couple is, of course, Attis and Cybele. This dyad creates a field of which two people can partake in the sense of being moved by its currents of energy and its inherent pattern of behavior. They would experience this field as a *vas hermeticum*, that is, as a space which enclosed them but which also contained object relations observable as a 'third thing' between them. The primitive form of the Attis–Cybele field, as portrayed in the myth, would tend towards fusion and literalization, an acting out or concretizing of the affects and feelings of desire. From this field, people make inappropriate sexual advances, or they make commitments that are not realistically in their best interest. Alchemically, this field is depicted as either a negative hermaphrodite or a dragon.

This primitive, literalized, form of the myth is in opposition to the 'third thing' experienced as an 'other' with its own dynamics linked to the projections and imagination of both people. Such an experience of the 'third thing' happens when both parties sense the mystery of which they are part and are willing to suffer not literalizing the fusion state, thereby gaining a new level of intimacy that also can be internalized as an intimacy with oneself. Alchemically, this condition is depicted as a conscious coital couple, shown in the eleventh woodcut of the *Rosarium* as being above water and with wings (see Figure 21, p. 199). The alchemists worked on such fields to transform them from a dominant fusion dynamic (in which one person fears or is overwhelmed by the emotions of the other) into a field that had a rhythmical dynamic of separation and fusion, with neither polarity dominating. The famous alchemical dictum of 'slay the dragon' represents this kind of transformation. The goal of this transformation was the *lapis*, that self-structure whose basic rhythm was the *coniunctio* purified of all negative fusion dynamics as well as its other side, soul-less distancing.

Desire, with its powerful, compulsive quality, is the single most dominant element which impedes the purification of the Attis–Cybele field. The overwhelming, compulsive quality of the field puts consciousness to sleep and seduces all other faculties into a merging fusion with the object. Yet in its transformed state – the transformation signified in one alchemical image by the cutting off of the paws of a lion – desire is the key ingredient. It is the fire which drives the process. The French psychoanalyst Luce Irigaray provides a profound insight into desire and the space or 'interval' in which union can be experienced when she says:

> Desire occupies or designates the interval. A permanent definition of desire would put an end to desire. Desire requires a sense of attraction: a change in the interval or the relations of nearness or distance between subject and object.
>
> (1987, 120)

In discussing desire, she speaks eloquently of the dynamics of the non-fused union state, the *coniunctio*. Irigaray notes that if a 'double desire' exists, that is, if a man and woman are capable of desiring and being desired, then:

> the positive and negative poles divide themselves among the two sexes . . . creating a chiasmus or double loop in which each can move out towards the other and back to itself . . . In order to keep one's distance, does not one have to know how to take? or speak? It comes down in the end to the same thing. Perhaps the ability to take requires a permanent space or container, a soul maybe, or a mind?
>
> (1987, 121)

Recognizing that the *coniunctio* is not without its dangers, Irigaray continues:

> The subject who offers or permits desire transports and so envelops, or incorporates the other. It is moreover dangerous if there is no third term. Not only because it is a necessary limitation. This third term can show up within the container as the latter's relationship with his or her own limits: a relationship with the divine, death, the social or cosmic order. If such a third term does not exist within and for the container, the latter may become *all-powerful*.
>
> (1987, 123)

In the initial four woodcuts of the *Rosarium Philosophorum* (see Figures 4, 9–11, pp. 105, 164, 168, 169), one finds this 'third term' to be the descending Holy Ghost. Later, the *coniunctio* forms and becomes the third thing itself, for it has internalized the rhythms of separation and nearness. But fusion, the collapse of the gap or interval, remains a constant threat. The seventeenth woodcut (Figure 27, p. 208) features a symbolic portrayal of the final overcoming of negative fusion states. All the woodcuts following the fifth address the issue of further transforming the *coniunctio* into a container–contained form that excludes the consummation of desire as its greater goal. This developed form of the *coniunctio* means the harmony between male and female polarities.

The *Turba Philosophorum*, an alchemical text written about 1300, represents a particularly fused and dangerous form of the *coniunctio*, reminiscent of the Attis–Cybele myth. A picture in the *Turba* shows a fusion state that takes place between a woman and a dragon (Figure 6). The woman represents the great goddess and the dragon represents the archaic drives toward fusion states, drives which overwhelm any sense of a 'creative interval' between people through which passion can have a mystery rather than an immediate outcome in action.

Figure 6 Coniunctio from the *Turba Philosophorum*

The text of the *Turba* has the following cryptic formulation:

> Nevertheless the Philosophers have put to death the woman who slays her hus-
> bands, for the body of that woman is full of weapons and poison. Let a grave
> be dug for that dragon, and let that woman be buried with him, he being
> chained fast to that woman; and the more he wounds and coils himself about
> her, the more will he be cut to pieces by the female weapons which are fash-
> ioned in the body of the woman. And when he sees that he is mingled with the
> limbs of the woman, he will be certain of death, and will be changed wholly
> into blood. But when the Philosophers see him changed into blood, they leave
> him a few days in the sun, until his softness is consumed, and the blood dries,
> and they find that poison. What then appears, is the hidden wind.
>
> (in Jung 1963, 14: paragraph 15)

In the first sentence of this cryptic statement, the alchemist is suggesting that
a prior process has occurred before the woman and dragon were chained together. 'Putting the woman to death' means that one has actively engaged the tendency to destroy the *coniunctio* and has overcome this tendency. Anytime one
engages a person who has had a terrible past experience with sexual or aggressive acts, in particular, incest violations, one will meet a strong resistance to the
formation of any union state. For example, an analysand dreamed that a man and
a woman were getting married, but she was doing everything she could to stop
the wedding, even to the extent of throwing eggs at them. The wedding would
represent her unconscious connection to me, the analytical transference. Her
behavior in the dream indicates how strong her resistance was to the establishment of a connection with me. She was unconsciously willing even to sacrifice
her most precious possession – the eggs, symbolizing her creativity and future
development – in order to stop the development of a field state of union with me.
In analysis, such issues must be recognized and actively confronted with interpretation. Whether it be the analyst's resistance to a union state, which also can
happen, or the analysand's, either must be confronted if the process is to continue. Either person's desire to remain unconscious can be represented by the
'woman who slays her husbands,' that is, destroys the active drive for union.

Sometimes, alchemical texts have repeated injunctions which act as devices
which function to overcome the resistance to the *coniunctio*. For example, in the
banners of the third woodcut of the *Rosarium Philosophorum*, called 'Naked Truth'
(Figure 10, p. 168), Sol says: 'O Luna, let me be thy husband,' and Luna says:
'O Sol, I must submit to thee' (Jung 1954, 16: paragraph 451). Both the repetition
and the naturalness of the metaphor function to spur on the act, 'psyching' oneself
up to deal with one's reluctance to engage in such potentially painful activity.

One has to learn how to enter and exit the field of union; and until one has
acquired experience enough in dealing with the area, one either does not enter at
all and thus remains narcissistically isolated or one attempts to enter and is immediately swallowed up by the field's magnetic energies and is fused to them. The
whole enterprise is extremely painful, old wounds being opened up and salted in
the process. But one finds one's way only through repeated excursions into that

territory, and through suffering the reopening of festering wounds so that they can, with time, properly heal.

The image from the *Turba* is an example of an extremely fused quality of the *coniunctio* which leads to the transformation of the dragon, the compulsive, concretizing/splitting quality of psyche. The woman has been slain by the 'Philosopher,' that is, by the alchemist. He has killed the desire to withdraw into unconsciousness and also the desire to destroy the union possibility within himself or his metal. Having died, she is now transformed. She is chained to the dragon which represents both the concretizing tendency toward fusion and as well the tendency to flee from this field experience. This archaic image of the interactive field quality feels 'death-like.' Anyone experiencing this interactive field quality may feel as if he or she is in a grave, always on the edge of being devoured by the death of unconsciousness. This very unnerving state constantly challenges one's faith. In this state, the 'weapons and poison' are always ready to re-appear, meaning that one feels in danger and tends to seek release through dissociating from the felt danger of attack. Whether it be through the dangers of being attacked by hatred, anger, or envy, one is always on edge in this field experience. Nearly everyone has areas of trauma within his or her personality structures, and everyone will thus have nearly instinctual reactions to avoid being re-traumatized. Falling back into unconsciousness through withdrawal or dissociation is a ready means of avoiding re-traumatization. Consequently, regression must be avoided, and thus the dragon is chained to the woman. This image represents a commitment to the process.

The slaying of the dragon indicates that the transformation of the impulse to concretize passions or the opposite, to flee from fusion states, has begun. The transformation point occurs when he is 'changed wholly into blood.' In other words, he becomes a tincture felt as passion, but the tincture is still not usable, still not safe. More must be done, and 'they leave him a few days in the sun, until his softness is consumed, and the blood dries, and they find that poison' (Jung 1963, 14: paragraph 15). The stress is upon drying, which means all unconsciousness must be exposed – water being representative of unconsciousness. This demanding task will stress anyone to the limit, for it requires that one experience such dreadful fusion states and be changed by them while experiencing the temptation to fall back into unconsciousness – the poison – so that one either fuses with the energies of the field which leads to acting out or else splits off from the experience. But if one succeeds, 'the hidden wind' appears. In other words, a higher, spiritual experience emerges out of the devastating fusion field. This aspect of the *Turba* (like the entire passage) is not simply some fantastic imagination but a metaphor for actual experience. One can experience being nearly devoured by states of passion, whether they be of hate or love; and at the same time, one can experience the field as nearly continuously killing any connection, with the result that one wishes just to avoid the entire ordeal. The last thing one expects to exist is a hidden, spiritual purpose to it all. Yet that is exactly what can happen.

Thus the *Turba*, one of the oldest known alchemical texts, can be seen as describing a dangerous form of the *prima materia* akin to that portrayed in the

Attis–Cybele myth. The dragon is the Attis component which is successfully transformed, as is the woman, Cybele, so that a spiritual orientation emerges.

The 'hidden wind' is the spiritual attitude that is necessary if one is to deal with the impossible fusion–distance dilemma that characterized the *prima materia* in the Attis–Cybele myth. In the *Turba*, as in alchemy in general, the wind, the spirit, ascends out of matter – the same result as in the eleventh painting of the *Splendor Solis* (Figure 7). The spirit is not imposed upon the transformation process as some set of rules or ethics. But as the alchemists insist that it takes gold to make gold, clearly some of this spiritual attitude must also exist before one can deal with such gruesome forms (Jung 1963, 14: paragraph 15) of the *coniunctio*.

HEROIC APPROACHES TO THE DESTRUCTIVE FUSION STATES

The Attis–Cybele myth, and with it the terrible forms of the Great Goddess that it embodies, were truly a problem for humankind as it evolved out of Neolithic culture and through the Bronze Age. The 'hidden wind' indeed proved too hidden, and the devouring quality of the unconscious, symbolized by the destructive aspects of Cybele, overpowered any potential for the development of consciousness. The Old Testament and the patriarchal religion of Israel arose at the time (about 1200 BCE) when the Great Goddess had an extremely destructive form. This new religion of monotheism was based upon experiences of the *numinosum*. But it was apparently impossible for the emerging patriarchal religion to use this vision to relate to the mysteries of union, the *hieros gamos*, that was the religious center of the cults of the Great Goddess. The dark, regressive pull of the unconscious was too strong; not enough 'wind' could relate to the older kind of vision and the mysteries of union. Instead, the Old Testament god, Yawheh, whose symbolic form was, among others, *ruach*, the wind, was created in the context of suppressing her worship and making the Great Goddess an object of contempt, derision, and hatred.

Was it necessary essentially to slay Cybele, to repress her totally so that a patriarchal ego, based upon the desire to order Nature, could emerge? In his *Symbols of Transformation*, Jung states the positive aspect of this development in which the hero, he who overcomes the Negative Goddess representing unconsciousness, emerges victorious. Jung considers the motif of sacrifice of instinctual libido, and he explains that the sacrifice is seen most clearly in the legend of Attis:

> Attis was the son–lover of Agdistis-Cybele, the mother of the gods. Driven mad by his mother's insane love for him, he castrated himself under a pine tree. The pine tree played an important part in his cult; every year a pine tree was decked out with garlands, an effigy of Attis was hung upon it and then it was cut down. Cybele then took the pine tree into her cave and lamented over it. The tree obviously signifies the son – according to one version Attis was actually changed into a pine tree whom the mother takes back into her 'cave,' i.e., the maternal womb. At the same time, the tree also has a maternal significance, since the hanging of the son or his effigy on the tree represents the

Figure 7 Eleventh painting from the *Splendor Solis*

union of mother and son . . . Again, the felling of the pine tree parallels the castration and is a direct reminder of it. In that case the tree would have more of a phallic meaning. But since the tree is primarily significant of the mother, its felling has the significance of a mother-sacrifice. These intricate overlap-pings of meaning can only be disentangled if we reduce them to a common denominator. This denominator is the libido: the son personifies the longing for the mother which exists in the psyche of every individual who finds him-self in a similar situation. The mother personifies the (incestuous) love for the son . . . The felling of the pine, i.e., castration, denotes the sacrifice of the libido, which seeks something that is as incongruous as it is impossible. The myth depicts [the] typical fate of a libido regression that is played out mainly in the unconscious . . .

The impulse to sacrifice proceeds in the above instance from the *mater saeva cupidium*, who drives the son to madness and self-mutilation. As a pri-mal being the mother represents the unconscious; hence the myths tell us that the impulse to sacrifice comes from the unconscious. This is to be understood in the sense that regression is inimical to life and disrupts the instinctual foun-dations of the personality, and is consequently followed by a compensatory reaction taking the form of violent suppression and elimination of the incom-patible tendency . . .

Transformation into the pine tree amounts to burial in the mother, just as Osiris was overgrown by the cedar . . . Attis is shown growing out of a tree . . . In the legend of Pentheus, which is bound up with the Dionysos myth, there is a striking counterpart to the death of Attis and the subsequent lamen-tation: Pentheus, curious to see the orgies of the Maenads, climbed up into a pine tree but was spotted by his mother; the Maenads cut down the tree, and Pentheus, taken for a wild animal, was torn to pieces by them in their frenzy, his own mother being the first to hurl herself upon him. In this legend the phal-lic meaning of the tree (felling = castration), its maternal significance (the tree 'bears' Pentheus), and its identity with the son (felling = slaying of Pentheus), are all present; at the same time we have the counterpart and complement of the Pietà, namely the Terrible Mother . . .

The essence and motive force of the sacrificial drama consist in an uncon-scious transformation of energy, of which the ego becomes aware in much the same way as sailors are made aware of a volcanic upheaval under the sea. Of course, when we consider the beauty and sublimity of the whole conception of sacrifice and its solemn ritual, it must be admitted that a psychological formu-lation has a shockingly sobering effect. The dramatic concreteness of the sac-rificial act is reduced to a barren abstraction, and the flourishing of the figures is flattened into two dimensionality . . . [But] scientific understanding makes for a deeper understanding of the phenomena in question. Thus we come to realize that the figures in the mythical drama possess qualities that are inter-changeable, because they do not have the same 'existential' meaning as the concrete figures of the physical world. The latter suffer tragedy, perhaps in the real sense, whereas the others merely enact it against the subjective backcloth of introspective consciousness . . . The essential thing in the mythical drama is not the concreteness of the figures, nor is it important what sort of animal is sacrificed or what sort of god it represents; what alone is important is that an act of sacrifice takes place, that a process of transformation is going on in the unconscious whose dynamism, whose contents and whose subjects are themselves unknown but becomes visible to the conscious mind by stimulating the imaginative material at its disposal, clothing themselves in it like the dancers who clothe themselves in the skins of animals or the priests in the skins of their human victims.

The great advantage of scientific abstraction is that it gives us a key to the mysterious processes enacted behind the scenes, where, leaving the colorful world of the theater behind us, we enter into the ultimate reality of psychic dynamism and psychic meaningfulness. This knowledge strips the unconscious process of all epiphenomenality and allows them to appear as what our whole experience tells us they are – autonomous quantities . . .

[Like all such animal sacrifices] the Mithraic killing of the bull is a sacrifice to the Terrible Mother, to the unconscious, which spontaneously attracts energy from the conscious mind because it has strayed too far from its roots, forgetting the power of the gods, without whom all life withers or ends catastrophically in a welter of perversity. In the act of sacrifice the conscious mind gives up its power and possessions in the interest of the unconscious. This makes possible a union of opposites resulting in a release of energy . . .

Comparison between the Mithraic and Christian sacrifice should show where the superiority of the Christian symbol lies: it lies in its frank admission that not only has man's animal instinctuality (symbolized by the bull) to be sacrificed, but the entire natural man, who is more than can be expressed by its theriomorphic symbol. Whereas the latter represents animal instinctuality and utter subjection to the law of the species, the natural man means something more than that, something specifically human, namely the ability to deviate from the law, or what in theological language is known as the capacity for 'sin' . . .

Through the sacrifice of the natural man an attempt is made to reach [the goal] of consciousness [being] in a position to assert itself completely and mold human nature as it wishes.

(1953, 5: paragraphs 659–60, 662, 669–70, 671, 673, 674)

Jung's approach to Attis–Cybele reflects the broad sweep of his libido theory. This heroic approach is necessary for addressing a life struggle in which libido does not flow well into outer or inner relationships, and in which strong characterological defenses exist against experiencing the depths the myth signifies.

As Attis is both fused in a love with Cybele, and unable to separate, so too is anyone who has not had a sufficiently good maternal bonding experience. Such a person is fused in a search for what has been absent, or not present enough in his or her early life. If a mother has been unable to 'see' her child's uniqueness, and instead only related out of a caretaking, mechanical mode, or out of a realm of what she 'should' do or what 'is right,' but not out of love and wonder, the child, male or female, will be deprived of an essential ingredient of its growth. Enormous frustration arises and, with it, a great deal of aggression that has no natural outlet. In the child's mind, he or she enacts aggressive attacks on the maternal body, for the child's frustration has no other outlet. But the child is also identified with the mother, fused in a bond of a promise of love, a promise that is the child's birthright, and one that has been met in instances that were all too few, yet tangible enough to lead to hope. Because the child is identified with the mother, the child's fantasized attacks also castrate itself. Thus, the symbol of the felled tree as both phallus and mother is not only a libido symbol, but a metaphor for experience. Not only people with pre-oedipal disorders are cast into these depths, nor are these depths only known in the defense systems of the borderline personality or the narcissistic character. Indeed, everyone, to one degree or another, suffers from wounds in these depths.

To one degree or another, everyone castrates himself or herself out of a terror of separating and reaching for the destined goal. He or she clings to a lesser form, whether it be a particular relationship or an individuation task. The hero who steals the fire or the grain from the gods suffers. Everyone fears taking hold of his or her power; everyone, in some depth of his or her being, enacts the drama of Attis and Cybele. Everyone suffers from a history of abandonment, perhaps not so severe as to undermine ego development as in borderline or other pathological structuring of psyche, but abandonment still exists as an awareness that one was not seen or loved. And when one dares to take up the mantle of individuation, the drama of Attis and Cybele comes forth. Everyone, to some degree, is caught in this web whereby separation leads to death, notably the death of the passion and the relational link that motivated one's separation, so that enthusiasm and passion turn to despair. In this same web, one is also caught in the demand to individuate and the equal or greater demand to stay merged with an inner loved object, either known, or more likely, never known enough. In this struggle, one more often than not takes up a compromise solution, a sort of partial castration through collective obedience in which the collective gains the projection of the desired mother. Those who are caught by the struggle between their individuation drives and an ego weakness based upon early fears or trauma will often unconsciously project the Terrible Mother on to an outer situation, and then subtly or not so subtly attack it. In turn, they are attacked, and while the attackers may have their own dark, shadow material, in fact the attacked person has inwardly acted out the Attis–Cybele drama and is crucified by its dynamics as well as by the outer emotional attack.

Whatever form the drama takes, it exists in everyone as an ontological state, not just as an image of the deep currents of the libido in their unconscious. In engaging these currents, not only on an individual conscious level but as a drama between two people, alchemy finds its greatest strength and mystery.

Clinically, the analyst meets two major reactions to the dynamic process represented by the Attis–Cybele myth, namely narcissistic structuring and borderline states. Both are reactions to what is felt to be an impossible fusion–separation drama. In the narcissistic character, fusion is maintained through controlling the object, while separation is also maintained through the narcissistic defense which wards off all affective involvement. In the borderline disorder the fusion–distance dilemma is resolved in radical shifts towards fusing with an object and, sensing the terror of loss of identity, recoiling into a distant state, with the object now carrying a projection of dread and extreme danger. At times, these oscillations combine, leading to the strange sense of bizarreness that can pervade work with borderline patients. Where these characterological defenses fail, psychotic areas emerge; otherwise they are hidden, to one degree or another, within the character structures. Psychotic process is a reaction to finding it impossible to negotiate fusion drives, neither to be able to separate nor to stay fused.

Jung's link between Pentheus and Attis is noteworthy in that Pentheus was ripped to pieces because he rejected Dionysos. But recognizing the 'mad god' within is the only way to deal with the Attis–Cybele drama, whereas rejecting madness is a way of heightening the drama. For this reason, the alchemical *prima materia* was most often denoted as chaos, and chaos is one of the best synonyms for inner states of madness.

CHAOS AND THE *CONIUNCTIO*

The dangerous aspect of the fusion states, as in the Attis–Cybele myth are, however, an essential feature of the transformation process. Whether consciously experienced or unconsciously affecting the ego, the *coniunctio* leads to a release of high-order energy into the conscious personality and with it a concomitant creation of disorder. Functionally, this disorder breaks down rigid defenses. That is why the *prima materia* is often referred to as the lead of Saturn:

> To the earlier alchemists especially, it is not quicksilver, but the lead associated with Saturn, which usually represents the prima materia. In the Arabic text of the *Turba* quicksilver is identical with the 'water of the moon and of Saturn.' In the 'Dicta Belini' Saturn says: 'My spirit is the water that loosens the rigid limbs of my brothers.' And the philosopher Petasios [says]: 'So bedeviled and shameless is the lead that all who wish to investigate it fall into madness through ignorance.'
>
> (Jung 1963, 14: paragraph 493)

The 'spirit [which is] is the water that loosens the rigid limbs of my brothers,' that is, which dissolves rigid character structures, is the madness experienced in the Attis–Cybele type myth of the son–lover. While this chaos results from experiencing the impossible passion described in the myth, by denying the pain of fusion and loss it can also be a defense. In either case, this chaos is especially seen in the *nigredo* – the sixth and seventh woodcuts (Figures 14 and 15, pp. 177, 178) – that follow the *coniunctio*, the fifth woodcut (Figure 12, p. 171) of the *Rosarium*.

In most of the versions of the myth Attis actually does go mad, or else Cybele is shown to be mad. Psychologically, madness can be a way out of an overwhelming state of mind and body. Madness is an inevitable result of the kind of fusion the myth demonstrates. One is so overwhelmed by feelings that to remain fused is impossible, but so is separation. Both options can lead to the creation of mad areas of psyche. In turn, these areas can become the *prima materia*.

Jung explains that the alchemists often speak of the *prima materia* in terms of the dangerous aspect of the son–lover myth:

> Venus, *regina, femina, virgo, puella praegnans* (whore) . . . Above all, the prima materia is the mother of the lapis, the *filius philosophorum*.
>
> (1963, 14: paragraph 14)

Jung cites the noted Rennaissance alchemist, Count Michale Maier, who in turn refers to the mid-fifteenth-century treatise of an author with the pseudonym 'Delphinas' to support his contention that the *prima materia* was the mother–son incest:

> the widow marries her son . . . But this marriage, which began with the expression of great joyfulness, ended in the bitterness of mourning . . . [W]hen the son sleeps with the mother, she kills him with the stroke of a viper.
>
> (1963, 14: paragraph 14)

Jung further discusses the link between the *prima materia*, death, and the son. The *prima materia*:

> is the earth and the serpent hidden in the earth, the blackness and the dew and the miraculous water which brings together all that is divided. The water is therefore called 'mother,' 'my mother who is my enemy,' but who also 'gathers together all my divided and scattered limbs.'
>
> (1963, 14: paragraph 15)

The dynamic of the Attis–Cybele myth is the *prima materia*; and the issue of an impossible fusion–separation dynamic, leading to an inner state of madness and self-castration, is an ever-present clinical reality. But the *prima materia* is also despised and easily dismissed. Fabricius notes: 'The *prima materia* is the chaos in which the stone is found . . . [I]t is so cheap and despicable that it is thrown out in the streets' (1976, 21). This potential for undervaluing chaos can be seen in the following example which highlights the difference between an alchemical approach and other possibilities to the dilemma of an impossible passion and its madness.

A man began telling me about the success he had in dealing with his sister over an inheritance. He was frightened of his sister who is five years older. In a previous session, I could determine that he oscillated between states of loving and hating her. But generally, this oscillation between opposites was difficult to perceive; instead, in relating to him I tended to feel confused. In a therapy group, other members tended to feel the same confusion and often lost interest or became sleepy when he spoke. In this session, as was commonly the case, he was ungrounded in the sense that he was disconnected from awareness of his body; he did not make contact with me when he spoke, and instead, he wandered into a series of mental associations that were often impossible for me to comprehend. When I asked him what he was saying, he did not know.

A field existed between us that was fragmented and through which it was extremely difficult, save for a few seconds duration, to focus upon what he was saying and to have any thoughts of my own. During this session, after I stopped to pause and reflect upon the extreme fragmentation I was feeling, and about his fragmentation as well, he stopped talking. I suddenly realized that he was so withdrawn and dissociated because he was extremely proud of what he had done with his sister. He had finally held his own, given her an ultimatum, and he felt good about it. But he could not communicate his pride to me because his need for mirroring – for me to see him as special in this act – was too terrifying. Communicating his pride to me would have meant that he had to face his need to merge with me, in both fantasy and affective experience, while I represented an omnipotent object.

This merger, in Kohutian, self-psychological terms, with a 'self-object' was overwhelming to him. Acknowledging this merger meant that he would have to feel needs that were unthinkable. When I could sort this state out for myself and tell him about it, for a minute or two the field between us became clear and related. As we then sat with each other and this clarity, he soon became anxious. We could thus both feel a connection, a sense of an energized space between us, but a space that frightened him as he felt the desire to fuse with me, indeed to merge into me. The space felt dangerous to him as his needs emerged, especially the needs to be embraced and to be seen as good. Consequently, as he shifted back to confusion and the field between us became fragmented, my capacity to experience him strongly diminished. In other words, psychotic process returned after the self-object status of our field began to feel too dangerous.

From a self-psychological point of view the problem is that a mutual self-object field is difficult to create, and therefore a fragmentation that can have psychotic features frequently occurs. As the analyst, I have to look to what I am adding to this self-object field. What is my resistance to mirroring him and to helping create the proper field quality of safety within the experience of being mirrored? Is it an issue of my becoming more empathic to the dangers which mirroring and associated exhibitionism present for him? In other words, the self-psychological approach treats the experience of chaos – to use a word that is a favorite of the alchemists – as the result of an *absence* of order rather than as an experience extremely important in its own right.

The alchemical approach would value the experience of chaos as something to be achieved. Rather than seeing the experience of chaos as the result of a fear of fusion, the way psychosis is often conceived of in psychoanalytic traditions, the alchemical approach values this experience and especially when it is the result of a previous operation. In other words, one does not only perceive chaotic areas, mad sectors in another person, but also one seeks to achieve the chaos of this state as a result of the *coniunctio*.

In the dynamics of the Attis–Cybele myth, the desire of the child has been tainted by the passions of the adolescent and then of the adult, and that desire has furthermore become subject to the taboo of incest. The result is that everyone, like the analysand, suffers from an impossible passion and its chaos which must be encountered if relationship is ever to be more than an economic joint venture or more than a place in which one can hide one's deepest fears and pathology.

The dynamics of the Attis and Cybele myth, with the twists and turns that it has taken since its inception at the beginning of the Neolithic Age, is thus the main focus for the alchemical *prima materia*. The myth underscores the treacherous nature of passion and begs for a wisdom that has rarely been seen in history. How does a man or a woman properly respect these energies? If a man fuses with them in the blindness and madness of passionate love, he becomes a man-boy. He is a fused being of opposites – a boundary-less infant-child-adolescent bursting with desire to reach fulfillment and bursting with despair of ever doing so. This boundary-less infant-child-adolescent is joined with an adult who has never truly become an adult and who can at best feign adulthood through rigid morals that condemn his 'other half.' The latter suffers the humiliation of never becoming the man that he could have become. And a woman's fusion with these energies renders her terrifying to men and women alike, for she has taken on an archetypal form that engulfs all object relations and renders her split between being young and old while these segments are, paradoxically, also fused. In other words, a more or less prominent bizarreness reigns. For in either sex, this fusion state is never seamless, never an amalgam of old and young in a symbolic third, but rather both at the same time. Often a slightly bizarre quality of a combination of charisma and humility exists along with a hidden madness which distorts reality so that the person tends at times to act in terribly destructive ways. In this mad state, a man or woman is forever caught in a double bind. If the person acts on passion, he or she only dies a meaningless psychic death, one that leads to no change at all, or the person causes untold suffering in others. And, if he or she does not act on the felt passion, he or she dries up into a premature old man or old woman, forever denying or fantasizing about this lost passion.

The Attis–Cybele myth portrays the *coniunctio–nigredo* rhythm far more deeply than any other union story because of its passionate portrayal of the devastating nature of the ensuing *nigredo* – suicide, madness, and self-castration. Dealing with the passions of the Attis–Cybele myth as the *prima materia* requires that anyone engaging the energies of madness possess a spiritual vantage point. The requirement that one possess a spiritual vantage point can be seen as underpinning the suppression of the negative form of the Great Goddess at the time of the emergence of the Old Testament rather than seeing this change in an overly simplistic framework of the patriarchy's suppressing the Goddess. The ninth painting of the *Splendor Solis* (Figure 8, p. 143) depicts a hermaphrodite which is devoid of an embodied or chthonic dimension, in distinction to the hermaphrodite of the tenth woodcut of the *Rosarium* (Figure 18, p. 183), which has been forged through the fires of successive *nigredos*. In the *Splendor Solis*, the hermaphrodite represents a spiritual self-image, a state that exists as an inner orienting center of great vitality and meaning. Subsequent alchemical operations further transform the image so that the 'lower waters' are included, as depicted in the eleventh image (Figure 7, p. 135) in which a spirit emerges out of these lower waters. But in between the spiritual hermaphrodite and this latter transformation is the tenth image (Figure 20, p. 198) – a madman dismembers a body that is reminiscent of the hermaphrodite. This transforming madness, indeed the madness of the Attis–Cybele myth, cannot be creative and contained unless a spiritual level

Figure 8 Ninth painting from the *Splendor Solis*

represented by the hermaphrodite first exists. The madman extracts this spirit, symbolized by the small golden head of the dismembered man, so that the spirit can be reunited with the body. Madness experienced in this way is the transforming agent of the alchemical process.

This transformative function of chaos is further noted by Jung in reference to the change in the symbol of the King in alchemy, representative of the collective's ruling attitudes:

In order to enter into God's Kingdom the king must transform himself into the prima materia in the body of his mother, and return to the dark initial state which the alchemists call the 'chaos.' In this massa confusa the elements are in conflict and repel one another; all connections are dissolved. Dissolution is the prerequisite for redemption. The celebrant of the mysteries had to suffer a figurative death in order to attain transformation.

(1963, 14: paragraph 381)

The experience of chaos is thus especially important; it is one of the most common attributes of the *prima materia* itself. Through a return to chaos, structures could be dissolved and then become a suitable *prima materia*. Again, Jung comments:

the essential feature of the prima materia is that it was defined as the 'massa confusa' and 'chaos,' referring to the original state of hostility between the elements, the disorder which the artifex gradually reduced to order by his operations.

(1967, 13: paragraph 552)

The link between chaos and a spiritual level of existence is a major aspect of the *prima materia* – the indispensable starting point for the *opus* – as seen in the alchemist's often repeated injunction: it takes gold to make gold. Aside from its significance for their actual work with material processes, on a spiritual or psychological level, this phrase indicates that the alchemist took illumination – spiritual gold – and the resulting formation of an internal self-structure as a 'beginning' condition. Many texts insist that the art is given by God and only known by one who has been transformed by the Spirit. The seventeenth-century alchemist, Gerhard Dorn says: 'It is not possible for any mortal to understand this art unless he is previously enlightened by the divine light' (quoted in Jung 1963, 14: paragraph 443). Since one often thinks of the creation of the self as an end product, relegating it to a beginning state may appear paradoxical. But it is not. For the self that can incarnate as a psychic center and create a sense of wholeness and especially a sense of meaning that had previously been non-existent has not necessarily developed the capacity to partake of the body or instinctual life.

Thus, as seen in the *Splendor Solis*, the *prima materia* may be the self in a certain spiritual condition that does not yet include a transformation of the body into a more subtle vehicle of consciousness, nor does this self-structure necessarily include an integration of the cultural and personal levels of repressed life hidden in the body. These domains would lead to a new self that is far more inclusive than the prior one, a self that could experience the fire of passion – to note a special alchemical concern – without melting into dangerous fusion states, or into withdrawal and denial. Starting with this spiritual self as a beginning, one can then further work on its transformation into an end product, the alchemical *lapis* that encompasses the body, instinctual processes and desire.

In the *Rosarium* the spiritual level that precedes the *nigredo* exists in the preceding image of the *coniunctio*. The descending dove, the spiritual dimension, has been incorporated in the rhythmical feature of the union state in which fusion and distance oscillate and unite. The nature of the *prima materia* as it links spirituality and passion is further explicated by De Rola who in his book, *Alchemy*, notes:

> the *Materia Prima* is said to have an imperfect body, a constant soul, a penetrating tincture and a clear transparent mercury, volatile and mobile. It bears within its breast the gold of the philosophers and the mercury of the wise.
>
> (1973, 10)

Spiritual illumination can yield a constancy of purpose, an inner personality or soul that has faith that a process and goal exist even amidst the 'darkest night.' Also, as a result of the experience of the spiritual self, the imagination gains a new clarity and fluidity; in alchemical terminology, one gains a transparent mercury. And the tincture, the penetrating substance, would refer to a self that at least has begun to achieve an integration of its sexual and aggressive nature to such an extent that its power may be brought to bear in a penetrating, imaginal manner. At this stage, one is no longer caught, for example, in a defensive, sado-masochistic cycle which preserves separation and flees from union.

The 'tincture' is a very important aspect of the *prima materia*, as Jung explains:

> The tincture is 'of a rosy colour' and corresponds to the blood of Christ who is 'compared and united' with the stone . . . The relation of the love-goddess to red dates back to ancient times. Scarlet is the colour of the Great Whore of Babylon and her beast. Red is the colour of sin. The rose is also an attribute of Dionysus. Red and rose-red are the colour of blood, a synonym for the *aqua permanens* and the soul, which are extracted from the prima materia and bring 'dead' bodies to life. The prima materia is called 'meretrix' and is equated with 'Great Babylon.'
>
> (1963, 14: paragraph 420)

But the 'imperfect body' – meaning the body in its form in which it is not a vehicle of consciousness, nor felt as a living presence that one is 'in,' and also not felt as a source of instinct and passion that can be consciously controlled – needs to be transformed into a subtle vehicle of awareness. For only then can the Philosophers' Stone be made, that is, a self in which spirit and body are united, with both functioning as a source of consciousness and neither given more importance than the other.

From the alchemical point of view, the *prima materia* which is revealed in a union state is a name for a certain pattern of psychic energy and associated structures that form an experience in which a numinous level of psychic life – as in spiritual illumination or the *coniunctio* – meets the world of separable, space–time events. Any number of affects, or states of mind, or patterns can be the *prima materia* as long as they occur at the interface where the *numinosum* meets embodied life.

The *prima materia* is, in this context, a set of patterns and their associated energy that emerge when the soul has a transcendent experience and then returns to the world of ego consciousness. The *Splendor Solis* identifies the primary material to be worked with as an 'ore,' a substance formed where heaven and earth meet (McLean 1981, 100). The chaos that is desired and sought after in this union is often affectionately called 'Our Chaos.' It is not simply a disordered state, but rather, it follows a previous union.

The Hermetic Museum (1678) includes an alchemical treatise entitled 'An Open Entrance to the Closed Palace of the King,' by An Anonymous Sage and Lover of Truth. The year of his writing is given as 1645, and he says he is 23 years old:

> Let the student incline his ear to the united verdict of the Sages, who describe this work as analogous to the Creation of the World. In the beginning God created Heaven and Earth; and the earth was without form and void, and the Spirit of God moved upon the face of the waters. And God said, 'Let there be light,' and there was light. These words are sufficient for the student of our Art. The Heaven must be united to the Earth on the couch of friendship; so shall he reign in glory for ever. The Earth is the heavy body . . . The Heaven is the place where the great Lights revolve, and through the air transmit their influences to the lower world. But in the beginning was one confused chaos. Our Chaos is, as it were, a mineral earth (by virtue of its coagulation), and yet also volatile air – in the *centre* of which is the Heaven of the sages, the Astral Centre, with which its light irradiates the earth to the surface . . . I thank Thee, O God, that Thou hast concealed these things from the wise and prudent, and hast revealed them unto babes!
>
> (Waite 1973, vol. 2: 167–68)

And in another section, as part of a description of the 'Appearance of Blackness in the Work of the Sun and the Moon,' he says:

> be doubly careful . . . and you will find that the earth has become quite dry and of a deep black. This is the death of the compound; the winds have ceased and there is a great calm. This is that great simultaneous eclipse of the Sun and Moon, when the Sea also has disappeared. Our Chaos is then ready, from which, at the bidding of God, all the wonders of the world may successively emerge.
>
> (Waite 1973, vol. 2: 188)

The anonymous writer differentiates between an initial, 'confused chaos,' and 'Our Chaos' which has been coagulated and is also volatile. The analyst can experience this differentiated quality of chaos in clinical practice when engaging the chaotic or mad parts of a sane person. Numerous preceding clinical examples have shown the existence of a confusing chaos, but when the analyst imaginally engages that chaos, it appears to become more congealed, as if containing a kind of elusive order. This order is 'volatile,' capable of escaping from awareness nearly as quickly as it was apprehended. This kind of chaos, 'Our Chaos,' is a result of a prior union – 'Heaven is united to Earth' – while the more primal, free-floating form of chaos, a true confused state, is met in practice when no real contact with the other person or with oneself exists. From the true confused state, the analyst can often deduce a pair of opposites. And from these opposites a 'third' form can emerge as the unconscious dyad or couple. The alchemical work then follows upon the discovery of this couple in a fertile state and its eventual death. This death leads to the Chaos or *nigredo* which the Sages call 'Our Chaos,' the result of a previous *coniunctio*.

THE CULTURAL IMPLICATIONS OF THE *CONIUNCTIO–NIGREDO* SEQUENCE

Thus, the Attis–Cybele myth embodies the fusion-death state that characterizes the *nigredo* aspect of the *coniunctio–nigredo* sequence recurring throughout the transformative process of alchemy. The myth depicts the shadow side of the process described in the *Rosarium Philosophorum*. The devastating and paralyzing states described in the myth are analogous to the *prima materia* of alchemy, the raw material of chaos, and the stormy affects of the mad parts of sane people. The ability to recognize and to tolerate the states described in the Attis–Cybele myth is required if the alchemical-psychological process is to succeed.

Jung identifies the psychological condition expressed in myths of the mother–son dyad, like Attis and Cybele, as the most significant condition for the continuing psychological development of humanity. As it undertakes the mandate of understanding the nature of transformation, alchemy focuses on this same dynamic, represented by the mother–son dyad. Jung writes:

> Alchemy is rather like an undercurrent to the Christianity that ruled on the surface. It is to this surface as the dream is to consciousness, and just as the dream compensates the conflicts of the conscious mind, so alchemy endeavours to fill in the gaps left open by the Christian tension of opposites. [The fundamental idea] of alchemy points back to the . . . primordial matriarchal world which [was] overthrown by the masculine world of the father. This historical shift in the world's consciousness towards the masculine is compensated first by the chthonic femininity of the unconscious. In certain pre-Christian religions the differentiation of the masculine principle had taken the form of the father–son specification, a change which was to be of the utmost importance for Christianity. Were the unconscious merely complementary, this shift of consciousness would have been accompanied by the production of a mother and daughter for which the necessary material lay ready to hand in the myth of Demeter and Persephone. But, as alchemy shows, the unconscious chose rather the Cybele–Attis type in the form of the *prima materia* and the *filius macrocosmi*, thus proving that it is not complementary but compensatory. This goes to show that the unconscious does not simply act *contrary* to the conscious mind but *modifies* it more in the manner of an opponent or partner. The son type . . . calls up another son . . . The mother, who was anterior to the world of the father, accommodates herself to the masculine principle and, with the aid of the human spirit (alchemy or 'the philosophy'), produces a son – not the antithesis of Christ but rather his chthonic counterpart, not a divine man but a fabulous being conforming to the nature of the primordial mother. And just as the redemption of man the microcosm

is the task of the 'upper' son, so the 'lower' son has the function of a *salvator macrocosmi* . . .

Although [this 'lower son'] is decidedly hermaphroditic he has a masculine name – a sign that the chthonic underworld, having been rejected by the spirit and identified with evil, has a tendency to compromise. There is no mistaking the fact that he is a concession to the spiritual and masculine principle, even though he carries in himself the weight of the earth and the whole fabulous nature of primordial animality . . .

This answer of the mother-world shows that the gulf between it and the father-world is not unbridgeable, seeing that the unconscious holds the seed of the unity of both.

(1953, 5: paragraphs 26, 29, 30)

Jung's basic point is that the Attis–Cybele myth indicates a fundamental shift in consciousness, a shift which has been stuck or stillborn since pre-Christian times. Christianity's attempt at a resolution resulted in transcendence. Alchemy, however, the subterranean undercurrent to Christianity, came closer to a resolution. Jung's suggestion that alchemy functions as a balancing factor to Christianity on a transpersonal plane in the same way that the dream functions for our conscious self on the personal level is an example of his extraordinary breadth of vision. This vision, according to von Franz, has resulted in a description of the relationship between the two worlds of alchemy and Christianity 'that cannot be bettered' (1975, 216). However, alchemy was a compensation not only to Christianity but also for all patriarchal religious thinking, including those Gnostic systems directed towards a spirit in the upper realm as known in ascent mysticism. In distinction to alchemy, these Gnostic systems usually oppose re-entering the life and realm of the chthonic spirit which is experienced as arising from below.

Throughout the centuries, the impulse in patriarchal Western culture has been to ascend and transcend, whereas the deficiency in the culture involves a lack from below – from underneath – from realms considered more base, primitive, and unformed. In these chthonic realms, a hitherto unknown, unintegrated, and unformed aspect of humanity lies waiting for a consciousness that is its equal.

Jung's understanding of the unconscious as a teleological entity, perpetually seeking to balance and harmonize the unfolding of incarnated life, is truly moving. And if one accepts Jung's proposition that alchemy holds the solution through compensation to the patriarchal suppression of the feminine and the denial of the chthonic masculine, the importance of alchemy for our troubled world becomes not only obvious but also pressing.

Whatever the path may now be to a new relationship towards the feminine and between the sexes, the attitude of consciousness towards this goal is one that can greatly benefit from the alchemical image of the *filius philosophorum*, the 'philosopher's son,' meaning the spirit born out of the alchemical art. In other words, what was once an unconscious compensation represented by the dynamics of the mother–son dyad can and indeed must now become a conscious attitude. Then, the greater depths of the feminine can be approached by a more capable ego, as it cannot be with a patriarchal or solely Apollonian attitude. Just as the ancient myth of Dionysos shows that this god, and perhaps this god alone, can coexist with the Great Goddess as Cybele-Rhea and survive amidst persecutory affects without being killed or reduced to a consort, so too a new kind of consciousness, yet to be achieved but envisioned by alchemy, is a necessary component of a future self-image.

8 The alchemical attitude to the transformation of relationship

THE UNDERLYING WISDOM OF ALCHEMICAL TRANSFORMATION

The core of the alchemical process of transformation is revealed in stories and images which provide insight into the transformative dynamics of seemingly irreconcilable states of opposites. Conflicting pairs of opposites, such as love and hate, despair and passion, or daring and cowardice, can be experienced within an individual or between two people as an unconscious dyad. Unless such opposites separate and combine in a fruitful way, releasing energy and creating consciousness, an ego, or a couple, can encounter conflicting states of mind and body that lead to stagnation and regression through which they lose energy and heart. For example, a male analysand has an intense and nearly automatic obedience to collective ideals or conventional standards of morality, yet an equally intense passion to act out forbidden energies. In effect, he leads a double life: the model citizen during the day, an obsession with prostitutes and child pornography at night. How can these opposites ever combine into a 'third' so that he is not constantly drawn by compulsion to one and then the other? How can his split internal structure heal so that such opposites no longer rule him? Even if the opposites in question are extremely split apart within the psychotic area, change always occurs through their union. But union is only the beginning of the alchemical process of transformation. For change in the internal structure to be stabilized requires the death of the union and the embrace of the subsequent *nigredo*. Through this *coniunctio–nigredo* sequence, the alchemical process works to create new and enduring form.

The goal of the process, as seen in the twentieth woodcut of the *Rosarium Philosophorum* (Figure 30, p. 213), is nothing less than the transcendence of such union–death cycles. In this last of the images of the series, the resurrected Christ figure symbolizes the stability and constancy of a self-structure even while, in the background (as shown in other variants of this woodcut), dissociative and violent processes still occur. Yet in this goal of the *opus*, a transformation of consciousness and structure is achieved that is capable of belief in the resurrection, not only the resurrection of a dead self, as in Christ, or the Egyptian parallel of the god Osiris, but also the resurrection of one's internal structure in whatever form it must take for continued individuation. Such faith is at the core of the goal, and this faith is achieved through what often seems to be an endless cycle of death and rebirth, of unions and their death.

The analyst in particular should note that in any process a union may occur without an unconscious and overwhelming *nigredo*. The relativization of the *nigredo* requires a high level of consciousness by both people, and especially a conscious suffering of the loss of physical union. Experiencing this pain, which is part of the alchemical imagery of 'slaying the dragon' or 'cutting off the paws of the lion,' can result in a union state that does not disappear into despair and confusion. But this conscious apprehension and minimization of the power of the *nigredo* are rare because, at other times in the process between these people, the *coniunctio–nigredo* sequence likely will appear once again, with the *nigredo* being a powerful and initially unconscious condition.

Three metaphorical tales embody the alchemical wisdom of the transformation of an interactive field: 'The Axiom of Maria Prophetissa,' 'The Axiom of Ostanes,' and 'Isis the Prophetess to her Son Horus.'

Like 'The Axiom of Maria Prophetissa' analyzed earlier, 'The Axiom of Ostanes' is an alchemical teaching that deals with the way the internal structure of an object changes. In particular, the enigmatic form of 'The Axiom of Ostanes' addresses the complexities of union, death, and the creation of a stable structure:

A nature is delighted by another nature, a nature conquers another nature, a nature dominates another nature.

The triadic formula of Ostanes underpins much alchemical thinking, from its earliest forms in Bolos Democritus around 200 BCE to the sixteenth century. Apparently, the fusion of Iranian and Greek-Egyptian ideas in Bolos of Mendes brought about the legends of Democritus collaborating with Ostanes – legends that no doubt took various forms, one of which is the story of the opening pillar and the triadic formula (Lindsay 1970, 158).

Bolos Democritus recounts his journey to Egypt to teach the lore of occult virtues, 'so that you might rise above multiple [diffused] curiosity and materials [or matter], *hyle*':

After learning these things from the master named Ostanes and aware of the diversity of the matter, I set myself to make the combination of natures. But, as our master had died before our initiation was completed and we were still all taken up in learning the matter, it was from Hades, as one says, that I tried to evoke him. I applied myself to the task, and, as soon as he appeared, I apostrophized him in these terms, 'Are you going to give me nothing in return for what I have done for you?'

I spoke in vain. He kept silent.

However when I addressed him as well as I could and asked him how I should combine the natures, he told me that it was difficult for him to speak; the *daimon* wouldn't allow it. He said only, 'The books are in the temple.'

Turning back, I then went to make searches in the temple on the chance of being able to lay my hands on the books . . . But despite all our searching we found nothing; and so we gave ourselves a terrible lot of trouble in trying to learn how substances and natures were united and combined in a single substance. Well, when we realized the synthesis of matter, some time passed by and a festival was held in the temple. We took part, all of us, in a banquet.

Then, as we were in the temple, all of a sudden a column of its own accord opened up in the middle. But at first glance there seemed nothing inside. However, [the son] Ostanes told us that it was in this column that his father's books had been placed. And, taking charge of the situation, he brought the thing out into the open. But when we bent to look, we saw in surprise that nothing had escaped us except this wholly valuable formula which we found there. 'A nature is delighted by another nature, a nature conquers another nature, a nature dominates another nature.' Great was our admiration for the way he had concentrated in a few words all the Scripture.

(quoted in Lindsay 1970, 102)

Lindsay notes:

A guiding principle of qualitative change, a formative principle, has been realized inside unitary process . . . What the alchemists were talking about was an omnipresent formative movement, which is shared by both men and the organic and inorganic objects of nature.

(1970, 144–45)

As Lindsay further explains,

The two materials, that of primary matter . . . and that of the alloying and transforming addition, must have something in common, some element of harmony. That is, they delighted in one another. But if that were all, a state of equilibrium was created and nothing happened; the first level was not transcended. So one nature must conquer the other. The conquering act was the moment of transformation, when the equilibrium was broken and a new relationship established. The new fused substance existed at a higher level and involved the creation of a new quality, which revealed itself in the colour-change. But that was not enough. The new state must be stabilized, so that it might provide the basis for yet another upward-movement. Hence, the third section of the formula: one nature must dominate another. The three stages of the alchemic act might then be defined: mixture on the original level, introduction of a dynamic factor which changes the original relations and creates a new qualitative level, then stabilisation of this level. In an Arab text . . . the process [is] described as three marriages, the two substances acting on one another being called male and female.

(Lindsay 1970, 116)

'The Axiom of Ostanes' as it functions in clinical practice is illustrated by a female analysand who, recalling the previous session, emphasized the way we discovered how her envy, and the envy of others, tended to spoil things and to cast gloom on her life. She told me how this day, as she waited in the waiting room, she wanted to say to me, 'How is it that I have this different, creative relationship with my daughter now? What has happened to allow it?' As she spoke, I felt a bodily tension, a desire to withdraw, and a sense that what she was saying felt odd. I was torn in two directions – to answer her and not to answer – and I would have liked to answer so that the painful feelings would leave. But I could not honestly answer her question without splitting myself away from my feelings. As I felt into this field more fully, trying to join my mind to my bodily and emotional reactions so that I would gain some image that made sense of the interaction, I recognized that she was genuinely asking for understanding and inquiry. Yet she was also communicating an opposite message that she did not want any reflections on my part but only to bask in the glory of her experience, turning it all back on to herself.

The axiom states that 'a nature delights in another nature,' an apt metaphor for the link that took place between our psyches in which I felt tormented and split. This state was an indication that our unconscious psyches were meeting each other and 'delighting' in a very unpleasant manner. A fusion state thus occurred.

I felt the conflicting nature of the opposites in the psychotic area to the extent that trying to formulate some answer quickly turned into a sense of emptiness and of having no answer. In the one state, I could give answers. I could say something like, 'You've achieved a lot by working so hard on your relationship with her, and it is bearing fruit.' In other words I could have mirrored her need to be seen as special and important; and while this reflection would have satisfied her, and the discomfort that I felt probably would have passed, I could not empathize in a fully embodied and genuine way.

Instead, as I intentionally engaged the field – feeling these shifting states and allowing myself to use the field as an object (as in active imagination), seeing and feeling the object, and then experiencing myself being in it – my perception of annihilating opposites emerged. These opposites did not come into awareness like the solution of a problem or like an understanding that was stable. Rather the perception was fleeting and difficult to maintain, and I could sufficiently communicate the perception to her to explain why it was impossible for me to answer her question.

Generally, the analyst does not 'deduce' an opposite quality from some state he or she experiences. For example, the analyst does not get very far by experiencing love and consciously wondering about hate or aggression. Such an opposite may often be present, but this cognitive approach is not the way to discover the opposite. Instead, the analyst must go though a state of 'unknowing,' that is, through as state of chaos in which he or she truly feels lost and without orientation. In this condition, the analyst may discover ways in which his or her mind and emotions cycle through different states and then recognize them to be opposites. But the states will usually not be clearly distinct, such as love and hate. Rather, as in this instance, they will be unique to the individual encounter.

The analysand and I felt an initial chaos, a state of bewilderment which, in addition to 'The Axiom of Ostanes,' could be reflected upon through 'The Axiom of Maria.' I could feel no sense of order but only conflicting mental and bodily

states without any meaning. Pain, absence of thinking, and a desire to flee dominated. Terribly conflicting states did not yield any sense of order, as is typical of
alchemical definitions of chaos. By consciously engaging this chaotic field quality, the One, and by discovering a container for its states in the oscillating nature
of the field in which I was alternately object and subject, opposites differentiated:
'Out of the One comes the Two,' states 'The Axiom of Maria.' The Two here was
a very unstable condition. In other processes, the Two can be far more stable; but
in this case, the split opposites created a state of Twoness that flickered in and out
of awareness.

With the self as the containing agent linking opposites, and this same linking
'seen' in the field, a new nature was perceptible, as in the next stage of 'The
Axiom of Ostanes,' 'a nature overcomes a nature.' In this process, the new nature
took the form of the analysand's terrifying background object. She was constantly under attack by this background form, which she recognized as her
ever-present maternal experience.

This 'presence' of a negative background object – a total opposite to the positive experience of a holding environment, of 'being backed up' – was chronic in
the analysand. The existence of such front–back splits is an archetypal patterning
of psyche. Many meditative systems attempt to constellate a positive background
object. As I could 'see' this background object, and she could also recognize it, a
new, and more stable consolidation emerged. This 'new nature' overcame the
previous nature. As long as the background object could be 'seen,' other forms of
splitting did not occur. But this state of imaginal awareness was highly unstable;
hence the last phase, 'a nature dominates another nature' had not yet occurred.
Instead, the analysand and I went through the first two stages repeatedly, in many
different life and transference experiences, hoping to gain more stability such as
she had done with her daughter. What is often remarkable about such a process is
that, in spite of the instability of the fleeting kind of order that appears, a process
of changing structure occurs which is, generally, quite a surprise and which certainly surprised both of us.

Essential and ancient principles of the transformation process are related in the
tale of 'Isis the Prophetess to her Son Horus' in which Isis reveals the secret of
alchemy. According to Lindsay, 'Isis plays only a small part in alchemic literature apart from [this] one work . . . There are two versions which do not differ
substantially. Passages from the second have been added in brackets':

> You, my son, you decided to set out for the battle with Typhon, so as to dis-
> pute with him the kingdom of your father. As for me, after your departure, I
> went off to Hormanouth, where the Sacred Art of Egypt is practised in secret.
> And after staying there a long time I wished to come back.
>
> Well, when I was about to leave, one of the prophets or angels who dwell
> in the first firmament caught sight of me [by permission of a favoring season
> and according to the necessary movement of the spheres]. He advanced
> towards me and wanted to mate with me in the intercourse of love.
>
> [He was just about to do as he wanted] but I refused to yield. I demanded
> first from him that he should tell me of the preparation of gold and silver.

He however exhibited a certain sign that he had on his head, and a vase that had not been coated with pitch, filled with transparent water, which he held between his hands. But he refused to tell me the truth.

Next day, having returned towards me, Amnael was seized with desire on my account and [unable to contain his impatience] he hastened to achieve the object for which he had come. But as for me, I deliberately took no notice [and I did not ask him about those things].

He however did not stop from trying to win me over and to invite me to the business, but I refused to let him take me. I triumphed over his lust till he was ready to show me the sign on his head and reveal to me, generously and without hiding anything, the sought-for mystery.

So he decided then to show me the sign and reveal the mysteries. He began by retailing the warnings and the oaths – and this is how he phrased it:

'I adjure you by heaven and earth, light and darkness. I adjure you by fire, water, air, and earth. I adjure you by the height of the heaven and the depth of Tartaros. I adjure you by Hermes and Anubis, and by the roaring of the serpent Ouroboros and of the Threeheaded Dog, Keberos, guardian of Hades. I adjure you by the Three Goddesses of Fate, by their Whips and by their Sword.'

When he had made me swear by all these words, he went on to enjoin upon me that I must never communicate the revelation to anyone except you, my beloved and legitimate son [so that he might be you, and you, he].

So go then, my child, to a certain laborer [Achaab] and ask him what he has sown and what he has harvested, and you will learn from him that the man who sows wheat also harvests wheat, and the man who sows barley harvests also barley.

Now that you've heard this discourse, my child, learn to comprehend the whole fabrication, *demiourgia*, and generation of these things, and know that it is the condition of man to sow a man, of a lion to sow a lion, of a dog to sow a dog, and if it happens that one of these beings is produced against the order of nature, he has engendered in the state of a monster and cannot subsist.

For a nature rejoices another nature, and a nature conquers another nature.

[So then, having shared in this divine power and been favored with this divine presence, illuminated in turn as a result of Isis's demand] we must prepare the matter with the aid of minerals alone without using other substances [and attain our goal by the fact that matter added was of the same nature as that which was prepared]. Just as I have told you, wheat engenders wheat, man engenders man, and similarly gold engenders gold.

See, there is the whole of the mystery.

(1970, 195)

The battle between Horus and Seth is the ancient struggle of these Egyptian gods in which Horus tears out Seth's testicles while Seth tears out one of Horus's eyes. In a man, the battle represents the classic 'shadow fight' between alternative attitudes: one emotional and violent, and often Evil, represented by Seth; the other spiritual and related, and Good, as represented by Horus. In a woman, the battle between Horus and Seth represents a conflict between internal attitudes, a spiritual, life-enhancing position, and a demonic force of death. According to Ogden, the conflict embodies the dynamics of projective identification:

> Projective identification is a concept that addresses the way in which feeling-states corresponding to the unconscious fantasies of one person (the projector) are engendered in and processed by another person (the recipient), that is, the way in which one person makes use of another person to experience and contain an aspect of himself. The projector has the primarily unconscious fantasy of getting rid of unwanted or endangered parts of himself (including internal objects) and of depositing that part in another person in a powerfully controlling way. The projected part of the self is felt to be partially lost and to be inhabiting another person. In association with this unconscious projective fantasy there is an interpersonal interaction by means of which the recipient is pressured to think, feel, and behave in a manner congruent with the ejected feelings and the self-representations embodied in the projective fantasy. In other words, the recipient is pressured to engage in an identification with a specific, disowned aspect of the projector.
>
> (1982, 1–2)

The process of projective identification can be gruesome: the object of the projection can feel as if his or her eye was torn out, with the eye being symbolic of consciousness. In response, the object tends to 'castrate' with emotional reactivity, especially the reactivity of rationality, defensiveness, and problem-solving. One therapist, for example, complained that she was anxious with a certain analysand. When the therapist and I probed deeper into the situation, she appeared to fear that the client would abandon her. The client was also demanding that the therapist solve his problems with anxiety. She was feeling anxious under the strain of this demand and the implicit threat of abandonment. So, she failed to deal with the data, the demand for omnipotence and the fear of abandonment. Instead she looked for solutions.

The analyst failed to 'see' that a young child was activated in the analysand, and that this part was itself under a terrible inner attack and was fleeing into omnipotence. The analysand urges the analyst to be omnipotent, and the analyst attempts to comply. In this inflated state, her eyes are torn out, and she makes a 'dog from a cat'; she gives a solution, falling prey to the compulsion of the field, rather than staying with the constellated field and its anxiety and abandonment issues.

So her analysand's emotional process effectively tears out her eye. But by granting him his wish for omnipotence, she is giving him a 'solution' that can do little but castrate him: 'I'll solve it for you, you moron.' Her 'solution' is not his own, and beyond that, it demands that he function at a level beyond his abilities, as he is subject to abandonment threats. So, in the metaphor of the tale, her eye is torn out, and his testicles are torn out.

But within such behavior between analyst and analysand exists Isis and the Angel, a potential *coniunctio*, in a sulfuric or compulsive form. After Isis resists his compulsion, the angel reveals the central mystery of alchemy 'like creates like,' with the injunction never to create through dissimilars.

In all human encounters, it is tempting to deny this wisdom. Every time a chaotic state exists, especially when psychotic areas are enlivened, the tendency is to switch to something known. Generally, it is also tempting to mirror one's need to be seen and to side-step other feelings of great discomfort. This act of side-stepping makes 'a dog from a cat.' Quick interpretations can violate the tale as well, especially when they increase the analyst's comfort level. From 'Isis the Prophetess to her Son Horus' the analyst and analysand further learn how neither acting upon nor speaking about felt desire can result in revealing a deeper wisdom. Both can know the mystery of the self within an interactive field in which the tale's crowning phrase, 'I am You,' can emerge.

The transformation process in alchemy depends on following the wisdom of these three parables. Inspired by such mythology, the Renaissance alchemist created in the *Rosarium Philosophorum* a treasure of images of field dynamics. The process of transformation entails the apprehension of an unconscious dyad from an initial chaos in which there is no sense of order or memory, and in which psychotic process can be the *prima materia*.

THE IMAGERY OF THE *ROSARIUM PHILOSOPHORUM*

The series of twenty woodcuts of the most famous alchemical text, the *Rosarium Philosophorum* (1550), can be seen as a process of entering a field between two people, experiencing field dynamics, and working with the transformation of the field itself. The goal is the creation of both an inner-individual and an outer-conjoined field quality which perseveres through any mental, emotional, somatic, or environmental trauma by means of a mind–body union that is so subtle as to be a source of true, imaginal perception. While this kind of stability is clearly an unobtainable goal, nevertheless, it indicates the value-system of this body of thought, and it further implies that the issue is not reaching perfection but being on the path of transformation.

The first ten woodcuts of the *Rosarium* are well-suited to describing an interactive field since they continuously work with the image of a couple and with the tenth woodcut, the 'Rebis' (Figure 18, p. 183), a hermaphrodite representing a union of the opposites. The stage depicted by the completion of the first ten woodcuts is called the 'Empress' or the 'White Stone,' which represents the creation of a self-structure that unifies mind and body. Most significantly, the structural gains represented by the 'White Stone' are capable of either persevering or being recovered amidst attacks of abandonment anxiety, panic and fear that an individual can feel as a psychic death. The Rebis can be an interactive, field quality between two people, or it can be an image of an internal self. The Rebis stands upon the moon representing the subtle body world – an indicator that this kind of embodied sight, an awareness of union states and their vicissitudes (in ensuing *nigredo* experiences) – now exists and will not be destroyed.

However, the alchemists recognize this creation to be 'watery,' not yet having the solidity characterized by the result of the next ten woodcuts, the *rubedo* phase. In the *albedo*, the field and a sense of self are often lost to awareness, especially under the impact of passion. The field can be recovered due to an essential element of faith achieved in the *albedo*, but in the *rubedo* the alchemist attempts to bring a kind of life and blood to the 'stone' that now has a deeper continuity and presence amidst intense emotion and body states. In the *albedo*, according to Jung:

> one does not live in the true sense of the word. It is a sort of abstract, ideal state. In order to make it come alive, it must have 'blood,' it must have what the alchemists called the *rubedo*, the 'redness' of life. Only the total experience of being can transform this ideal state into a fully human mode of existence.
>
> (McGuire and Hull 1977, 229)

In alchemy, the work with 'redness' must be founded on a prior illumination or solar phase: 'And so he which knoweth not the beginning, obtaineth not the end, and he which knoweth not what he seeks is ignorant also of what he shall find' (McLean 1980, 19). This illumination descends into the body, and as a result, the 'White Stone' can be created through working with the opposites as in a conjoined field experience and an unconscious dyad. The *Rosarium* states:

> Whereas it has been said, that Luna contains white Sulphur in it . . . yet the form of fire is hidden in it under the whiteness. Therefore it is possible for all Silver to be made Gold. Whereupon the Philosopher says, 'It is not Gold unless it has first been made Silver.'
>
> (McLean 1980, 80)

This stress upon making silver, the 'White Stone,' before gold is essential to the alchemical way, for unless body-awareness and the imaginal world of the subtle body are recovered, the spiritual path of the *rubedo* will only lead to more mind–body splitting.

The ten woodcuts of the *rubedo* do not lend themselves to a field interpretation as readily as the first ten, although several of them, especially the eleventh woodcut, 'Fermentation' (Figure 21, p. 199), can be seen as representing possible field dynamics. The *rubedo* stage, however, goes beyond the relating and the imaginal seeing of lunar, feminine life and eventually regains the solar, spiritual vision that was a prerequisite. Initially this vision was disembodied, a result of the *unio mystica*, and quite ignorant of embodied life and the feminine mysteries of the *coniunctio*. Spirit is still a danger to the 'White Stone,' for the spirit can be used to escape from the relatedness and embodiment that bring with them the dangers of fusion and identity loss. These states attend the levels of engagement with the 'Other' that the alchemist intends to overcome, especially the impossible passion described by the Attis–Cybele myth. Reconciling this state of passion may well be the meaning of the most mysterious image of the entire series, the eighteenth woodcut in which the green lion devours the sun (Figure 28, p. 210).

Thus, not only spirit but also the dangers of passion can cause the process to regress away from embodiment. Passion, most prominently featured in the eleventh woodcut, the 'Fermentation,' is the focus of the *rubedo* stage. In the twelfth woodcut, 'Illumination' (Figure 22, p. 201) and in the eighteenth woodcut,

'Mortification of the Celestial Marriage,' the solar life is continually sacrificed in the service of creating a new self-structure that does not flee from the body and which is also stable under the impact of the passions and spiritual vision.

Especially important is the nineteenth woodcut in which the soul is crowned by large figures (Figure 29, p. 212), whereas in other renderings of the *Rosarium* the crown is far too big for the soul. The meaning of this image is that the person must recognize that the source of illumination lies outside his being (McLean 1980, 129), an important issue in terms of the ways the *numinosum* is experienced. The *numinosum* always has a transcendent aspect, a Self which cannot be embodied, felt within, while it also is capable of indwelling and creating a self. These two aspects of self, immanent and transcendent, are not confused in the alchemical tradition. While these sources of blessing and meaning have a substantial similarity, they are experienced in realms having far different scales. With this knowledge, the alchemist never fails to know his place in the Cosmos, and inflation no longer betrays him.

Generally, the *Rosarium*, in its *rubedo* state, consolidates a self that can live without fusing with others and which experiences a passion for linking – with others and with one's self – that is not disowned from one day to the next in fear of engulfment and contamination.

Transformation of interactive processes furthers this result in which one gains a self sensitive to both 'lunar' and 'solar' modes of relating and experiencing the *numinosum*, for the scrolls on this image of 'Coronation' read:

> Truly, the moon is the mother; and the father by the son was created; whose father is the son. The dragon dieth not except with his brother and sister; and not with one alone but with both of them.

The transformation of the dragon, the image of the death of a field characterized by concretization of thoughts and projections and by a dullness of vision, is accomplished through imaginal work on the unconscious couple, 'brother and sister,' apprehended within the subtle body field. Thus, even though the *Rosarium* sets out experiences of transcendence that go beyond conjoined field notions, they are reached through working with the unconscious dyad.

The unconscious dyad exists in a medium, the subtle body, which is central to alchemical ways of thinking. Jung has underscored this role of a medium for projections: 'It is this medium, the subtle body which unifies spirit and body, through which the psyche can have very real effects, through which psychical reality is known' (1988, 432). The effects of one person upon another are so strong that the object frequently prefers to 'not notice' them. Jung further states:

> If somebody has an intuition that you have a certain thought, you are most probably made to think that thought. Intuition seems to work through the sympathetic system, and being a half-unconscious function, intuitions also bring out an unconscious effect in the object of the intuition. In dealing with intuitives, you notice that they can intuit a thing in such a way that it is shot into your backbone, into your spinal cord, and you must admit that you thought it,

though afterwards you will realize that the thought was surely not your own . . .

(1988, 616–17)

And Jung also notes that:

> A projection is a very tangible thing, a sort of semisubstantial thing which forms a load as if it had real weight. It is exactly as the primitives understand it, a subtle body . . . It is interesting that the alchemists described the making of the stone as a projection. That is to say, it is something that is detached from one; you detach something and establish it as an independent existence, put it outside yourself. Now, that may be quite legitimate inasmuch as it is a matter of objectifying psychic contents; or it may be most illegitimate if it is used for magical purposes, or if it is a simple projection where you get rid of something . . .

(1988, 1495–96)

This capacity to 'objectify psychic contents' rather than 'get rid of them' is part of the mystery of projection and underlies the capacity to feel certain states of mind and imagine them to be part of an interactive field. One can imagine 'throwing' them into the field.

The field is affected by the inner life of each person. For example, a man dreamed of having sex with a woman, but he could see, in a mirror, that his penis went right through her and came out her back. He had very little sexual sensation as she was nearly insubstantial. Whatever this image was referring to in his life, it was also representing the interactive field between us. He could be very engaging with an energy that was present and clear, but any connecting energy that arose between himself and me would fade into insubstantiality. This rhythm between the opposites of power and insubstantiality, with each ruling in an alternating manner, was the rhythm of the interactive field between us. In projective identification, I could feel both of these states. But what did I contribute? I faded out with him unless I held on to my attention very tightly. But this very act precluded my experiencing him. So, I would go through a similar rhythm of loosening my conscious attention and allowing whatever might emerge, and then focusing in a controlled, intense way. Thus, these opposites defined our field; we both contributed, even though his dream initiated the awareness of the opposites. He recognized that these qualities of opposite and conflicting states existed within him, but only when I pointed them out. So, I could see the opposites as an unconscious dynamic between his ego and his feminine side, and I could even make a case for this relation dominating the interactive field, much as an analyst can think of his or her countertransference as a reaction to the analysand's transference. But could I really know whether or not this sequence of events was true? Could I know that my internal ego–anima connection did not equally or even more strongly affect the field than did his? I could only determine that a relational field quality dominated our work. We could both imaginally experience this quality, individually and interactively, but when my awareness floated back and forth between the opposites, as did his own, we experienced ourselves as also in the field. Thus, the space we occupied could have the nature of the alchemical *vas* if we allowed it to, for we actively had to intersect the field to discover this quality of space. If we did not act in this way, then the space remained Cartesian, a three-dimensional world of 'his' process and 'my' process and their interaction. However, this Cartesian space does not have have texture or spirit; it is not a plenum, but empty. The alchemical path recognizes that observing and experiencing the field affords a way of transformation.

THE *PRIMA MATERIA* OF THE TRANSFORMATION PROCESS

In the 'Mercurial Fountain,' the first woodcut of the *Rosarium* (Figure 4, p. 105), the object of transformation – unification of mind and body through working with an unconscious dyad – is represented in an abstract form. The double-headed serpent and the lower, Dionysian waters are both 'starting points,' forms of the alchemical *prima materia*. The serpent, Binarius, represents the anti-worlds in mad areas of psyche. And the Kwakiutl myth of Sisiutl (p. 106f.) further amplifies this image, demonstrating that experiencing the confusion, fear, and mindlessness of the annihilating anti-worlds can lead to vision, to being able to 'see,' a sacred goal of working with the *prima materia*.

The upper level, the dyadic world of the Binarius, and the lower waters of the Fountain, the passions and body-states of the ecstatic Dionysos, himself a mad god, are identical. The inscription on the Mercurial Fountain indicates that Mercurius is *animalis*, *vegetabilis* and *mineralis*, which is repeated at the level of the Binarius. *Vegetabilis*, Jung notes, should be translated as 'living' and *animalis* as 'animate,' in the sense of having a soul or even in the sense of 'psychic' (1954, 16: paragraph 402). Thus, the three qualities of the triune god of alchemy are equivalent to matter, soul and spirit. The three streams flowing out of the fountain are, as McLean notes, synonymous with the Lunar, Solar, and Middle stream, the Water of Life as they are found in Tantrism (1980, 119). Combining solar and lunar within a field of the 'third' is the leitmotif of the entire process. Its success or failure cannot be guaranteed, for the 'waters' dealt with are described as follows:

> No fountain and no water has my like
> I make both rich and poor men whole or sick
> For deadly can I be and poisonous.

> (Fabricius 1976, 18)

The upper and lower forms of the *prima materia* are two aspects of the same phenomenon, the way that spirit and matter are two sides of the same coin. The one is felt through the mental-spiritual realm, the other through embodied life and the somatic unconscious, the subtle body. But these experiences are split at the level of the heart chakra, as in the Tantric thought which influenced the *Rosarium* (McLean 1980, 119). In other words, the *Rosarium* represents spirit and matter as modes of experiencing life that have become contradictory and mutually exclusive. The idea is that the development of consciousness throughout the history of patriarchal and solar-heroic life has resulted in this split, which must now be healed. A simplified way of describing the split is to speak of mind–body splitting, but actually two major human modalities of perception and cognition are not joined in a rhythmic harmony as they must be. The *Rosarium*, and perhaps Renaissance alchemy in general, is about healing this split, which is first illustrated in the nineteenth woodcut (Figure 29, p. 212). The way of healing in the *Rosarium* is through dealing with pairs of opposites, usually represented as sun and moon, or brother and sister, pairs seen as opposing qualities of the subtle body, or within an interactive field.

The *Rosarium* offers yet another vantage point on the double-headed serpent, one that is especially important in the *rubedo* phase as characterized by the last ten woodcuts. For the serpent exists at the level of the brow chakra, which means that the Binarius is centered at a level of spiritual vision.

The transcendent vision that the alchemist Albertus believed was necessary for his work – 'Unless the soul shall come forth from the body and shall ascend upward into heaven, you shall profit nothing in this Art' (McLean 1980, 110) – inevitably incarnates back into a life of ordinary space and time. In its link to the *numinosum*, the soul, which is capable of spiritual and physical experience, has reached beyond its temporal existence; but upon its return to embodied life and the ego, the soul encounters overwhelming anxieties. As a result, the person will experience an intense state of confusion and split opposites, as if a remembrance of the Order and Light of the *unio mystica* took place but was then totally lost in an opposite state of terror and total disorientation. If one does not become so overwhelmed at this juncture that one becomes acutely psychotic, these swings between anti-worlds will eventually calm down, and as a result, a process of the incarnation of the *numinosum*, which can eventually lead to the creation of a stable inner, spiritual self, will begin. This psychic self-structure is one of the alchemists' starting points, as embodied in their belief that it takes gold to make gold. When Jung (1988) deals with the body in his analysis of Nietzsche's *Thus Spake Zarathustra*, he says that a person has to have spirit to put into the body before he or she can enter the body and experience its subtle nature. If this spiritual beginning is absent, entering the body does not result in transformative experience, such as subtle-body awareness and mind–body union.

Thus, the psychotic anxieties represented by the double-headed serpent, or the same anxieties of the madness of the Dionysian realm, need not be considered within a developmental paradigm as, for instance, a defense against identity loss in fusion states. These anxieties certainly can serve this function of avoiding deeper levels of pain, but the *Rosarium* recognizes this level of anxiety as a necessary concomitant to the experience of illumination. When a person is experiencing psychotic levels, such as the intense swings between opposites in the Binarius, he or she can be calmed and the state can become creative if another person relating to them creates a sense of containment. Such positive support can only occur if that person knows the level of psychotic anxiety as a result of illumination and is able to empathize with the one suffering the intense anxiety state, but such empathy must be accompanied by remembering the illumination that preceded this present experience of loss. The suffering subject has no aware-ness of this spiritual level, but the assumption that can be made, in the alchemi-cal way, is that it does exist as a precursor of the chaos being experienced. Thus, in the fateful seventh woodcut of the *Rosarium*, known as the *impregnatio* (see Figure 15, p. 178), the soul ascends to heaven and leaves behind a dead her-maphroditic being. From a conscious point of view, a person or a couple exper-iencing the dynamics represented by this woodcut will only know a terrible state of disorientation and loss of any form of inner or outer connection. Yet from a deeper vantage point, this lost connection, the soul, is said to be in the process of being impregnated by a higher form of consciousness.

This alchemical approach is 'non-reductive' and spiritual in the sense that dis-ordered states of mind are not seen as remnants of developmental failures of personality. The role of spiritual awareness proves especially important when analyst and analysand encounter the last ten woodcuts of the *rubedo*. For then analyst and analysand must 'add' not only passion and embodiment, in the sense of living the self in the real world (which is not yet part of the *opus* in the *albedo* phase of the first ten woodcuts), but they must also add spiritual awareness, the experience of which has been somewhat dulled or lost in the embodiment process. The lunar level of the *albedo*, the 'White Stone' created through the tenth woodcut (see Figure 18, p. 183), in which a self-structure uniting opposites has been achieved (albeit in a 'watery' or unstable form, still subject to being temporarily lost through intense affects), must be joined with spiritual awareness. This inclusion of spiritual life can become a problem, for it can be employed to flee from the world, relationships, and the body. Spiritual life can become a safe haven from intense conflict, loss, and abandonment, as it has in many spiritual disciplines that the West has incorporated. So when the life of the spirit is re-incorporated, it must be done without losing the embodied, lunar sight and sense of self created in the *albedo*. This incorporation of spirit in an embodied way is accomplished in the *rubedo* stage through a keen awareness of the need to sacri-fice solar awareness, that is, the kind of illumination and knowledge that the soul gains in its intuitive or spiritual mode. In the process of this sacrifice, one further enlivens the 'White Stone' until it transforms into its final 'Red' form which inte-grates spirit, passion, and embodied life including behavior in the world.

DISCOVERY AND RESISTANCE TO EXPERIENCING THE UNCONSCIOUS DYAD

The second woodcut of the *Rosarium*, the 'Left-hand Contact,' features the first image of a couple, the alchemical Sol and Luna (Figure 9). The 'left-hand con-tact' is referred to in Tantrism as 'sinister,' because it represents a linking that all but leaves out conscious reflection and control. In a sense, both people's uncon-scious forces combine while involving incestuous energies. These unconscious forces are the early familial connections that one has internalized, particularly the unspoken, unconscious, and forbidden linkages between family members. The potential for misuse of these energies in analysis and in personal relationships is

Figure 9 'Left-hand Contact': second woodcut of the *Rosarium Philosophorum*

very real. For this reason, in the second woodcut, the descending dove, representing the illumination by the spirit or the link to a higher consciousness, must be
present. This link is 'added' to the encounter, and only in the fifth woodcut, the
'Conjunction' (Figure 12, p. 171), is this control integrated into the field's own
dynamics. In the first four woodcuts, and especially in the second, a kind of 'external' awareness, something like a spiritually informed superego, is brought to bear.

The analyst and analysand may encounter unconscious dyads in seemingly
mundane, everyday encounters. For example, in a common interaction, a wife
may say something somewhat critical to her husband. The criticism is not intense,

and he can easily allow the 'sting' in it to pass and even see the value of what she has said. Or else he can react angrily at 'her tone' or her 'negativity.' But what if he delays having such reactions and instead waits, allowing himself to experience his feelings. The alchemist Geber quoted in the *Rosarium* says: 'There are three things necessary for this Art, that is Patience, Delay, and Aptness of Instruments' (McLean 1980, 96). As the husband looks within himself, he may see that he is upset and angry; but he may then search further for the reasons that he feels this way. As he searches in this way, all the while maintaining emotional contact with his wife by noting that he needs to experience his feelings, he may come up with something new. Rather than feeling worn-out notions of being attacked or diminished, he may feel that she is feeling contemptuous of him. The word 'contempt,' like finding the right word in a poem, may thus appear. He may ask her if this word makes sense: 'Were you feeling contemptuous of me?' And suppose his wife, perhaps after a bout of resistance which he does not allow to detract him from his search, agrees that she did feel contempt for him.

This process may have required a degree of perseverance and gentleness on his part that was not easy to manifest. For still under the sting of feeling attacked, if he is to induce her to look more deeply, he must also protect her from his own anger as he inquires about her reactions, never knowing if he is right, but perhaps open to discovering his own darker qualities. To encourage another person to connect to an unconscious part of themselves is not easy, even if that part has just been activated. In the instance of a woman's contempt for a man, this connection can be particularly difficult to achieve, for such negative reactions can work their controlling ways while in the background, never spoken yet having a silent and substantial controlling effect. But if he has succeeded in this effort at discovery, he may then look further into his feelings and recognize that being treated with contempt – which he now recognizes to be a long-standing pattern not only with his wife but also with previous women in his life – makes him very angry.

So where does this exchange leave this couple? The wife has revealed her contempt, and the husband has recognized that he is very angry. She could now 'work on her contempt,' see how it links to her early object relations and feelings about men. In turn, he could further look at how his intense anger is also related to his early experiences and to women in general. In this way, they could both begin to work on their shadow qualities.

This mutual discovery is the beginning of an alchemical process of transformation. But how do they enter into the realm of the subtle body, into a place where transformation can occur? They began in a state of dealing with emotions that they would each feel to be repulsive. Surely they would not consciously subject each other to destructive states of rage and corrosive states of contempt. The alchemists spoke of a 'repulsiveness' in this beginning or Chaos which must be found and which is not necessarily obvious. The husband's insistence on stopping, waiting, and feeling was an act of penetrating a chaos that could have easily been side-stepped. The wife's readiness to listen, reflect, and acknowledge her contempt was similarly a response that could have been easily side-stepped. Had either of these two people been unwilling or unable to be conscious of their shadow side, then they could not have entered the realm of the subtle body. In alchemy, from a state of repulsiveness, the *opus* could begin. In the alchemical text '*Novum lumen*,' the 'ignition of the art,' is explained as follows:

> To cause things hidden in the shadow to appear, and to take away the shadow from them, this is permitted to the intelligent philosopher by God through nature . . . All these things happen, and the eyes of common men do not see them, but the eyes of the mind and of the imagination perceive them with true and truest vision.

(Jung 1968, 12: paragraph 350)

Thus, an imaginal act can now take place. They may now 'decide' to go further. I emphasize 'decide' because one of them must take the lead to ask the questions: 'What is our unconscious dyad now?' 'What is moving us?' This act is always accompanied by resistance. Both people must give up control at this point. For it is no longer 'my anger' or 'my contempt' or 'your anger' or 'your contempt,' but now both people must lose such protective vantage points and instead enter a field with its own life. But even more is at stake, for this act is also an entrance into a *liminal* space in which equality and an absence of hierarchical relating exists. In this space, collective norms such as the incest taboo vanish, and according to Victor Turner, 'a gross quantum of affect – even of illicit affect –' arises (1974, 257). Such a space reveals passions, especially those known through incestuous drives. Within it, 'his anger' and 'her contempt' are associated with parental figures and early, incestuous feelings. Such issues make the 'move' to an unconscious dyad an act that usually has a certain illicit sense to it, along with a loss of power and control.

If they choose to enter this space, the couple may then consider that they have two states between them, anger and contempt. What if they try further to imagine that between them, metaphorically speaking, exists a couple – a woman with contempt for a man and a man with intense anger towards a woman? They may try, that is, to separate from their individual identification with these affects, and they may instead imaginally 'thrust them' into the space between them and begin to feel them as a pair of affects that they are both in, but which they also can both observe.

If a couple allows such a dyad to exist, each may feel that he or she is in a 'space of relations' in which each is moved by energies not previously experienced. The space becomes enlivened. Not only may both people feel the rhythm of the *coniunctio*, but also each may identify with either side of the dyad. The man can begin to feel his deep-seated contempt for the woman's masculine side, and the woman can feel an intense anger at the man's feminine side. Thus, the sense of a field between them allows them to experience a fluidity of identity and of active and passive roles. Furthermore, their individual consciousness expands for they have to face how deep structures within each of them have such powerful attitudes. And all the while they may experience how the field itself exists and also how it carries their conscious thoughts like the sea carries its waves. Through this experience they may begin to know that they are part of a mystery, for anger and contempt are only words now, merely forms that clothe a far deeper mystery of opposites. The alchemists would speak of Sol and Luna, and the couple would be clear, as is the case in the *Splendor Solis* and in the *Rosarium Philosophorum*, that their active and passive roles change.

In such a way from a simple remark – a criticism that could easily be side-stepped as hundreds of such remarks were, no doubt, previously by this hypothetical couple – they may enter into a realm of mystery that can enliven and challenge their relationship. For the field has its own currents, its desires and movements towards union, and with this dynamic the magnet-like power of the *coniunctio* draws in many facets of their unconscious life that each may well wish to keep unconscious. From a dry encounter, their 'earth,' as the alchemists would say, has become 'foliated,' enlivened so that their bodies now attract; and they feel they exist within a mystery that was always there, yet hidden in its very simplicity.

By entering a field with its defining and fluid dyadic forms, both people in a sense not only submit to a higher authority but also must trust the other not to misuse his or her power. If they succeed, they will in the process usually feel closer together than ever before. In effect, they will share a mystery; in a small yet significant sense, they will have been initiated together into the mystery of their relationship.

PREPARING FOR THE *CONIUNCTIO*

After the 'Left-hand Contact' in which both people may more or less sense the incestuous energies but tend to keep them from conscious awareness, the *Rosarium* follows with the third and fourth woodcuts which are especially important as they lead up to the transition to the liminal space of the *coniunctio*. The third woodcut, 'Naked Truth,' depicts the couple with their clothes off, and their incestuous passions are more evident (Figure 10). Sol says: 'O Luna, let me be thy husband,' while Luna exclaims, 'O Sol, I must submit to thee.' And the descending dove bears the inscription: 'It is the spirit which vivifies.' A variant of the pictures states: 'It is the spirit which unites' (Fabricius 1976, 34).

Instead of being directly connected by their left hands, the potentially sinister, incestuous contact, Sol and Luna are now connected by a rose which each respectively holds in hand – Luna, the white, and Sol, the red. Thus, they have been separated from the passion of incest, whose energies can now be more openly shown, to each other. The injunctions of Sol and Luna are to overcome resistance to relating.

Whereas in the 'Left-hand Contact' each rose had two heads, in 'Naked Truth' each rose has one head. Sol and Luna are overcoming their ambivalence and their tendency towards splitting. The two roses of the dove have become the *rosa mystica*, the rose symbolizing the *unio mystica* of love on the 'spiritual' level of incest. The text accompanying the third woodcut of the *Rosarium* reads:

> He who would be initiated into this art and secret wisdom must put away the vice of arrogance and must be devout, righteous, deep-witted, humane towards his fellows, of a cheerful countenance and a happy disposition, and respectful withal. Likewise, he must be an observer of the eternal secrets that are

revealed to him. My son, above all I admonish thee to fear God who seeth thy attitude and in whom is help for the solitary, whosoever he may be.

(McLean 1980, 24)

The third woodcut is a litany against the destructive aspects of narcissistic structures. One cannot enter creatively into an interactive field without doing harm unless one is able to accept the often shocking awareness of one's unconscious, shadow qualities which can accompany the process and disrupt one's narcissistic equilibrium.

Figure 10 'Naked Truth': third woodcut of the *Rosarium Philosophorum*

In the next image preparing for the *coniunctio*, the fourth woodcut, 'Immersion in the Bath' the experience of the 'lower' Dionysian-Mercurial waters takes place (Figure 11). At this stage, both people are able to experience erotic energies and, through the spiritual intelligence represented by the descending dove, to know that a mystery is at hand greater than any they may imagine. Dealing with projections at this stage can destroy the awareness of the field, while too much fusion, which interpretation can help to separate, can also undermine the process. The *Rosarium* proclaims: 'This fetal water (*aqua foetum*) contains everything it needs' (Fabricius, 1976, 64).

Figure 11 'Immersion in the Bath': fourth woodcut of the *Rosarium Philosophorum*

Having survived the processes of the third and fourth woodcuts, one is able to approach the main transformative sequence of the *Rosarium*, the *coniunctio–nigredo* sequence of the fifth through the seventh woodcuts, met again in the last ten woodcuts of the *rubedo* phase. In the alchemical way of transformation, becoming depressed or suffering is not a sufficiently creative *nigredo* state; rather, one seeks a death of structure that follows a union state, the *coniunctio*. The previously cited hypothetical example of a husband and wife interacting would probably result in a *nigredo* state. That is, after their encounter, it is highly likely that during the next days they would feel somewhat estranged. Unless they could remember that they had previously been in the liminal space of the *coniunctio*, their experience would degenerate. That degeneration would include returning to a married life of projections and deceptions and, eventually, to yet another return to a sacred space and a possible new beginning of their *opus*. One finds such beginnings over and over again, until some stability, as in 'The Axiom of Ostanes,' is achieved. This stability is represented in the fifth woodcut, the 'Conjunction' (Figure 12).

In the fifth woodcut, the field is represented by a dyad that is largely in the unconscious – Sol and Luna are depicted as being under water. In this field quality, the existence of the dyad must either be inferred or else 'seen' though an imaginal penetration. This first image of union in the *Rosarium* is introduced as a vision.

To explain the intermediate nature of the *coniunctio* is difficult. In the archetypal image of the *coniunctio*, two substances combine and energy is released. This process can be compared to the modern concept of cold fusion, notably the experiments in Utah in which substances were said to have combined in a fusion reaction, giving off energy even while applying none of the extreme heat used in conventional atomic reactions.

The ancient traditions, upon which alchemical thinking is based, expect the creation of something new out of a union experience. For example, the union state of mind and body is said to create the *pneuma*, the substance which alchemical thought insists permeates the universe and of which the stars are made. This *pneuma* is said to exist within an infinite set of tensions that link all life and matter, a set of connections that are the basis of the notion of *relations per se*. While the *pneuma* always exists, the alchemical idea is that it is also created by the union experience. Rather than the release of energy discussed in cold fusion, a very subtle, usually unseen substance, the *pneuma*, is released by the union experience. In the alchemical process of transformation, one is thought capable of developing one's senses to the point of being able to see this level of existence, to see how one is connected to another human being and to the cosmos. Couliano discusses this development of the senses:

> The [intermediary between soul and body] is composed of the same substance – the spirit (*pneuma*) – of which the stars are made and performs the function of primary instrument (*proton organon*) of the soul in relation to the body. Such a mechanism furnishes the conditions necessary to resolve the contradictions between the corporeal and the incorporeal: it is so subtle that it

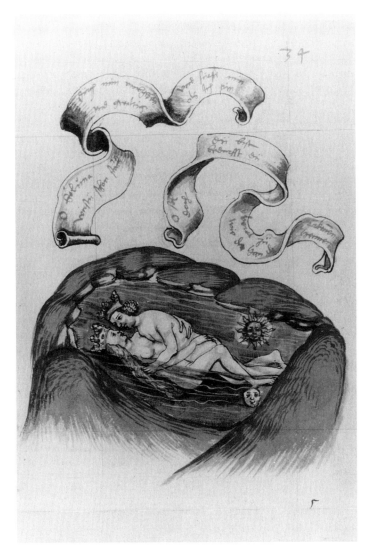

Figure 12 'Conjunction': fifth woodcut of the *Rosarium Philosophorum*

approximates the immaterial nature of the soul, and yet it has a body which, as such, can enter into contact with the sensory world. Without this astral spirit, body and soul would be completely unaware of each other . . . For the soul has no ontological aperture through which it can look down, while the body is only a form of organization of natural elements, a form which would disintegrate immediately without the vitality ensured it by the soul. Finally, the soul can only transmit all vital activities, including movement, to the body by means of the *proton organon*, the spiritual apparatus located in the heart . . .

The body opens up to the soul a window to the world through the five sensory organs whose messages go to the same cardiac apparatus which now is engaged in codifying them so that they may become comprehensible. Called *phantasia* or inner sense, the sidereal spirit transforms messages from the five senses into *phantasms* perceptible to the soul. For the soul cannot grasp anything that is not converted into a sequence of phantasms; in short, it can understand nothing without phantasms . . . The *sensus interior*, inner sense or Aristotelian common sense, which had become a concept inseparable not only from Scholasticism but also from all western thought until the eighteenth century, is to keep its importance even for Descartes and reappear, perhaps for the last time, at the beginning of Kant's *Critique of Pure Reason*. Among philosophers of the nineteenth century it had already lost credence, being changed into a mere curiosity of history limited to books specializing on the subject or becoming the butt of ridicule . . .

(1987, 4–5)

Thus, the *coniunctio* is more than an amalgam of two things, more than an intertwining of projections from one person to another, and more than a state in which projections penetrate another person and, in Jung's metaphor, actually lodge in the spinal cord of the recipient of the projection. In other words, the *coniunctio* is a phenomenon that is beyond both projection and introjection. The alchemical concern lies in making the *coniunctio* and its products more conscious, more stable, and more incorporative of states of mind usually disowned by collective life – notably the emotions and dangers of incest and, in a larger sense, passion.

When the *coniunctio* is seen, which is to say when its presence is known in the here-and-now – whether that seeing be through one's eyes or through feeling or sensing or hearing – the death that follows is often a powerful transforming agent. The kind of imaginal penetration that can 'see' – which is to say somehow to perceive the nature of forms that operate within a relationship, the forms I have spoken of as a 'background object' or the forms taken by mind–body splits or vertical splits, or the nature of an unconscious dyad – is actually present to most people. Its existence has been denied, for what this kind of vision knows is generally not acceptable to the rational world. And its existence has also often been denied because what has been seen, the background of violence and incest desires that an adult would prefer go unseen or the texture of lies that undermine a family system, is too dangerous for the growing child to own. When a child sees a terribly dangerous image lurking behind a parent who is acting as if that image is not present and, for that matter, who does not know it exists, the child has little recourse except to join in denying its existence. But because the child is closely linked to the child archetype, this psychic structure can see and survive. Thus, the young child both sees and denies his or her sight. In the process of denial, the negative qualities of the object are incorporated, with the result that the child's unconscious becomes structured by dangerous, attacking forces, and the heroic aspect of the emerging ego, the child archetype, tries to battle these forces.

Thus, the drama of disowned vision is played out as an internal drama, projected outwards again and again, but in a distorted, paranoid form that can be denied by the object and which the subject also hopes is not true. A game of deception ensues, and psychoanalytic approaches occupy themselves endlessly with the subject's internal object world, with the ways it is structured by mythical patterns or developmental arrest, and with the projections it emits. Once this projection analysis is the focus, the reality of vision easily becomes a possible side-issue and is usually discarded as a part of paranoid process. The alchemists speak of real and fantastic imagination, for the imagination has a trickster-like quality that easily can be used, along neurotic lines, for the purpose of self-deception.

Typical of an imaginal process that is central to the transformation of the unconscious dyad is the refrain found in 'Light of Lights,' quoted in the *Rosarium Philosophorum*:

> The dragon dies not unless he be killed by his brother and sister, and not by one only but by two at once. Sol is the brother and Luna is the sister.
>
> (McLean 1980, 49)

The importance of this refrain for the alchemists is underscored by its repetition in three more places within the text of the *Rosarium* (McLean 1980, 21, 31), including the banners of the nineteenth woodcut (Figure 29, p. 212) (McLean 1980, 109). This refrain is the essence of the transformation process: the apprehension of an unconscious dyad, especially of the union of opposites and the death of the union, has the power to kill the dragon, symbolic of the unconscious in its literalizing, compulsive, and trickster-like capacity to lie and practice self-deception.

For example, the hypothetical husband–wife, with their rage–contempt dyad, could transform their relationship field by focusing upon the shared nature of their dyad, of Sol and Luna together. This focus would mean that more and more unconscious material from either person could be tolerated by the other without reacting in angry, defensive ways or withdrawing. Instead of triggering the other into a reaction, one person's nastiness through this process could trigger a caring for soul: one's own and that of the other. Every upsurge of emotion and argument becomes a *prima materia*, something interesting to be seen with care rather than something to be reacted to and treated as an enemy. In this way, the dragon, representing the unconscious as it is experienced between them, dies repeatedly, and more and more unconscious material can be integrated in the process. But in this alchemical approach, such death and transformation happens not through Sol alone, nor through Luna alone, not with interpretive, rational understanding alone, nor with empathy and feeling alone. Instead, if its existence is to be known, the union of Sol and Luna must be experienced within the subtle body, an interactive field that must be imaginally entered.

Transformation thus requires that two states combine, and that the combined state itself transforms. In Mylius's version of the first woodcut, the alchemists drink from the Mercurial Fountain (Figure 13). To drink is to incorporate, and that is how any relationship of depth proceeds. Each person incorporates a quality of the field they both create. But the union state is often far from blissful. The *Rosarium*'s portrayal in the first woodcut (Figure 4, p. 105) is a wonderful rendering of the opposites in union as they oscillate in a field with its own rhythm,

Figure 13 Mylius's version of the first woodcut of the *Rosarium Philosophorum*

and in which neither the engulfment of fusion nor the threat of abandonment because of the loss and fear of connection is dominant. Rather, throughout the process the recognition that the combining of psyches also incurs states in which fusion, loss, and madness are intertwined within the vicissitudes of passion, acts as a powerfully transformative container.

9 Union, death, and the resurrection of the self

THE *CONIUNCTIO–NIGREDO* SEQUENCE IN THE *ROSARIUM PHILOSOPHORUM*

The transformation process of alchemy, as portrayed in the first five woodcuts of the *Rosarium Philosophorum* focuses upon discovering the opposites that comprise an unconscious dyad between two people and then relating to the union of these opposites. The union state of the fifth woodcut followed by the death of that union, depicted in the sixth and seventh woodcuts (Figures 12, 14–15, pp. 171, 177, 178), forms the essential *coniunctio–nigredo* sequence, the central transformative dynamic through which a self is eventually created. In the process of this development, interactive fields can change from forms that tend towards a literalization of its contents into forms that rhythmically structure union and separation and retain this stability amidst a variety of relational, internal, and environmental disturbances.

The alchemical path of transformation, portrayed in the woodcuts of the *Rosarium*, describes a pattern of transformation which occurs continuously in the unconscious as it strives throughout a lifetime to create a self. The unconscious, according to Jung, puts forth:

> a bewildering profusion of semblances for that obscure thing we call . . . 'self.' It almost seems as if we were to go on dreaming in the unconscious the age-old dream of alchemy, and to continue to pile new synonyms on top of old, only to know as much or as little about it in the end as the ancients themselves . . . It is easy enough to say 'self,' but exactly what have we said? That remains shrouded in 'metaphysical' darkness . . . True, [the self] is a concept that grows steadily clearer with experience – our dreams show – without, however, losing anything of its transcendence. Since we cannot possibly know the boundaries of something unknown to us, it follows that we are not in a position to set any bounds to the self . . . The empirical manifestations of unconscious contents bear all the marks of something illimitable, something not determined by space and time. This quality is numinous and therefore alarming, above all to a cautious mind that knows the value of precisely limited concepts . . .
>
> All that can be said about the symbolism [of the self] is that it portrays an autonomous psychic fact, characterized by a phenomenology which is always repeating itself and is everywhere the same. It seems to be a sort of

atomic nucleus about whose innermost structure and ultimate meaning we know nothing.

(1968, 12: paragraphs 247–49)

The self of alchemical transformation, as depicted in the *Rosarium*, has the quality of 'non-locality' of the field which embraces not only the individual but also all of humanity. The self is like the electron of physics that is everywhere and only localized when attended to in a particular space–time situation. This alchemical attitude of embracing humanity and nature is more than a wishful fantasy; it is a psychological and ethical attitude of care for others and society, a concern that is enlivened by the self. The self embraces an ethic of being 'socially useful' (Adler 1964, 254). But the self that is finally 'resurrected,' as depicted in the twentieth and last woodcut of the *Rosarium*, 'Resurrection' (Figure 30, p. 213) also retains a 'mystical' element, for it is a creation that knows of a transcendent light and thrives upon its wisdom, and it can retain stability and mature within the emotional intensity of passion and relationship. Thus, the self of alchemy is embodied and sexual, living and thriving not only through the spirit but also through the passions.

The alchemical attitude attends to the transformation process of various union states through both a 'solar' and a 'lunar' consciousness. Lunar consciousness can be too undifferentiated, too unformed, too imaginative in an undisciplined way, and overly empathic; solar consciousness can be too penetrating, too destructive of the sensitivity of the watery, lunar creation, and fixated upon being 'right' rather than submitting to relatedness, body awareness, and the demands of a larger whole. Reconciling these two forms of consciousness is necessary to create a relationship that can survive as a living and functioning entity amidst negative emotions and especially abandonment threats.

Jung quotes the alchemical maxim: 'Take the foul deposit that remains in the cooking-vessel and preserve it, for it is the crown of the heart' (Jung 1954, 16: paragraph 496). The foul deposit of the pain and grief of human interactions, especially those which deny the absence of relationship and seek to force some connection, and those in which psychotic levels of transference and countertransference dominate, become the crown upon which a new heart connection could grow. This growth can be reflected in terms of the imagery of the *coniunctio–nigredo* sequence: the despair, abandonment, and suicidal nature of the *nigredo* of the sixth woodcut, and the even more troubling state of absolutely no contact, of living in 'parallel universes' of the seventh woodcut.

The sixth woodcut of the *Rosarium*, 'Coffin of Putrefying Conception,' depicts the regal couple, Sol and Luna, as dead, having melted into a single being with two heads (Figure 14):

> Here King and Queen are lying dead
> In great distress the soul is sped.

In effect, the unconscious dyad is dead: the marriage bed has turned into a coffin of 'putrefying conception,' indicating how the death is believed to be a source of

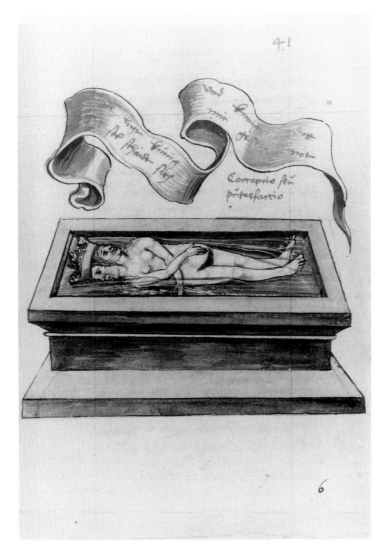

Figure 14 'Coffin of Putrefying Conception': sixth woodcut of the *Rosarium Philosophorum*

new life for the interactive field. The event is also named 'conception or putre-faction,' reflecting the alchemist's insight into the enigmatic and paradoxical nature of the 'black' transformation process: a building up by building down, a putrefying movement of creation. 'The corruption of one is the generation of the other,' says the *Rosarium*. 'When you see your matter going black, rejoice: for that is the beginning of the work' (Fabricius 1976, 102). The 'building up and building down' is a good image for ways that the opposites of life and death find harmony in the transformation process. At the outset of the work, these opposites, as states within the field of the double-headed serpent, were totally opposed to and annihilating of each other. Jung concludes about the sixth woodcut:

> this death is an interim stage to be followed by a new life. No new life can arise, say the alchemists, without the death of the old. They liken the art to the work of the sower, who buries the grain in the earth: only to awaken to new life.
>
> (1954, 16: paragraph 467)

The seventh woodcut is called the 'Extraction and Impregnation of the Soul' (Figure 15). Out of the decay of the corrupting body, the soul, in the shape of a

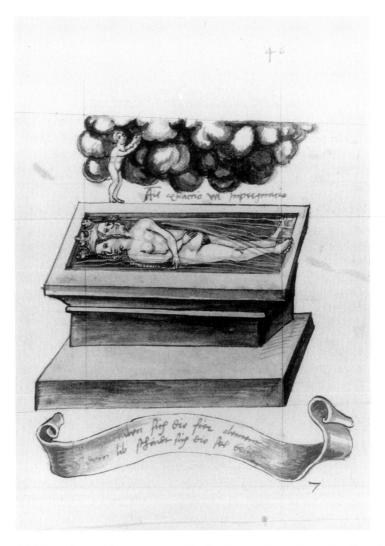

Figure 15 'Extraction and Impregnation of the Soul': seventh woodcut of the *Rosarium Philosophorum*

homunculus, ascends to heaven in order to receive its 'impregnation.' In the *Rosarium* text, the torments suffered during the 'extraction of the soul' form part of the *iterum mori* – the 'reiterated death' – which belongs to the experience of the interactive field at this stage of the work. This experience can be extremely trying, causing both people to want to give up or somehow to escape the process. To continue takes courage and will.

The dissociative nature of this field experience is represented by an alchemical author called Hermes, the King, who says:

> Know my son that this, our stone, which has many names and various colors, is arranged by and composed of the four elements. These we should separate and cut up in their limbs, dividing them into smaller and smaller pieces, mortifying the parts, and changing them into the nature which is in it [the stone].
>
> (McLean 1980, 45)

And the depressive quality of the field quality represented by the seventh woodcut is seen in the words of the alchemical author Sorin:

> Divide the whole thing, rub it frequently until death reigns from the intensity of blackness, as a dust. This a great sign in the investigation of which not a few have perished.
>
> (McLean 1980, 45)

And again, the necessity of reaching this 'blackness' is recognized by Hermes who says: 'Take his brain, grind it up with very strong vinegar, or with boy's urine, until it turns black' (McLean 1980, 45–46). These images characterize the dark, dangerous, and potentially fruitful nature of this field experience which appears to thrive upon the torments and mad states of mind of the seventh woodcut.

Jung likens the seventh woodcut to a schizophrenic dissociation (1954, 16: paragraph 476). This woodcut represents a field quality that is the most difficult to deal with without violating the wisdom of the aphorism to create 'like from like.' In such violations, the analyst often takes the lead in creating the monstrosity of a delusional transference and unworkable psychotic field. Knowledge and experience with the nature of the opposites in a mad sector, and especially with the bizarre quality of their fusion or the double binds they infuse in the field, are essential for properly dealing with this stage of the *Rosarium*. However, one can experience such states both as a *prima materia* and as associated to a *coniunctio*. Both phases are part of the alchemical process of transformation: the one connected to apprehending the chaos of the double-headed serpent, the other an agent for transforming rigidity and allowing a new self to emerge. The former requires seeing and experiencing the opposites; the latter requires this and more – remembering or discovering that a union state has preceded the *nigredo*. The *Rosarium* thus insists that a great mystery is at work during this most difficult of stages. For now the soul, the agent of linking and psychic reality, is being renewed, even while the field experience itself is barely tolerable.

The eighth, ninth, and tenth woodcuts of the *Rosarium* represent a qualitative transformation of the interactive field in which it is not only re-animated but also

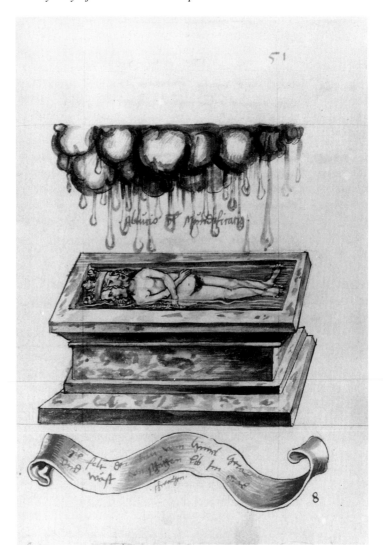

Figure 16 'Falling Dew': eighth woodcut of the *Rosarium Philosophorum*

its structure is changed into one in which negative fusion states, to a considerable degree, are no longer so problematic. This state still requires the *rubedo* stage for its fulfillment, but in the *albedo* considerable gains are made.

The suffering of the *nigredo* is finally relieved in the eighth woodcut, 'Falling Dew' (Figure 16), by the heavenly dew or 'philosophical humidity . . . falling as clear as a tear' (Fabricius 1976, 112). The dew is also said to have a miraculous effect, not only to cleanse but also to fertilize the hermaphroditic corpse, leading to an incipient pregnancy:

Here falls the heavenly dew, to lave
The soiled black body in the grave.

'The falling dew,' Jung maintains, 'is a portent of the divine birth now at hand.'
For Jung, the dew:

> is a synonym for the *aqua permanens*, hence for Mercurius. The whitening
> (*albedo* or *dealbatio*) is likened to the *ortis solis*, the sunrise; it is the light, the
> illumination, that follows the darkness.
>
> (1954, 16: paragraphs 483–84)

By experiencing the *coniunctio* and resulting *nigredo* over and over again, a new
state could be reached, the 'whitening' of the *albedo*. This new state was part of
the qualitative transformations of alchemy which were signified by color
changes. In the *albedo*, the despair, madness, and fears of abandonment were
overcome to the extent that these states no longer created a radical splitting from
union or a regressive fusion into total identity loss (Schwartz-Salant 1995b, 35).

The falling dew leads to the revival of the regal couple in the ninth woodcut,
'Return of the Soul' (Figure 17). As Jung aptly puts it, 'the reconciler, the soul, dives
down from heaven to breathe life into the dead body' (1954, 16: paragraph 494).
Fabricius describes this return of the soul in terms of the changes in an individual:

> As a result of the preceding operations of ablution, calcination, and incinera-
> tion the gross body has finally taken on a 'soulish' and 'spiritual' form,
> becoming a *corpus mundum* – a 'purified body' – capable of sheltering soul
> and spirit or even drawing them down to itself . . . The soul returns with the
> spirit in the figure of the homunculus, who is bisexual and represents the uni-
> fied anima and spiritus.
>
> (1976, 124)

The same can be said of the field; it is renewed and takes on a form that
is purified.

The tenth woodcut, 'Rebis,' depicts the realization of the '*white coniunctio*,'
that is, the conjunction striven for in the previous woodcuts (Figure 18). The
hermaphrodite can be seen to represent a field quality in which a structural state
exists that allows for a connection between mind and body, or between conscious
and unconscious, even amidst states of impending loss and abandonment. The
connection to one's own heart and the imaginal link to another person through the
imagination of heart (Corbin 1969, 219–22) no longer vanishes. The hermaphroditic figure stands on the lunar crescent, signifying a foundation that is rooted in
change, but also overcomes the death-like state of abandonment.

Jung was very negative about the image of the 'Rebis' as it appeared in the
Rosarium (1954, 16: paragraph 533). He believed it was a monstrosity and represented ways in which the alchemical mind was ignorant of projection and stuck
in sexuality. I have argued elsewhere (Schwartz-Salant 1984, 1989) that Jung is
wrong on this point and that he was, as is evident from his remarks on the 'Rebis,'
reacting to Freud's emphasis upon sexuality. While I still hold this view, I also

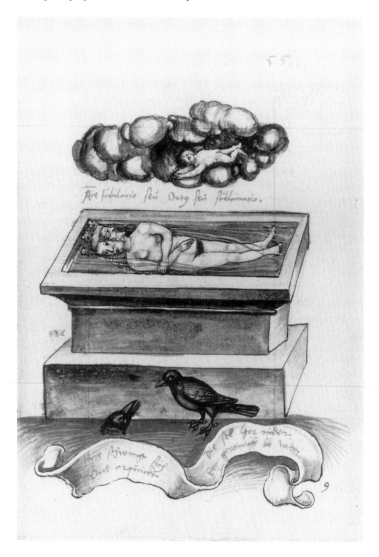

Figure 17 'Return of the Soul': ninth woodcut of the *Rosarium Philosophorum*

think that Jung's intuition has value, for sexuality and passion have not yet been dealt with in the *albedo* phase of the *Rosarium*. These fires of human life began the transformation process in the 'Left-hand Contact' of the second woodcut (Figure 9, p. 164), but they then stimulated the creation of a psychic self, the 'White Stone' which lacks passion and an integrated sexuality. Or as Jung said, the *albedo* phase of transformation still lacks 'blood' which is symbolic of a passion for life:

> [In the] state of 'whiteness' one does not *live* in the true sense of the word. It is a sort of abstract, ideal state. In order to make it come alive, it must have

Figure 18 'Rebis': tenth woodcut of the *Rosarium Philosophorum*

'blood,' it must have what the alchemists called the *rubedo*, the 'redness' of life. Only the total experience of being can transform this ideal state into a fully human mode of existence. Blood alone can re-animate a glorious state of consciousness in which the last trace of blackness is dissolved, in which the devil no longer has an autonomous existence but rejoins the profound unity of the psyche. Then the *opus magnum* is finished: the human soul is completely integrated.

(McGuire and Hull 1977, 229)

Finally, in the *rubedo* phase, this state of the self as a field quality is further enhanced by becoming an individual and transcendent self-structure as well.

UNION–DEATH DYNAMICS IN ANALYTIC PRACTICE

In dealing with the *coniunctio–nigredo* sequence in analytic practice, the analyst must thus be alert to the darker forms of union. For example, the so-called negative transference can be such a union state forged through hatred and envy. Yet it is also a union state in which fusion drives and individuating tendencies towards separation are intertwined. If seen as a *coniunctio* and respected as such, the negative union state can develop along the creative lines set out by the *Rosarium*. In other words, if the analyst only looks for positive union states that 'feel good,' he or she will never be working within an alchemical spirit and will not help the analysand to work towards mind–body linking or the creation of a self. These same remarks are of course true for any couple attempting to embrace the depth and mystery of relationship.

The following, extensive clinical material illustrates the union–death dynamic in the *albedo* phase of the first ten woodcuts. This case also highlights errors that occurred in the *nigredo* stage and the process of repair that then took place. The material is taken from the fourth to the sixth years of my work with a female analysand suffering from relationship issues related to early physical and sexual abuse (Schwartz-Salant 1990). During the first four years the theme of incest and its devastating effect never arose; it had also been hidden in a number of her previous analyses. One of her initial complaints was that her previous therapist told her that he found her spiritually but not sexually attractive. This judgment was a grave injury to her, and when she spoke about it, she was in a state of mind–body splitting and mental blankness. But most significant for our later work was my willingness to side-step these dissociated states of mind and instead focus upon her statement as an injunction to me not to reject her.

After four years, she began recalling memories of being sexually abused by her older brother, and much earlier by a nursemaid. At this time, we explored the sado-masochistic nature of her inner life, first as it expressed itself in brutal self-attacks for what she took to be her role in the incest episode and then in even harsher attacks that she had made it all up and was really crazy. As this theme of incest gradually became more central to our work, I found myself internally resisting the possibility that it could really have happened to her. She then began a session with a question: 'What do I do with my feelings when I feel no connection with you?' It was as if she had said, on the one hand, that she had no feelings at all and then that she had said, on the other hand, that she had feelings. The confusion and emotions that accompanied the posing of this question were so charged that I tried to avoid the effects and contradictory nature of her communication; but I only felt challenged and angry. I was bewildered by the strength of my reaction, but I mostly side-stepped it and focused upon a sense of being irritated with her. I took this feeling, along with my tendency to dismiss her question as unimportant, as representing an induced reaction to her masochism. I challenged her by insisting that a connection did exist between us, but it was on a sado-masochistic level; and I focused the session on exploring these dynamics as they were developing within projective identification. I thought a good deal had been accomplished, but the result was the emergence of a psychotic transference.

In subsequent sessions, the analysand was blank, withdrawn, and terrified. She took anything that I was saying to her or had said to her in previous sessions in a very literal way. For example, at one point in the previous session, while engaged in what I took to be a mutually enlivened field through which I was experiencing introjects from a projective identification process, I said: 'You expect me to hate you and find you a disgusting whore.' I experienced this fantasy as pressing into my awareness during the session, and I believed that I had sufficiently processed it internally so that I could share it as an imaginal process and thus bring it to her awareness in the here-and-now of the analytic session. My shocking language was cast in the material of many previous sessions in which we had dealt with her self-attack stemming from memories of her brother's sexual abuse of her. I had come to believe that by now she knew she was an incest victim, but I was soon to learn that while this knowledge had been assimilated by her normal neurotic ego, it had not been assimilated at all by her more psychotic parts. Thus, with the interactive field enlivened, I believed I experienced the analysand's sado-masochistic couple in which her inner sadist was blaming her for the incest and, in effect, accusing her of being a whore. I thought I was bringing this dynamic out and into consciousness by giving it voice. In fact, I was revealing my inexperience (at that time) both with the anti-worlds of the opposites in psychotic processes and with countertransference tendencies to avoid these areas by creating meaning. Furthermore, if I had recognized that the sado-masochistic couple was not 'hers' but 'ours' and that this couple was a negative form of the *coniunctio*, I would have provided a far better container for the analysand, and the *nigredo* that followed would have been less severe and less dangerous. However, this awareness only came to me several months after my inappropriate intervention.

Countertransference errors are extremely common when dealing with the *nigredo* that follows a *coniunctio*. A (sado-masochistic) union state had preceded this session, but my desire to avoid the blank and dark states of mind of the *nigredo* caused me to not remember, to believe in the existence of and not a preceding state of connection. This connection was now totally absent from the analysand's awareness; and if I had been more conscious, I would have recognized that this connection was also absent from my awareness. I forced a connection. Contradicting the wisdom of the 'Tale of Isis to her Son Horus' to create 'like from like,' I erred in trying to create order and meaning in a chaotic, meaningless state as a defence against that condition.

In his investigation of alchemy, Jung mentions that the *nigredo* 'brought about a deformation and a psychic suffering which . . . [compared] to the plight of the unfortunate Job' (1963, 14: paragraph 494). The alchemical writer Olympiodorus notes the pain, struggle, and violence of the *nigredo*, saying that 'all the while [a] demon . . . instills negligence, impeding our intentions; everywhere [this demon] creeps about, both within and without, causing oversights, anxiety, and unexpected accidents' (Jung 1963, 14: paragraph 493). And the philosopher Petasios says: 'So bedeviled and shameless is the lead that all who wish to investigate it fall into madness through ignorance' (Jung 1963, 14: paragraph 493). If the alchemists are correct, investigating the difficult experiences associated with the *nigredo* will bring about levels of psychotic transference and countertransference, and ignorance will rear its head anew in each case.

In *Mysterium Coniunctionis*, Jung records various alchemical texts that depict the *coniunctio* and its results. In a sense, the alchemical texts are like X-rays that show what lies beneath the surface of phenomena that are often dealt with through a personal historical perspective. According to Jung, the *coniunctio* has undesirable results at the beginning (1963, 14: paragraph 152). He explores the nature of one of these negative images, the rabid dog, in a way that I find particularly insightful as it relates to the clinical material under discussion:

> The infant hermaphrodite, who is infected from his very cradle by the bite of the rabid Corascene dog, whereby he is maddened and rages with perpetual hydrophobia; nay, though of all natural things water is the closest to him, yet he is terrified of it and flees from it. O fate! Yet in the grove of Diana there is a pair of doves, which assuage his raving madness. Then will the impatient, swarthy, rabid dog, that he may suffer no more of his hydrophobia and perish drowned in the waters, come to the surface half suffocated . . . Keep him at a distance, and the darkness will disappear. When the moon is at the full, give him wings and he will fly away as an eagle, leaving Diana's birds dead behind him.
>
> (Jung 1963, 14: paragraph 182)

Jung views the source of madness, the rabid dog, not only as dangerous but also as the source of a new spirit, the eagle that ascends from its transformation.

Jung links the rabid dog to chaos or the *prima materia*, or to lead which 'contains a demon' that drives the adept mad (1963, 14: paragraph 183). Elsewhere, Jung refers to the enemy of the new birth as the 'thief' (1963, 14: paragraph 193). In clinical practice, this dangerous quality takes various forms, including incest. The alchemical symbolism of transforming the rabid dog or thief can reflect the arduous process of creating an analytic container for the anxieties, shame, panic states, and associated opposites split in a mad way that accompany the return of the experience of incest abuse. The 'thief' represents an experience of losing, over and over again, any seeming gains in awareness or linking with the person. The miraculous transformation into an eagle can appear in terms of an idealized transference as a manifestation of the spirit archetype (Schwartz-Salant 1982, 43–44). When the analyst works with the unbounded, chaotic and extremely distrustful states of mind to which imagery such as the rabid dog refers, he or she can experience the emergence of both a creative, idealized transference and the extreme vulnerability that accompanies such transference as a quite miraculous occurrence. At this point, however, the analysand had no perceptible idealization.

The analysand, largely through my blunder, thus entered into her psychotic part, but with a certain degree of containment. She was filled with distrust and terror toward me. Yet, largely through the sane part of her being, she also knew that she had to work things out with me; an alliance did exist. She had written up the session which began with her question about feelings and her connection to me, and her belief that I had said that I hated her. At this point, I was still (foolishly) committed to helping her more normal ego qualities recognize the distortions of her psychotic part. I was looking 'at her' – not 'my' or 'our' – psychotic distortions, trying to help her sort out reality. When we finally went back to her initial question, I told her that I felt angered by it, which I experienced as an attack upon our work. I had tried to forge a connection that did not exist, which I could now see was a hostile act on my part. Only after this kind of exploration, in which I began to reflect upon the validity of her perceptions, did she find some relief. Now, a space was reconstituting in which she could again work on her incest issues and her psychotic qualities which had been manifesting as extreme splitting, withdrawal, reality distortion, and suicidal drives.

If I were to foster the integration of her psychotic part rather than to fortify her normal-neurotic ego, I would have to acknowledge openly the truth of her perceptions, even if these perceptions could be seen as partial and distorted. Such acknowledgement can help the analysand to risk recognizing and expressing perceptions such as feeling hated by the analyst. My analysand, I later learned, was terrified that such an assertion would lead to my decision to terminate the analysis.

The reality distortions that stem from the psychotic part would appear to make the act of acknowledging the truth of the analysand's perceptions quite hazardous. The analysand could use such a procedure to reify further his or her distortions. But my experience is that, unless a schizophrenic process is at work, this concern usually does not prove to be problematic and is often based upon the analyst's introjection of the analysand's fears of being abandoned for having been confrontational. Unless the analyst finds a way to mirror the accuracy of the soul's vision, he or she will rarely succeed in helping the analysand integrate the depth of his or her being that is trapped in psychotic distortions.

In a subsequent session, the analysand said:

> I cannot trust anyone. I'm in a cold, withdrawn place and I am terrified of the power you have over me. If I tell you anything of what I thought last night you can annihilate me in an instant. I have never before felt the total power you have over me and it terrifies me. I just want to withdraw and totally leave everything, this process, life.

At this point, her terror now centered upon what I had said when we went over the session, for I told her that she 'heard' me say that she was a disgusting whore. I explained that I did not actually believe that she was a whore but that I was playing out a fantasy with her, a process of which I thought she was aware while it was happening. She listened intently, and I thought I was making progress in helping her to see her reality distortions. In the next session, I learned that it was not the 'whore part' that got to her but rather that I had said that 'she "heard" me say' what I said, implying to her that I had not said it at all and that she was psychotic. She felt that I had annihilated her perceptions, and she was left not knowing what to believe or trust.

She was especially terrified by the possibility that I thought she was crazy. She felt that now I was just soothing her and lying to her. As I again explained that I had actually said what she believed I had said, but that she had taken it in the wrong way, it was becoming clear, even to me in my absurd attack on the psychotic elements between us, that I was having little effect. I then asked myself: Where is she correct? She believed that I had said what I did because I really felt that she was a disgusting whore, but that I was now denying this feeling. Her belief could stem from her psychotic part or from a trickster-like force dominating our process – Mercurius in his demonic form, like the rabid dog. Or was her belief rooted in a perception of my own mad parts, with which I have had, when with this analysand, too little awareness?

I did deny her perceptions, as when I did not accurately hear and process her question concerning what she should do with her feelings when she felt no connection to me. When I insisted that only a change of form in the connection had occurred, I denied what she experienced, namely a space in which she had absolutely no link with me or with herself.

After another session, feeling the stress of my work with her, I recorded the following imaginal process:

> I want to thrash her, drown her in a stormy sea, throw her body to and fro in the waves until she will stop this torture of me with her withdrawals and masochism, leaving me always the guilty party. More and more I feel as if I have committed incest with her. I feel as if I am her guilty brother who did it to her and then denied it. I feel the edges of losing the as-if. Did I do it or didn't I?

I recognized that unconsciously I may have felt this identification for some time, namely that I was her older brother, the one who had incestuously violated her. As a consequence of denying this level of psychotic countertransference, I had been forcing interpretations and trying to feel empathic and related to her, rather than feeling the air of unreality which actually pervaded our work.

CONTAINING PSYCHOTIC PROCESS THROUGH THE FIELD QUALITY OF THE *CONIUNCTIO*

After these attempts to sort out our process together, she asked the inevitable question: 'Does this mean that I have been putting these reactions into you?' How easy it would have been to say, 'yes!' Clearly, projective identification had occurred, but I also knew that, in becoming aware of the psychotic countertransference, I was opening up to a much larger realm that seemed to have a goal or purpose; a classical projective identification approach would kill that awareness. The experience of the larger domain of the interactive field, which included my own incest fantasies, created a sense of meaning. This area was no doubt in need of exploration, yet it soon began to feel too airy and non-substantial, and I turned back to a projective identification view, psychological parts which I put into her and she into me. In turn, this projective identification approach felt too small, as it foreclosed a sense of meaning. In this way, an emergence of the awareness of the oscillation between developmental and mythical levels resulted. Such oscilla-tions characterize the interactive field experience when it is enlivened. One's sense of space changes, as in the alchemical saying: 'This stone is under you, and near you, and above you, and around you' (Jung 1963, 14: paragraph 45).

We could understand our interaction as inclusive of a 'third thing,' a mythical realm that had been ordering and weaving together the psychotic parts of our psy-ches. To reveal this realm, we could look at the background of our psychotic episodes. They always were preceded by an unconscious union state, usually (I discovered by going over her dreams) indicated by themes of a wedding. Then, a devastating *nigredo* would set in. For example, a wedding dream preceded the session in which I had insisted that we had a connection. I recognized that my periodically difficult times with this analysand had always been preceded by such dreams; at this point, I found that I could document four previous ones, and there may have been more.

The symbolism of the *coniunctio* is extremely varied and subtle, usually not nearly so overt as the marriage and wedding imagery in this particular case. Instead, one must often deal with obscure images of union, and it is easy at times to overlook images that can imply the existence of the *coniunctio*, such as fight-ing animals, or dream motifs such as a fire starting in the cellar, a burglar break-ing in, or the analysand's father dying. Jung also refers to the imagery of a flash of lightning and a 'stone birth' (Jung 1963, 14: paragraph 376). But such images can easily be taken as representing only the analysand's intrapsychic existence, or as reflecting childhood material emerging through the transference. What is often seen as developmental arrest is actually a result of a *coniunctio* occurring between two psyches, and the negative transference–countertransference is a union state that is very tempting for the analyst either to side-step or to interpret defensively.

In this case, the alchemical metaphor 'our' *nigredo* had been found and grad-ually contained. Could we then, having gotten our bearings, imaginally deal with the material that had devoured us, and do so without losing feeling? Sometimes, at her urging, the analysand and I, went back to the fateful session in which I sought to deal with our relationship in terms of a sado-masochistic quality. I was perplexed and at times felt persecuted by her insistence that we still had unfin-ished business, although by now I had learned to respect her resistance to going on until we had cleared up what had occurred in that session to her satisfaction.

Whereas she previously rebelled at my saying that 'she heard me say' what I had said, now she was deeply upset at the content as well. She believed I really felt she was a disgusting whore. I felt anxious about her dropping more deeply into a psychotic state in which suicidal drives mounted from her despair over the loss of her capacity to think and from her fear that she was psychotic. She felt that she would never emerge from this state. I tended to recall to her that at the time I had believed that we were in tune together, that she understood that I was role-playing with her, and that I was not at all conscious of feeling that she was in any way disgusting. In fact, I had believed that a totally opposite state prevailed, a state in which I felt a deep kinship with her, a common effect of the *coniunctio* (Jung 1954, 16: paragraph 445), as if she were an intimately known sister with whom I had a right to say or feel whatever I chose. I only now learned that this belief was my own and not shared by her. She, however, felt no right at all, and if anything, felt totally in my power. She could sense, but only barely feel, a deep anger. Through these so-called kinship feelings, our psychotic parts were secretly dominating the interactive field, and a sado-masochistic dyad was being acted out, rather than enacted. So I had to ask myself: 'Did I believe she was a disgusting whore?' I had to recognize that in some place, in some way, I could say 'Yes,' for to the extent that I felt I was her brother in incest, I also experienced her as seducing me.

The imagery of the whore is found in alchemy. The *nigredo* emerges from this image, the whore as the dark side of the moon wounds the sun (Jung 1963, 14: paragraph 21). Yet I was driven to recognize that this imagery was also pertinent to my own psychotic sector, structured by such mythical forms as the Attis–Cybele myth.

When my normal ego state was strongly affected by this archetypal pattern, I felt in danger of being overwhelmed by the analysand's needs and desires. Engulfment and a loss of my autonomy felt very real, and I could have split from this psychic reality and laid the confusion and distress totally at my analysand's door. However, through being able to relate imaginally to the presence of this archetypal sector and its associated ego state, I could now begin to see my projection on to her, even though I had not consciously felt her to be seductive or dangerous. It then became clear to me that, through the constellation of this archetypal pattern, I would see her as a whore and both hate her for the power she had over me and also desire to fuse with her to neutralize that power and to regain a sense of love. Thus, an unconscious dyad, analogous to the Attis–Cybele fusion state, began to become clear.

In terms of the *Rosarium*, this dyad was present during the initial session; it was a 'left-hand contact' (the second woodcut Figure 9, p. 164) in which our unconscious psyches were fused through desire while simultaneously fighting off any affective contact. If I had been more experienced at the time, I might have been able to handle this field quality far better than I did because I would have been more aware that the *nigredo* has its own dynamics which are very strong and which induce states of madness.

Once this madness was gathered up, our process could continue in a less stressful and conflicted way. The *Rosarium* indicates the condition of 'Naked Truth' as the field quality of the third woodcut. I had to recognize and take responsibility for my subjective errors with this analysand. At times, this procedure was narcissistically humiliating; I was shocked at the ways in which I had been and still was unconscious. But this procedure allowed us to continue in a useful way, and indeed to experience the nature of our emotional connection.

The analyst can understand the analysand in various ways such as through empathy, reflections upon one's own experience, and knowledge of developmental or archetypal patterns. The analyst can make interventions and interpretations based upon such understanding. But imaginal sight – the mainstay of the alchemical way – will only be available to the analyst when he or she consciously sees through the eyes of his or her own complexes. So I had to engage the quality of mutual unconsciousness in this case and, as a result, I came upon levels of my own psyche that I had often encountered, but not with the archetypal and autonomous quality I now had to face. The imaginal perceptions that the analyst may have will be reliable only if he or she processes them so that they make sense from both developmental and archetypal points of view. This dual vantage point will underpin the analyst's perception. In this case, I had to see the extreme distress and madness that encompassed my analysand's split-off part in defense of her experiences of being incestuously violated. For example, I could focus upon the Kleinian paranoid-schizoid position and my analysand's difficulty of entering the depressive position, but it was also important to see her inner madness as a result of the *coniunctio* that had occurred in the analytic process.

Unless I recognized and took responsibility for levels in myself in which an Attis-like myth functioned, my analysand would be left feeling delusional, her vision denied. As a result, she could have no clear idea of what was occurring between us. Instead, her vision would manifest through bodily pains and distress about that particular sado-masochistic session. It took considerable courage for her to contain her confusion and discomfort rather than to disengage from her vision and to become her compliant, arid and competent self. Consciousness of this archetypal level and its overwhelming nature for me was the key to entering a heart-centered link with her which could perceive her process. Prompted by her concerns, which could so easily be reduced to paranoia, I also had to recognize that I actually spoke of her as a whore not merely as an actor in her drama. By first unraveling my feelings in this vulnerable, personal way, I was then able to sense the underlying archetypal dynamic that could weave together these states of desired fusion, withdrawal, and hatred.

The qualities that often create the greatest difficulties in analysis are precisely those that go back to ancient substrata of the mind, such as the son–lover mythologem, a major form of the *prima materia*. In the ancient substrata of the mind, the analyst must confront shadow qualities that are not capable of being integrated into the ego sphere, but which must instead be seen, felt, and experienced as devotees of a god or goddess would experience that deity's rite. The scale of such phenomena is far larger than that of the ego; the act of imaginally perceiving and experiencing their numinosity is significant.

The errors that an analyst commits can be a result of his or her insufficient personal analysis, or they can be part of a trickster-like quality of the unconscious that will have its way with the analyst, perhaps for the sake of increasing his or her own consciousness. The wounds that the analyst inflicts upon analysands, and vice versa, are part of the evil that the analyst experiences as he or she engages the unconscious. The analyst must take responsibility for this evil without wilting under its weight. The analyst cannot ascribe all of his or her errors, insults, and serious injuries to the analysand as part of a process of 'older' wounds reappearing in the transference; and the analyst must also wonder about how these negative experiences might be created in the analytic process and about his or her associated responsibility for them. Creativity has an intense shadow, and if the analytical process is to be a creative endeavor, the analyst must expect the strong shadow side that inevitably appears.

Near the end of the two-year span of the clinical case that I have been citing, the analysand's rage was mobilized by what she perceived as my lack of connection to myself. This issue surfaced after yet another dream of a wedding. This time, we both wondered what would happen next. Two weeks later, her rage came as never before, and with it came intense despair and hatred of me for not being connected to her and also for not just letting her die. She was filled with hatred for what she experienced as my torturing her with our process and for my faith in that process.

In subsequent sessions, the analysand listened with her head turned away, risking not trying to connect to me through visual contact. In this way, she could hear if I were well-connected or not – to her and to myself. At this time, her madness emerged ever more forcefully. At times, I was anxious about it, for her madness did not have the form of a child-part lost in overwhelming anxieties and rage, but instead it felt like a mass of formless fury aimed at me.

She dreamed of an insurance man who was named John Hinkley, the deranged would-be assassin of American President Ronald Reagan. It became clear that her insurance against loss and abandonment was to come from being mad. The pain of the loss of connection with me was mounting to a new level of intensity. She felt she knew union – with me and with herself – at moments probably linked to her wedding dreams, but we had no continuity and no embodied sense of linking. A soulless state tortured her, and its lack of containment was, at times, very anxiety-provoking for me. Jung's alchemical research suggests that an unconscious process was also at work, in which the desired heart-connection was being sought and, perhaps, wrought (1954, 16: paragraph 482).

Several months later she had another dream of a wedding; this *coniunctio* and resulting *nigredo* were the most devastating yet. She spoke now of feeling 'totally dispensable.' However, in spite of the dream's intensity, and while suicidal thoughts and emotional isolation were still present, she was now far less schizoid. She felt as if the young part of her that had hidden as a child in hopes of not being found was now also part of the material in her process. Previously, this part was only felt through an interactive field of non-linking. This new spiral downward contained the previous material but included an important structural change as well. Feelings of withdrawal and unrelatedness still plagued her, but they were less intense in general, and they were particularly less intense while she was with me.

In the next session, she said that during the previous session she was different. When I told her that I also felt her to be different now, introverted and reflective rather than withdrawn, she responded by saying that she, too, noticed these changes. When she left my office she said goodbye. Previously she had said nothing, but had just left.

The union state thus acts like a magnet which attracts split-off schizoid states of mind, levels of soul abuse that can often be too awful to contemplate. The *coniunctio* sets in motion a process that sweeps the analysand–analyst dyad along as if a current in a vast sea were engaged, and the individual psyches bob up and down with newly integrated pieces of the unconscious. At times, the analyst will be mistaken if he or she only pays attention to this deeper movement, especially when countertransference acting-out has been the issue, as was the case in the fateful session with which I began this clinical analysis. However, had we not addressed the larger movement beneath us, the container that was created would have been far too small for the analysand's process. This smaller focus would have forced her into guilt or else accusations and away from a sense that we were in this together, weaving our story which in some ways matched or recreated her early life history but was its own creation as well.

In this case, we could gradually recognize the purpose of the *nigredos* to be the dissolution of the analysand's (and my own) rigid defenses against madness, and more importantly, the dissolution of defenses against the underlying pain and vulnerability that her abused soul suffered. As a consequence, it gradually became clear that this process was not only hers but also ours, through which we were changing together.

As the analysand gradually became more able to connect with her split-off soul, her withdrawal lessened, and a heart-centered imagination became possible. I was then able to feel an aliveness in my heart and less drive to enforce control and connection through knowledge or interpretation. This process is difficult to describe because it exists within an imaginal reality in which one's attention flows through the heart and out towards another person. In the process, imaginal sight emerges. This sight can be experienced through the eyes, through the body, or through feeling, but this level of perception gently penetrates in ways that a discursive process fails to achieve. To the abandoned soul, knowledge without heart feels like abandonment. The heart offers a way to connect without violating the soul.

The *nigredo* states that continued to emerge were difficult to manage, especially as they plunged the analysand ever more deeply into states of distrust. Yet these states always proved to be rooted in the process of creating a new analytical container, for example, for incest violations by other family members which she feared I did not really believe occurred. For the analysand, dealing with her persecutory doubts was like the motif in the alchemical text to which I previously referred: keeping the rabid dog at a distance. Through this process, like the dog transforming into an eagle, a creative, idealized transference did finally begin to arise.

My analysand suffered terribly when her heart-connection and my heart-connection with her were absent. The loss of heart was the main abandonment issue in our work, as it had always been in her life. The psychoanalyst Harry Guntrip refers to the 'lost heart of the self' (1969, 97) in the schizoid personality, and this metaphor well describes the schizoid quality in everyone. What was remarkable about the process of unions and ensuing *nigredo* states was that this process continually integrated the heart.

The *coniunctio–nigredo* sequence of the fifth, sixth, and seventh woodcuts (Figures 12, 14–15, pp. 171, 177, 178) dominated this case. Empathy was impossible in the field represented by the seventh woodcut, except the empathy of recognizing that there was none. This form of empathy did little to remove the pain felt within the field, but I could eventually respect the process as having some mystery beyond conscious awareness. The field quality of the seventh woodcut is characterized by three facets:

1. Both people experience being in parallel universes; no meaningful connecting is possible.
2. Either person or both people tend to act impulsively and automatically, as if a mechanical quality takes over. The analyst especially tends to talk in a stilted and forced manner, devoid of feeling. If the analyst delays such intrusions into the process, he or she is soon grateful for having been saved from an ensuing humiliation.
3. A subtle sense of bizarreness can be present. If the analyst really focuses upon the person a feeling of oddness will manifest.

The seventh woodcut depicts the physical and psychic agony of the field quality, and unfortunately, in many instances, the analysand carries most of the suffering. Generally, analysts are in a power position by virtue of the imbalance in the analytic situation, and consequently their splitting defenses are usually far more serviceable than are the analysand's. While analysts can remain relatively 'untouched,' were they to enter into the truth of their pain, they would find it to be, in fact, no less than that of their analysands. The analyst and analysand must suffer the pain of non-linking and the total absence of a heart-connection. Only the experience and endurance of this suffering by both people can bring on the falling dew of the eighth woodcut (Figure 16, p. 180) with its renewal of the unconscious dyad and of the field experience.

In my process with this analysand, the interactive field was enlivened and empathic connection was again possible. Moreover, the capacity for my own imaginal sight of her psychic life was enhanced, and she too could begin to trust her bodily and imaginal perception. The 'return of the soul,' symbolized by the ninth woodcut (Figure 17, p. 182), meant that a more stable sense of linking existed, and with it a renewed awareness of the 'third area' as a space with its own process and mystery. In this case, the subtle body experience was more present to both of us. Furthermore, at this stage a new capacity for imaginal sight came into existence, a capacity for vision that was no longer disembodied. This experience culminated in the kind of field qualities signified by the 'Rebis' of the tenth woodcut (Figure 18, p. 183).

When two people constitute a field with this quality, they can experience the devastating fields of the sixth and seventh woodcuts without their connection being destroyed by splitting and defensiveness. Both people are more capable of retaining a sense of self while also experiencing how this self-state is fluid and needs to be recovered through mutual exploration.

At this point, analyst and analysand have achieved something of great value, hard-won through many trials of the *nigredo*. In alchemical language, however, the Rebis is still 'watery,' fluid, and easily lost. With this stage, analyst and analysand believe that union can be regained, both as an internal state and as a field quality. In a sense the first nine woodcuts are a process leading to the creation of faith in a conjoined process that can be used and respected.

Most significantly, the Rebis signifies an interactive field quality of kinship. Kinship denotes that special condition in which abandonment and loss still exist, but are no longer major issues, and a fundamental trust in the presence of the other is stabilized. Moreover, in kinship with another person, the other takes us in, cares about us in a reflective way that is undaunted by narcissistic needs and envy. As one analysand put it, 'I feel like I'm your creative project.' And I felt that I was his as well. Although the Rebis has a very positive quality of linking opposites, creating the energy of kinship, and representing a shared self within the interactive field, it can dissolve under the impact of the passions; and without the integration of a wide range of desires this image can degenerate into a dangerous fusion state.

PASSION AND THE TRANSFORMATION OF THE INTERACTIVE FIELD

In Freud's discovery of psychoanalysis, the passions, as in the 'Left-hand Contact' of the *Rosarium* (Figure 9, p. 164), were the focus of the analytical process. Psychoanalysis addressed the *nigredo* in its characteristically reductive way by seeking earlier causes for its phenomenology and implicitly included the *coniunctio* as the linking process of the transference–countertransference. But the emphasis on passion then diminished as the formation of narcissistic and borderline disorders, which defend against psychotic levels and fears of engulfment in early states of passion, were addressed. Thereafter, the relations to objects became paramount, and with this change in focus, passion left center-stage of psychoanalytic thinking, while any direct encounter with the energies of the *coniunctio* was rarely the focus of psychoanalytical thinking. With the advent of object-relations theories, interpretation of the transference and the analysis of characterological defenses were clearly the chosen paths of psychoanalysis. Furthermore, the transference and the notions of fields which have arisen in the last decade in psychoanalysis do not include the usefulness or necessity of experiencing the passion of an interactive domain and its transformative significance.

Psychoanalysis has always had a dual focus upon the transference as an experience and upon the transference or countertransference as a form of projection to be analyzed as a source of information about the analysand's process. But with the possible exception of the work of Sandor Ferenczi (1938, 1955), psychoanalysis has seldom focused upon the transference relationship as an enlivened field quality characterized by passion. In any event, it is reasonable to see psychoanalysis as beginning with a *rubedo* experience in Freud's discovery of incest experiences or fantasies, developing through a phase like the first ten woodcuts of the *Rosarium*, and culminating with the tenth woodcut in which psychic death through splitting and other schizoid defense mechanisms is addressed. Throughout the process, the goal of psychoanalysis has been to help a person gain his or her own capacity to relate to the unconscious. This conscious–unconscious relationship is symbolized in the *Rosarium* by the hermaphrodite of the Rebis holding three snakes in one hand and the fourth snake in the other hand.

The energies of passion known in the *rubedo* have been cut up and diminished in modern times, for example by Freud's notion of infantile and genital sexuality. While Wilhelm Reich's (1973) heroic ideal of embracing all of the libido in the orgasm remained just an ideal, for Freud, repression and sublimation of infantile sexuality were necessary and inevitable. These energies cannot be fully known in the flesh, and when such knowledge is attempted, the energies often move towards a sado-masochistic level in which the ego attempts to transcend the limitations of the flesh.

Containing passion and relating to it are essential skills for anyone wishing to deal with the complexities of union states and with associated abandonment issues and their powerful, related emotions. Without passion, any relationship risks decay into mechanical behavior and resentment. The alchemical text, the *Splendor Solis*, contains a great deal of wisdom about such issues.

For example, the sixth painting of the *Splendor Solis* refers to the stage in Virgil's *Aeneid* in which Aeneas, who is helped by Cybele, is able to pass safely through Hell (Figure 19). Only someone who can experience passion without losing consciousness and structure has the capacity to deal both with the soulless states of abandonment that Hell represents and with the overwhelming emotion symbolized by its fires. Such a passage through Hell is essential for the existence of a stable, individual self. Without such a passage, the self is forever guarded by a variety of narcissistic and schizoid defenses, among others.

In the *Splendor Solis*, several paintings follow the sixth image which depicts the theft of the branch, and they lead to the birth of a hermaphrodite, which represents a self-symbol that has not been linked to the chthonic dimension of the body. Addressing the chthonic dimension in a powerful way, the tenth painting shows a wild-looking man with a sword who has cut off the limbs, shown in their white and blood-reddened dismembered condition, of another man (Figure 20). Remarkably, this dark shadow quality achieves the dismemberment of the rigid body and psychic self-image. This figure represents the integration of those aspects of our being that are capable of psychotic acts which stem from an inner identification with the animal life of the unconscious. When this identification is activated, that is, when it is not consciously suffered and sacrificed but is instead acted upon in a grandiose and delusional way, this shadow shows its psychotic quality. But when this identification is integrated to the extent that it determines a border that one cannot cross without doing violence either to one's own soul or to that of another, and when one suffers the frustration of non-identification with these energies, then this shadow becomes more creative. Most remarkably, the shadow then becomes the sacrificer of rigid structures, leading to the eleventh painting of the the the *Splendor Solis* in which the body is transformed and the spirit is experienced as ascending from the depths of the body (Figure 7, p. 135). This transformation represents the creation of the self within a subtle-body realm in which matter and spirit are no longer separated but linked in a field of new

Figure 19 Sixth painting from the *Splendor Solis*

perceptual capacity. The subtle body is a potential container for passion, and achieving this container in a stable form is a main goal of the transformation process in alchemy. The subtle body or interactive field evolves towards structures that contain passion in an essential aspect of the *rubedo* stage of the last ten woodcuts of the *Rosarium* in which issues of union, death and passion are considered in greater detail than in the *Splendor Solis*.

Figure 20 Tenth painting from the *Splendor Solis*

The *rubedo* stage of the *Rosarium* begins with the eleventh woodcut, 'Fermentation' (Figure 21). This woodcut represents a stage in which the interactive field has become enlivened in a new way. Both passion and spirit are the enlivening elements, although the text makes it clear that fermentation is added 'a little, and then little again' (McLean 1981, 69). The field's existence is now more directly felt and seen, as is implied by the fact that the couple, representing a once totally unconscious dyad, is now no longer under water.

Figure 21 'Fermentation': eleventh woodcut of the *Rosarium Philosophorum*

The transformative power that attends such fields is important to recognize, but intense resistances to such fields, especially in cases in which the incest taboo has been actually or emotionally violated by a parental figure or sibling, can emerge and must be respected. I certainly failed to have this respect for resistance in the case I have discussed in this chapter. In previous publications, whose content can be seen as reflecting the field dynamics of the eleventh woodcut, I have written about such clinical interactions. In one particular case (Schwartz-Salant 1989, 144–57), fifteen years after a crucial session in which the enlivened interactive field became a stimulus for an imaginal process, the analysand still considers it to have been a transformative event in her life which enabled her to make significant changes both internally and in her life circumstances. The imaginal experience of the field connected her so much more deeply to her unconscious that even today she can draw upon this invaluable source. In this woodcut, the field is as alive as the unconscious in a vital active imagination, only it is now part of a shared process with another person which gives it a spontaneity that can be enduring.

But the field's enlivened nature can also be misused – inferred to exist as a useful entity before it has been created as a result of the *coniunctio–nigredo* sequence – as I did in the case I have discussed in this chapter. I wrongly assumed that the analysand and I shared an imaginal process that could contain the statement that she expected me to see her as a whore. But in the other case to which I have alluded, and in which an imaginal interaction has a more directly positive outcome, the interactive field was a container which could form and hold seemingly shocking statements that proved creative.

In the eleventh woodcut, the field's own dynamics manifest in a reversal of gender roles: the woman is now atop the male. Culturally conditioned male–female role reversals, especially in the forms of active–passive, are often keenly evident in this stage of the process, signified by the eleventh woodcut (Schwartz-Salant 1992). Each person can 'penetrate the other,' and can do so in a way that can be startling and throw one out of a position of power and knowledge over and over again. Such engagements are only successful if they are played out against an awareness of a field with its own dynamics. This situation is parallel to active imagination in which one dialogues with an image in the unconscious. The field takes the place of the unconscious, and the image is the unconscious dyad.

The dangers of the energies of passion are now lessened by the fact that a psychic self-structure has been achieved in the tenth woodcut (Figure 18, p. 183). Within the experience afforded by the field quality of the eleventh woodcut (Figure 21, p. 199), the analyst and analysand can now know the rhythm of the *coniunctio* in which it is a 'third thing' that can be imaginally sensed and related to as if a vision were present. The process is far more conscious than it is in the *coniunctio* of the fifth woodcut (Figure 12, p. 171), for now the experience of the *nigredo* has resulted in the assimilation of incestuous, and thus compulsive, material.

Clearly, a 'shadow side' of this process is always a 'wild analysis' in which anything can be said. Such behavior is usually a defense against one or the other person's anxiety and, in turn, can often hide sado-masochistic drives. These dangers exist for those who have not passed through the *albedo* phase, and especially the inflation-cleansing state of the *mundificatio* (Jung 1954, 16: paragraph 502). The *albedo* stage of the *Rosarium* creates a psychic self that is the orienting center for the *rubedo* phase. Without this experience of the self and its function as a center of one's being, the *rubedo* stage cannot be successfully entered which, I believe, is an essential part of alchemical wisdom, as revealed in the next four woodcuts.

Passion, which historically is always followed by tragedy and death (as seen in Denis de Rougement's *Love in the Western World* [1983]), can become a creative factor in the *rubedo*. But in a remarkable change from the *albedo* phase, the union state now need not immediately lead to a devastating *nigredo*. The ensuing imagery of the *Rosarium* indicates the way and the wisdom of this process.

The twelfth to fifteenth woodcuts of the *Rosarium* and their accompanying texts accomplish two goals. On the one hand, they illustrate ways in which solar-rational awareness and illumination can be destructive and how, at times, they must be sacrificed. On the other hand, they represent the same *nigredo* sequence as seen in the *albedo* phase, with the main difference that the hermaphrodite in the sarcophagus is winged. Just as the *coniunctio* in the eleventh woodcut is an aerial creature, so too these states of *nigredo* are more capable of being conscious

Figure 22 'Illumination': twelfth woodcut of the *Rosarium Philosophorum*

to the participants and readily reflected upon than blindly suffered as is often the case in the *albedo* phase.

The twelfth woodcut, 'Illumination,' shows the sun, signifying illumination and rational thinking, dying in the well of Luna which represents being, imagination, and emotional awareness (Figure 22). In an analytical process, the analyst is often the beholder of consciousness, gained for example from his or her reflections on projective identification or dream analysis. Equally, the analyst 'knows' a great deal from a life-long study of forms of the transference and countertransference and from the many cases that he or she has fitted into a diagnostic schema. However, such forms of awareness, 'solar forms' in the alchemical metaphor, are easily misused by an analyst defending against being re-traumatized, that is, defending against his or her early wounds being inflamed by the interaction with the analysand, and especially by the analysand's awareness.

Before awareness can be creatively sacrificed, as is the situation in the twelfth woodcut, it is obviously necessary to have such analytical knowledge. The sun voluntarily enters the well, signifying that the analyst may have a considerable array of understanding, and may even have a solar-spiritual capacity through which he or she imaginally holds to an awareness, but at this stage the awareness is given up. This act feels dangerous to the analyst, for he or she is then without defense and instead in a state of unknowing. While the seventh woodcut (Figure 15, p. 178) forces this condition in the *albedo* stage, this condition is voluntarily entered in the twelfth woodcut.

This act of sacrifice is the epitome of a voluntary death of narcissism in favor of creativity. It is possible to differentiate a creative endeavor into narcissistic and more authentic forms. In the former, a person essentially shows what he or she already knows. In the latter, this demonstration is consciously given up and the creative process seeks out what is not known. While such a sacrifice also plays a role in the *albedo* phase, as it does in any analysis, it is especially important in the *rubedo* phase, for in dealing with passion, any clinging to knowledge is dangerous. This kind of narcissistic attitude is easily overwhelmed by passion and can lead to regressive and destructive fusion states in which either the unconscious dyad is acted out or it is split and its presence denied.

Thus, this sacrifice precedes the *nigredo* stages of the thirteenth and fourteenth woodcuts (Figures 23–24), for as a result of the winged and 'red' passionate nature of the unconscious dyad, the suffering of non-action and unknowing can easily be side-stepped and the process endangered. Solar awareness is both the sacrificed and the sacrificer: the analyst and analysand must consciously sacrifice what they know in service of experiencing once again a deadness and lack of connection, as in the sixth and seventh woodcuts (Figures 14–15, pp. 177, 178). The point is that with the addition or presence of passion, these states of 'absence' or despair are very easily circumvented in a kind of manic behavior which is the negative aspect of the winged nature of the hermaphrodite. Thus, in the *rubedo* stage, 'death' is not so evident and is not forced upon the consciousness of analyst and analysand, as it is in the *albedo* stage; rather in the *rubedo* stage, the lunar nature of the 'death' of linking, its emotional texture, must be sought after through the sacrifice of solar awareness.

Now that a 'lunar foundation' – a stability and access to imaginal sight – exists, as seen in the creation of the Rebis, the *rubedo* stage works by transforming the solar forces out of their negative, compulsive form. An underlying dyad is always the focus, and through this dyad change occurs: 'The dragon dieth with the sun and moon, not by sun or moon alone.' And with the death of the dragon – yet again symbolizing the literalization of fusion drives – an individual self that survives the heat of passion eventually will emerge, resurrected from its dissolution under the impact of desire and death.

As in its parallel, the sixth woodcut, a *nigredo* then sets in again in the thirteenth woodcut, 'Nourishment,' and this death is part of transforming Sol (Figure 23). An

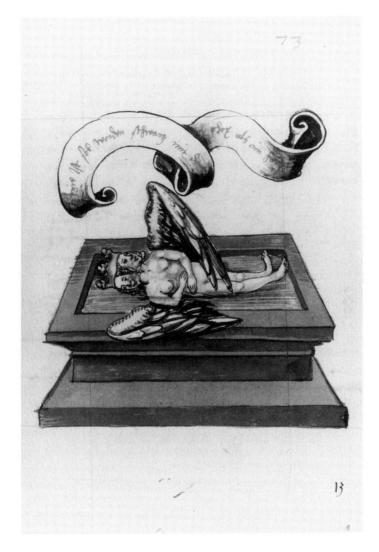

Figure 23 'Nourishment': thirteenth woodcut of the *Rosarium Philosophorum*

accompanying text speaks of the red sulfur digested by the silvery moon. The condition of the dead hermaphrodite is called *nutrimentum* or 'nourishment.' In other words, the *nigredo* stage is now felt more consciously in its function of transforming the potentially invasive and compulsive nature of consciousness. Despair and the pain of abandonment alone are no longer the main focal point.

The importance of the transformation of consciousness cannot be overemphasized. The modern world highly values achievement and 'doing' in distinction to 'being.' For the analyst to possess a genuine state of awareness about his or her analysand's process – an awareness gained, for example, from the transference or dream interpretation – and to sacrifice this consciousness is far from a simple matter. Such an act of sacrifice flies in the face of collective values and the narcissistic enhancement such an act of 'knowing' elicits. Furthermore, sacrificing consciousness about another's process can lead to a regression into a 'watery' stage unless the analyst knows he or she is giving up something that feels quite precious for a still greater goal. When this awareness is present, the interactive field is further enlivened, and the mystery of relationship is served, a mystery in which the analyst knows that he or she can become the receiver of the analysand's consciousness as readily as he or she is the source of awareness about the analysand.

In the fourteenth woodcut, called 'Fixation,' the hermaphrodite is no longer winged, and instead a naked woman ascends to heaven (Figure 24). In the corresponding seventh woodcut of the *albedo* phase of the *Rosarium*, the ascending soul was masculine, and the field capacity conveyed a loss of any solid penetrating capacity, leaving both people in a state of emptiness and deadness. The fourteenth woodcut signifies an end of the totally lunar life of the previous field qualities, especially of the *albedo* phase, and it indicates the beginning of a new solar life of the hermaphrodite. Consciousness, with its potentially compulsive and soul-killing element is transformed. The self that eventually resurrects requires this transformation for its eventual stability amidst change.

Similar to the eighth woodcut (Figure 16, p. 180), the *Rosarium*'s fifteenth woodcut, called 'Multiplication,' features a descent of rain from heaven (Figure 25). In the fifteenth woodcut, as Fabricius notes, the solar sulphur is no longer 'fermenting' in the stone or 'nourishing' it, but 'fixing' it by 'multiplying' in its earth. These woodcuts are therefore all transformations of the male element, the active and aggressive 'sulphur' which is penetrating but which can also be corrosive. The alchemists saw that suffering the awareness of these negative qualities could result in a falling dew, a rain that causes a multiplying effect of the product, the stone (Fabricius 1976, 154).

This state of multiplication is not a fanciful wish, but a result of experience, for when a strong self quality exists in a person, it has a 'multiplying' effect on others. In analytic practice, the analyst's self, if it has been forged in the heat of processes such as the *Rosarium* describes, will have such an effect. This effect can be called 'introjection'; but introjection is only an abstract term for a poorly understood process. Instead a mystery of transmission is involved, and alchemical thinking thrives on such realities.

The alchemical process thus attempts to create a self-structure which is also a field quality, an essence of relations *per se* that has a capacity for active

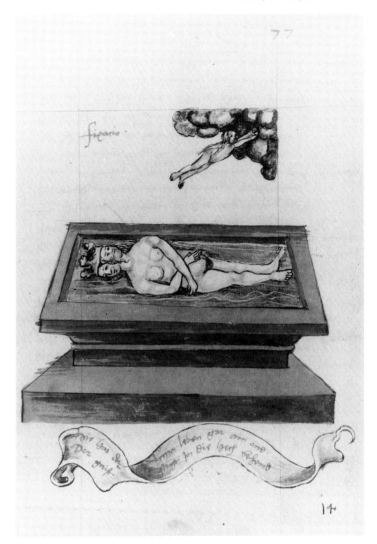

Figure 24 'Fixation': fourteenth woodcut of the *Rosarium Philosophorum*

penetration and active reception. These qualities are no longer split as in cultural allocations of the one to men and the other to women. Transcending this split is a clear goal of the alchemical process.

MUTUAL TRANSFORMATION OF SELF-STRUCTURES AND THE INTERACTIVE FIELD

Similar to the eighth woodcut, the sixteenth woodcut, called 'Revival,' shows the soul diving back (Figure 26). The motto explains:

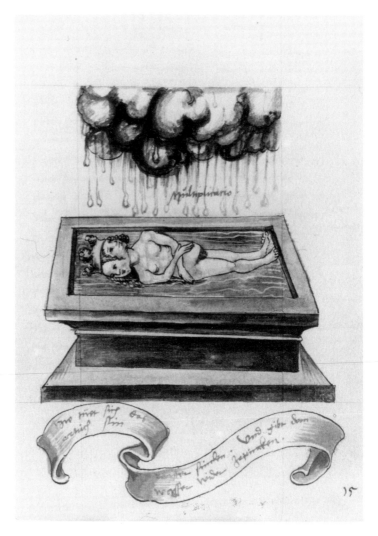

Figure 25 'Multiplication': fifteenth woodcut of the *Rosarium Philosophorum*

> Here comes the soul from heaven,
> glorious and clear, truly
> Reviving the philosopher's daughter.

The female half is revived in the sixteenth woodcut. The stage has been passed in which the stone reaches its 'third degree of preparation' and 'the body is converted into spirit' (Fabricius 1976, 158). A major goal of the *rubedo* stage is the embodiment of the self and a field quality, through which the presence of the body as the vehicle of perception is sought.

Thus, the *rubedo* is moving through stages of integrating passion and spirit by sacrificing their power-oriented features, with the result that a new power is

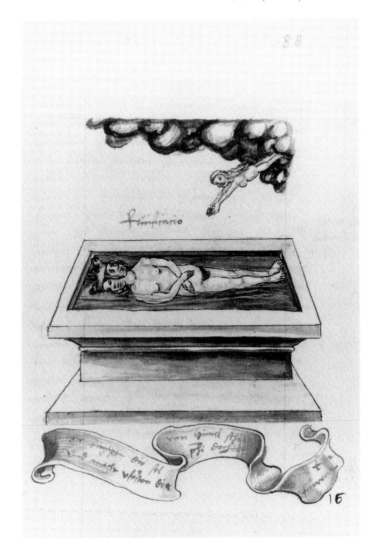

Figure 26 'Revival': sixteenth woodcut of the *Rosarium Philosophorum*

added to the 'White Stone' of the *albedo* stage. A stronger, spiritual quality and a more stable structure are being forged. This state is a goal that may be known in any relationship from time to time, but which usually vanishes as stress and shadow contents become too pressing for the people involved. For the alchemists, this state is realizable as a stable interactive field that is forming and continuing to 'redden' as it becomes more conscious and allows for both spiritual and imaginal vision.

The seventeenth woodcut, 'Perfection,' shows what is known as the third conjunction, the result being the hermaphrodite now on the solar hill (Figure 27). The

Figure 27 'Perfection': seventeenth woodcut of the *Rosarium Philosophorum*

Three and the Four are united, symbolizing a conscious–unconscious union; but
now the lion, the symbol of incest, is in the background, and the three-headed serpent is about to die. The woodcut also shows a self-nourishing process in the pel-
ican. The couple is triumphant. The incestuous aspect of the solar marriage, represented by the lion, appears behind the hermaphrodite. An accompanying text in
the *Rosarium* reads:

> I [Luna] am the crescent, moist and cold moon, and you, O sun, are warm or
> moist (or else dry). When we have copulated in equal rank in our house, which
> cannot take place except by means of a gentle fire, carrying with it a heave

[fire], we must nestle in this and become like the dwelling woman and her husband of noble origin . . .

Sol replies to Luna:

> If you will do this and will not do me any harm, then my body shall change once more; afterwards I will give you a new power of penetration by means of which you will become mighty in the struggle of the fire of liquefaction and purgation. And you will go out of this without diminution and darkness . . . and you will not be fought because you will not be rebellious.
>
> (McLean 1980, 101–02)

Sol acknowledges the power of Luna. Masculine, solar life finally recognizes the power of the feminine not only to harm but also to transform. Furthermore, the solar life of the masculine recognizes how vital it is to the transformation of the feminine. This recognition holds for men and women and also for these powers as opposites within an individual or within an interactive field.

A most significant issue represented in the seventeenth woodcut is that the hermaphrodite stands upon the triple-headed serpent, Mercurius, which is now transforming itself. This image represents a field quality which not only overcomes unconscious fusion states that passion can promote but also ends the deceptions of projective identification. Two people can now experience a field in which passion exists, in which paranoid elements no longer dominate, and in which active and passive roles readily change.

In the eighteenth woodcut, 'Mortification of the Celestial Marriage' or 'Green Lion Devouring the Sun' (Fabricius 1976, 170), this process of the transformation continues as the the solar life of rational and spiritual understanding is again sacrificed in the service of creating a new field structure (Figure 28). The goal symbolized by this woodcut is to create a field that can exist in a stable manner within the passions represented by the Attis–Cybele myth. This stability would express itself in an experience of self and other that does not flee from the body, that maintains imaginal sight, and that is stable under the impact of the passions and spiritual vision. To accomplish this stability, as McLean notes, the alchemist must be willing to sacrifice all that he or she knows, all the structure and knowledge that has been gained. He or she must risk meeting the dissolving, devouring aspect of the unconscious, the Green Lion (McLean 1980, 129).

The eighteenth woodcut represents a stage in which one or other is willing to sacrifice safety in consciousness by accepting shadow motives for acts that were actually destructive. To accept the shadow, to acknowledge one's undermining or malevolent behavior can be very dangerous, for the other person can then do actual harm. For example, one is vulnerable to all manner of rejection and scorn, narcissistic injuries and abandonment that threaten the stability of the self. The eighteenth woodcut represents a field quality which is conducive to risk while faith exists that one can survive such attacks as a vital, embodied self. The point is that one would risk one's solar self, knowing that this risk was a way in which the soul and truth were honored. Only by facing and overcoming the dangers of the

Figure 28 'Mortification of the Celestial Marriage': eighteenth woodcut of the *Rosarium Philosophorum*

'Green Lion' can one avoid becoming rigid or invulnerable in the process of denying the 'object world' its power to injure. This level of strength could experience the passions represented by the impossible fusion state of Attis and Cybele without being emotionally overwhelmed by those passions.

In the nineteenth woodcut, 'Assumption and Coronation' the soul is depicted as uniting with the Holy Trinity (Figure 29). The soul is not only crowned by images of larger people, but in other renderings of the *Rosarium*, the crown is far too large for the soul, meaning that the person must recognize that the source of illumination lies outside his or her being (McLean 1980, 129). This issue is important in terms of the ways in which the *numinosum* is experienced. The *numinosum* always has a transcendent aspect, a Self which cannot be embodied, felt within, while it also is capable of creating an immanent self. These two aspects of self, immanent and transcendent, are symbolically evident in the nineteenth woodcut, along with a lunar, subtle body life. Experience shows that the two aspects of self have a substantial similarity, but these sources of blessing and meaning are experienced in realms of far different scale. Knowing this difference between immanence and transcendence, the alchemist never fails to know his place in the Cosmos, and grandiosity no longer tempts or betrays him. In the spiritual life of relationships, the same level of consciousness is essential.

Throughout the *Rosarium*, work on an interactive process furthers the creation of a self that is sensitive to both 'lunar' and 'solar' modes of relating and experiencing the *numinosum*. Even though experiences of transcendence that go beyond conjoined field notions are set out in the *Rosarium*, the transformation process that realizes the mysteries of the solar phase of the *numinosum* continually thrives within a field of relations.

The twentieth and last woodcut of the *Rosarium* represents the 'Resurrection' of the glorified and incorruptible body of Christ (Figure 30). While this is the ultimate goal, I have seen this image of the resurrection body in dreams even near the beginning of an analysis. One such image was brought to my attention by a man who had the following dream:

> I am – or I also see myself – in a coffin. I am covered by layers of a woman, books and rocks. I see myself pushing them off, and as I do I see that I have a perfectly clear, luminescent body. It is radiant and I am jubilant at the sight.

At the time of this dream, the analysis had been dealing with a major trauma in this man's early life, the loss of his father's love and attention. At 4 years of age, his father became withdrawn and depressed and essentially 'disappeared' after he had known him as a deeply loving person. His father then 'gave him' to an uncle for his education. He lost his father's passion and genuine interest; he felt this as a terrible betrayal for he had loved him deeply.

His entire life of relationships with men and women had always been schizoid, covered over by intellectualizations (the books in the dream), masochism (being subject to the 'anal rocks' in the dream), and seduction (layered over by the feminine in the dream). In actual life, he either was with two women during a given time span, or he was with one woman in a way that had an 'in and out' quality.

The resurrection body, the luminous body of the dream allowed an interactive field to exist between us in which he could 'use me' in Winnicott's (1971) sense of 'object usage,' that is, without fear of destroying me. He could have his reflections, and I could have mine, unfettered by the distortions of projective and introjective mechanisms. This state was present from the beginning of our work, in spite of the many layers of schizoid process that would otherwise deny the existence of the luminous body. In this case, the field quality appeared early on, certainly in the transference, perhaps indicating the potential in our process for recovering the passion he so desperately needed. At times, the unconscious shows

Figure 29 'Assumption and Coronation': nineteenth woodcut of the *Rosarium Philosophorum*

a possible goal very early on in a process, and then one has to work to achieve it in a stable way.

To engage the irrational depths of relationship in the *rubedo* stage is to transform passion from an immanent danger to the soul into a creative fire of change towards greater intimacy and individuality. Within the context of a spiritual awareness that knows both an immanent and a transcendent form, the interactive field between people becomes a source of a self that is both shared and individual, a state that is a welcome paradox which helps to overcome the narcissism plaguing both relationship and the entire culture.

Figure 30 'Resurrection': twentieth woodcut of the *Rosarium Philosophorum*

The twentieth and last woodcut of the *Rosarium* is different from all of the preceding woodcuts, for 'Resurrection' portrays the emergence from the grave of a single human being (Fabricius 1973). Prior to this woodcut, when an image such as the 'Rebis' of the tenth woodcut (Figure 18, p. 183) defines the interactive field, a person has achieved a connection between the conscious and the unconscious that can exist amidst threats of object loss and abandonment. But this creation is still not a self-image in the sense of the twentieth woodcut. While in both the tenth and seventeenth woodcuts (Figures 18, 27, p. 183, 208) the hermaphroditic image emerges as the result of a process of union and death, this image primarily represents a connecting link. Whether as a link between the conscious and the unconscious or the mind and the body – in an individual or as a field quality between people – the accomplishments of the tenth and seventeenth woodcuts are not representative of an orienting center, the self. That is the crowning achievement of the last woodcut of the series.

A self-structure also exists within the entire process – for example, the alchemists insist that it takes gold to make gold – but the self is lost and gained as the different qualitative states of the *Rosarium* are encountered. In the 'Resurrection,' a new kind of stability is finally achieved, a self that is both immanent and transcendent. Whereas one's orientation may have earlier stemmed from a conscious–unconscious connection or from a shared, interactive field through which the connection was forged, now a different, qualitative experience also exists. Now, an inner 'other' is felt and known as the center of one's being, but it is also felt as 'outer,' as transcendent. To the person experiencing this quality of the self, the dual features of immanence and transcendence are in no way contradictory or polarized. And the self that is finally created in the *Rosarium* is not merely a source of identity; it is an ongoing guide – felt in time and space rather than inferred from dreams or intuitively sensed – and it is known as one's final cause. The self that emerges in 'Resurrection' is a guide towards fate that can break with collective conventions if that proves necessary. This self is a center and circumference of being that differs in significant ways from the self of Christianity or any other religious construct that favors a spiritual over a bodily life.

The last woodcut of the *Rosarium*, 'Resurrection,' is thus the crowning achievement of the *opus*. Whereas in the prevailing Christian belief system the resurrection is an act of faith, in Renaissance alchemy the resurrection is an ongoing, personal and interior experience. The Christian self-image is primarily a spiritual construct, whereas the alchemical self-image has both a spirit and a body. Rather than a self that is confined to spiritual matters and flourishes only in an atmosphere of repression in which the passions must be sublimated and relations between people carefully proscribed, the alchemical self is wrought both individually and in relationship's fire of passion and madness.

Suffering through numerous sequences of union–death states and wrestling with mad sectors that always bring a person to the edge of his or her courage and strength, the alchemical process also leads in the twentieth woodcut to an ongoing awareness and experience of the 'intermediate realm' of the subtle body. Without the subtle-body/interactive-field concept, human life becomes either sterile – as when it is focused upon a world of material things – or spiritualized in a world of mind–body splitting. Surely, Western culture has exhausted these options.

The twentieth woodcut of the *Rosarium* signifies the existence of the subtle realm in which a self can flourish, a self that combines both spiritual and physical attributes and which draws upon the transcendent as well as one's most intimately personal experiences. Because 'Resurrection' signifies the creation of an ongoing faith in the existence of the self within a subtle-body realm, it is a marvelous term for this end phase; indeed, it signals a faith kindled and sustained by experience. The motto accompanying the woodcut says:

After my passion and manifold torments I am again risen,
Being purified and cleansed from all spots.

The *nigredo* ceases to be catastrophic and, most significantly, this positive development occurs within not only an individual but also a relationship.

Maintaining a self-structure is very difficult when someone is confronted with an emotional attack from another person or from collective attitudes. The individuals involved in a relationship suffering from betrayal have difficulty maintaining a sense of self and conscious awareness of their field experiences. The self-structure of alchemy offers stability amidst such chaotic experiences, but this alchemical self-structure is not granted by grace. Nor is it the result of a mystical vision. Such illumination merely accompanies the beginning of the process by which the state of 'Resurrection' is created. Ultimately, only the experiences of union and death, forged through suffering, vision, and courage, can create the alchemical self.

10 Appreciating the mystery of relationship

The twenty-second and final painting of the great alchemical work, the *Splendor Solis*, depicts a mythical scene which symbolizes the essence of the alchemical understanding of transformation both individually and in relationships (Figure 31). Dominating the painting is the image of the setting sun, looking to its left with a sober and mature expression. The painting's foreground contains both the burned and broken trees of a devastated landscape and the new growth of emerging plant life. In the background of the painting is a celestial city elevated on a hill with a soaring steeple arising from the cluster of buildings. In front of the city is a lake with a solitary house on the left shore. The lake forms into a stream which flows to the painting's foreground. This painting contains many elements symbolic of a transformed consciousness.

The setting sun, ready to meet the earth in a final, grand union, is a purified sun, analogous to the transformed consciousness of the alchemical process (McLean 1981). The burned-out landscape, the result of too much fire – as in passions gone wild and becoming destructive – is a reminder of how essential death is to the alchemical process. The sober and mature expression on the sun's face reflects the experience of the trials and torments of change.

The sun's meeting the earth parallels the union of this transformed consciousness and ordinary day-to-day experience. While the sun represents consciousness, it is also a major symbol of the self and the crowning achievement of the creation of a particular kind of self-structure. The alchemically born self of the *Splendor Solis* is not only personal but also connected to the transcendent. New life has been forged in the alchemical fires of coagulating and dissolving old forms of being which, to be transformed, must die, be reborn, and die again. This death–rebirth sequence in the alchemical process of transformation constitutes the continual distillation in which a purified consciousness and self-structure are eventually created.

The sequence of a new kind of order and then the death of that order is the fundamental dynamic of alchemical transformation. Alchemical thinking reflects the fact that no matter how exalted the stage of any process in life, that stage lives within the context of whatever despair and failure accompanied its creation. Thus, in the last image of the *Splendor Solis*, two states – a created self and its purified consciousness – are joined not only with life and the body but also with a history of despair and failure.

Figure 31 Twenty-second painting of the *Splendor Solis*

The combination in the picture's foreground of a death-like quality with emerging plant life – signifying new growth – characterizes a mature consciousness for the present. The here-and-now of existence is not idealized in terms of 'what can be.' Instead, the experiences of failure, death, and loss of opportunity are never forgotten. At the same time, the new growth emerging in the here-and-now is also recognized. As old forms of existence are outgrown, the experience of their devastation and their previous but outgrown usefulness imbues the present with depth and maturity. Behind everything else in the picture, and signifying what can be reached for in yearning for transcendence, is a celestial city – the true, transcendent home of the self.

Relationships are not only forms of exchange of energy and function between people but also living structures which regulate a person's sense of identity and well-being. Two people, or a single person doing creative work, or a person and a collective organization inevitably create a relationship which has its own character and dynamism. Once this relationship is consciously entered, each person's autonomy is reduced to the extent that the interests and feelings of another must now be considered along with one's own. This conscious entry into a relationship can be experienced as an act of freedom in the sense of an expressed intention to love another person or to be loyal to an organization or to one's own creative process. However, when the parties concerned lack a sufficient sense of individual identity to remain separate and viable in their own right, the conscious entry into a relationship can be felt as a danger and a trap, even a form of slavery.

As living forms of exchange, relationships mediate between a person and his or her unconscious psyche, spiritual reality, family system, workplace, and cultural life. All of these forms of exchange are the bases of relationships which span a broad spectrum of experience from the 'profane' of compulsive, automatic behavior on the one hand to the 'sacred' of reflective life and a concern for soul on the other. If the form of exchange is primarily one in which two people exploit each other to meet narcissistic demands, then the relationship is reduced to providing an arena for enacting sexual, aggressive, and economic needs. Relationships, however, can also dignify and modify each person's behavior towards the other, forming invisible yet powerful containing structures which are living realities that can themselves transform from states which create compulsive and unreflective behavior into states which create and foster care for the soul.

Containment in relationship serves a variety of purposes, not all of which encourage and create new growth in the participating partners. A relationship can easily serve the status quo, secretly encouraging each person to avoid change, thereby creating a container which manifests as a fused, co-dependent structure. Basically, co-dependent relationships are forms of security that stifle growth, either in a personal relationship or in a corporate relationship in which an individual is part of a rigid and domineering organizational structure which, in exchange for the promise of security, demands nearly total obedience in attitude and perhaps even in thinking. Such co-dependent relationships, whether personal or corporate, invariably serve to facilitate any variety of addictive, habitual, or other soul-killing behaviors.

As each partner colludes with the other, this collusive state is a container that allows for stasis and encourages a fear of change. Such containing qualities are extremely seductive, for any relationship – even a destructive one – is always experienced as an entity larger than either of the partners. Consequently, a fused relationship has a power which becomes something like a god-image that is secretly served, with potentially devastating consequences, and may exhibit a very unified supportive appearance while actually harboring a sado-masochistic unconscious dyad in which the partners subtly if not blatantly undermine each other. To leave a co-dependent relationship and to seek out other relationships with positive containing qualities can be felt as dangerous and is often tenaciously resisted. Generally, by protecting each partner from knowing his or her madness, static relationships reduce the likelihood of either partner's being truly overwhelmed by that madness.

Individuals who have achieved considerable spiritual integration while on a solitary path may nevertheless discover themselves to be quite childish or extremely defensive when they enter a relationship with another person. Because they experience a relationship as dangerous and threatening, they no longer feel safe enough or separate enough as a self to risk encountering the depths and powers of their inner spiritual life. They require the toughening process of the *rubedo* stage of alchemical transformation if they are to avoid the tragedy of either an unwillingly lived solitary life or a creatively or spiritually impoverished life lived within a relationship. While a relationship based on compromise may protect individuals from dangerous states of mind and can sometimes appear adequate enough to serve their purposes, over time such a relationship steals away resolve and enthusiasm and encourages cowardice in the face of one's own depths and in the face of life itself.

All people need a partner in the effort to individuate if this integrative path is to include love, aggression, and bodily life, along with a spiritual focus of values and goals. Rarely, if ever, can a person enter the path of creating and transforming a self without the fire and challenge of an ongoing relationship. As the path of a relationship leads through new creations of experience and aspirations, it becomes more than a rendition of past history. Any deep relationship has its elements of heaven and hell; but when it is a process characterized by a stability of trust and meaning, hard won through many trials of betrayal and failure to meet the demands of intimacy, a resilient container is created which better enables each partner to live through the turmoil, tragedies, joys, and difficulties of life. When partners know and experience each other through chaos and destructiveness as well as through beauty and growth, they create a container which encourages and supports the process of individuation and which becomes each person's most sacred possession.

Unless a person meets the needs, demands, and consciousness of another person in the intertwined province of a relationship, he or she will always stay on an overly spiritualized or superficial level of consciousness. Relationship with another person inevitably brings out one's negative side – the childish, regressive yearnings which cause one unconsciously to feel that one's partner is a great danger, a force attempting to separate one from one's internal maternal or paternal images. A deep relationship can disrupt such inner fusion states and force a person to recognize those regressive aspects of himself or herself that do not want to change and which are often projected on to the partner in an attempt to disown them.

Whether a person is expressing his or her rage and hatred toward the partner for not embodying idealized parental images or is behaving in a way that creates the illusion of the idealized parent in the experience of the partner, this person can endeavor to use the relationship to embark upon the hard work of integrating such dark, shadow sides of the ego personality. Unless a person knows these dark and destructive sides of his or her being, the ego is always in a weakened condition which makes relating a dangerous venture. Thus, instead of enhancing one's awareness, relationship obscures consciousness and fosters regression. However, without a relationship, analytic or personal, it is very difficult to come to terms with the shadow aspects of one's being.

Many people regularly contact a spiritual state through prayer or meditation, but this state may in fact be experienced as an 'outer' reality that is transcendent rather than as an inner reality that is embodied. The embodied, incarnated state exemplifies the self of alchemy – for example, the self signified by the twenty-second painting of the *Splendor Solis* or the self of the twentieth woodcut of the *Rosarium Philosophorum*. Such an embodied spirituality requires an awareness of evil, of those renegade, anti-life qualities of one's being that are primarily out to destroy and undermine the courage to live and grow. Without the integration of the darker, destructive elements of being, one's spiritual aspects often remain merely a potential reality. When transformed, however, such destructive elements provide a grounding counterbalance of limitation to the infinite spiritual dimension of the psyche.

As containers for the integration of shadow elements, relationships are thus important vehicles for the creation of consciousness, an invisible presence that guides and nurtures the soul. However, in order for this state to exist, relationships themselves must transform from states of early union into more mature forms that have an awareness of the power and reality of a dyad which defines the unconscious side of the relationship.

The union state that exists in relationships generally involves the unconscious elements of each party rather than the more conscious elements. Consciously, two people may seem to be loving and cooperative even while their unconscious dyad, which may be the major locus of the union between them, can behave in significantly different ways from the conscious image and values to which both people adhere. By its nature, the 'dark' couple underlying the 'conscious' couple is strange and usually unpleasant. For instance, the dark couple may be like two vicious animals locked in a life and death struggle, or as described in the *Turba Philosophorum*, two lovers locked in an embrace – one a human being, the other a serpent. Unfortunately, the energies of such conflicts are often so intense and so rejected by the conscious partners that they are virtually uncontained. Therefore, they subtly and gradually infiltrate the environment, affecting others, notably children in a family system. Acquiring the vision to see the forms of their unconscious dyad requires the partners to strive to absorb the narcissistic injury involved in admitting the existence of such vicious and unpleasant qualities within themselves without rebelling in defense and accusation of the other.

This act of growth and maturity requires that both sides are able to suffer narcissistic injuries without reacting with power positions of blame, anger, or withdrawal. Seeing the unconscious dyad and recognizing its power begins a process of discovering that we have been acting in ways that are, in fact, unconscious, driven, and destructive, even while believing that the exact opposite is true.

Relationships can only mature if they change, indeed only if they encompass a rhythm of death and rebirth. Accordingly, relationships follow the same logic as the alchemical process. Thus, a society's continuing narcissistic preoccupation not only renders union states and change of any kind inadmissible to conscious life but such narcissistic preoccupation also stands squarely against the transformative potential of the experience of the death of structure inherent within relationships. Western culture is, in fact, dominated not only by a fear of death but also by a fear of the death of relationships. For example, the very possibility of losing a job, a marriage, a friendship, or a connection to a professional organization may by itself become a terribly powerful stress factor.

The same reflections hold for individuals and the workplace. A work environment always has a kind of culture or attitude that distinguishes it from other such environments. But the culture, especially of a large corporation, also has a shadow side, an unconscious set of values that do not stand out in the light of everyday activity, as can be seen in the particularly negative underside of tobacco companies which have lied for years about the unhealthy effects of cigarettes. Anyone working for such a company would be involved in a relationship that had a conscious aspect, perhaps one filled with loyalty and good feeling; but he or she could also be subject to another unconscious aspect, perhaps a very dark dyad in which the powers of evil are present. Relationships between two people or between people and institutions only grow and mature through the partners' becoming conscious of the existence and relative autonomy of the unconscious dyad in which they are participants, for this dyad always affects both people in something like the way deeper currents in an ocean affect the waves on the surface.

Both the unconscious dyad within a relationship and the levels at which people consciously know and experience their relationship vary in intensity. On the one hand, a person in relationship to a large corporation or to his or her boss may feel no conscious sense of union with that institution or person in authority. In such impersonal situations, even while a person may feel nearly insignificant amidst the mass of employees, he or she may have a strong unconscious dyadic link with fellow workers or with the institution itself. On the other hand, one may imagine a very strong bond between people or between a person and an institution characterized by love, fidelity, and a variety of other powerful emotions. But in all relationships, regardless of the level of awareness and intensity, both partners will at some point inevitably experience a death of the union state, for that is Nature's way, as the alchemist's would have it; and rather than resist this death, the alchemical attitude welcomed it as a vehicle of growth and change.

The union of different states, usually dominated by unconscious factors either within the psyche of one person or the union of the psyches of two people, is characterized by the creation of something new that is often only glimpsed by the conscious personality as a fleeting, special moment. In this epiphany, people can suddenly experience themselves in a non-ordinary state, as if space and time were suspended and a different kind of energy and sense of expansiveness had appeared. Then, this vision usually departs as quickly as it occurs. That the created state is more than an amalgam of the parts that are joined is a central aspect of the mystery of union.

In an alchemical way of thinking, the locus for the transformation of the self is the depth and mystery of a relationship engaged within an interactive field which is both conscious and unconscious and which is structured by an unconscious dyad. Finding this dyad as a 'third area' between the two partners requires the surrendering of ego control and the establishment of trust in a mutual process that is both frightening and exhilarating.

Always, the key issue in discovering the transformative mystery of relationship and of the self is intention. Are two people willing to enter these turbulent waters in which each person's individuality and consciousness are subject to the magnifying power and intensity of the 'third area'? While such a commitment to personal transformation invariably wounds one's narcissism, this sacrifice is indispensable to the creation of a relationship with a sacred significance.

Success in the venture of discovering and experiencing a 'third area' is often fleeting. Yet, like the alchemical elixir, a glance and an emotional or physical register of the presence of the field has a strong effect. Relating to the depths of a 'third area' is like noticing an animal or bird move in a forest – no sooner has one seen it than it may vanish. When walking in the forest and hearing a bird's song, one may look into a particular tree to find the bird only to find that the song has vanished, perhaps to reappear elsewhere. But is it now the *same* bird? Even though uncertainty always hovers, that one did unquestionably hear 'a bird's song' keeps one linked to this experience.

The art of relating to 'third areas' is to listen over and over again, to glimpse a fleeting vision, and to trust the imagination. Generally, two people can pin down the source of the imagery of the 'third area' better than can one person alone, for one person will too easily reify a perception, and hold on to an image or idea rather than feel it dissolve into confusion and disorientation. Two people are more likely to move from the question 'Where did the bird go?' to the suspicion 'Perhaps it was never there.'

And it is important to remember that more than apparently harmless creatures lurk in the forest. If they are to succeed in establishing the existence of a 'third area' with its own process, two people must enter a domain in which madness is an ever-present feature. We all have mad areas, areas of our personality in which we behave in soul-killing ways toward ourselves and toward others. The madness that arises within our psyche and the regressive narcissistic structures that become dominant in response to this madness are perhaps the greatest obstacles to change in relationships.

Grasping the existence of a mad area of psyche requires the same alertness and tenacity required by hunting for scarce game. But in the case of the psyche, the hunt is not for a 'thing,' an image, for example, so much as it is a hunt for the atmosphere *around* the image. The object of the hunt – and the metaphor of a lion hunt is found in alchemy – may become invisible as readily as it appears, anew, as though for the first time. From an alchemical point of view the value of hunting such a mysterious 'thing' or 'animal' lies not so much in the hunting itself as in the activity's capacity to lower the intensity of one's focus to include the space around the perception, around the sought-after 'thing' or 'animal.' In this imaginal act of lowering one's 'solar' focus and raising, in its place, a kind of 'lunar' sight, the interactive field itself becomes the object of attention. When the space *between* perceptions becomes the area explored, acceptance of confusion and loss of focus becomes a natural part of the process at hand.

In seeking the life and process of a 'third area,' it is better to steer a middle course between the objectivity of the scientific method and the subjectivity of the imagination, that is, between dealing exclusively with projections and dealing exclusively with interactive fields. Such 'dual focus' requires that a person be willing to glimpse the life of the 'third area' and to reflect upon its chaotic or orderly process in terms of projections reflected within a developmental schema, and also with the imagination focused upon the field itself. Neither focus can dominate the other, for both are necessary and have their place. But if the focus that is brought to bear upon a relationship is to penetrate the unknown, 'to look without seeing' or 'to see without looking,' then the scientific approach – emphasizing how failures in development and associated 'fixation points' are being replayed in the here-and-now – may be limited by its own methodology. The scientific way, with its attempt at objective certainty, can act as a shield against being re-traumatized by the partner's projections and vision when it refuses to recognize the validity of mad parts of the psyche. Then, the alchemical way of seeing internal states in the partner or imagining their existence through imaginally perceiving one's own interiority becomes the focal point of a conscious effort to transform 'lead into gold.' Yet without the scientific approach, the imaginal way of alchemy degenerates into generalities which lose the particularity of the individuals concerned.

If the process of discovery contains the rhythm of both the 'scientific' and the 'imaginal,' and if the fleeting nature of imaginal perceptions is trusted without being reified, then two people experience their relationship as a vessel containing both of them. Both people attempting to glimpse the mystery of their relationship are, alternatively, scientists and alchemists, perceiving on the one hand with objectivity and on the other hand with the vision of the imagination. When two people acknowledge that each is both rational and mad, they are prepared to enter the 'third area' that has its own mystery and that is far larger than both of them together.

A person dealing with 'third areas' has to learn to 'see' differently, to see through the eyes of the unconscious, and especially through the vision of the self. If two people within their interactive process recognize the necessity for a more encompassing form of vision, they will be moving towards the creation of selves which can simultaneously see both opposites.

In relationships, two people can learn about the efficacy of passion in finding a way between such opposites. The passion for the creation of soul in relating and the passion for creativity itself are driving forces that can transcend the madness of double-bind communications and the madness in which people hide in order to avoid the challenge of individuation. The alchemical way of transformation, which embraces the dangers and healing qualities of passion, can reveal both the cowardliness of timidity in the face of desire and the madness that accompanies the enactment of passion with all its creative and destructive energy.

Sensitivity to the 'third area' and its processes is thus the key to the mystery of relationship. Above all, both people must be prepared to deal with their mad parts that distort and deny the other's reality. Entering the unknown reality of the unconscious and risking the experience of madness, either one's own or that of the other, is a courageous act often rewarded by momentary awareness of a numinous energy within the shared field. This can be lasting for those who choose to remember and, through remembering, renew the experience.

Exploring and engaging one's madness in relationship to the madness of another within the context of an interactive field experience is extremely challenging in both analytic and non-analytic relationships. The analytic model must overcome two fundamental realities which can limit the depth and range of the relationship: first, the basic inequality of the relationship because of the existence of an inherent power difference between analyst and analysand; second, the possibilities for intimacy and commitment in non-analytic relationships which are beyond the capacity of the analytic model. Despite these limitations, the analytic or clinical relationship has distinct advantages over the non-analytic or personal relationship in terms of its capacity to build a containing presence that is sustainable amid the inevitable clash of blaming and counter-attacks which inevitably occur when mad parts of sane people are activated within the interactive field.

Analysis is relationship seen under a magnifying power usually absent from daily discourse; it is also relationship in which the partners meet to work toward the goal of creating a self through enhancing awareness of both unconscious processes and the function of Eros over destruction. An analytic relationship provides the safety of boundaries and focused interest that allows for the discovery of, and relationship to, a 'third area.' A non-analytic relationship does not have the same feature of containment possessed by the analytic form in which anything said is respected and reflected upon, even if very nasty and accusatory statements are made. Furthermore, the analytic relationship has boundaries which are not to be crossed. The analysand and analyst are not friends in the world, and definite procedures define their meeting. Such limit-setting gives a sense of safety and reliability that non-analytic relationships only rarely achieve.

The major boundary challenge within non-analytic relationships is that each person must respect the relationship enough to refrain from compartmentalizing it into certain areas that it serves while seeking other levels of intimacy elsewhere. Such loose boundaries never create a safe enough space for the act of discovery of a common interactive field. But even if the boundaries of commitment are secure, will and desire are required to explore sensitive areas in which either person may be emotionally out of control, and indeed mad. While one partner may be the focus of exploration, there must be an implicit belief that whatever is discovered about his or her unconscious psyche will soon be pertinent as well to the other partner. Only in this way is it possible for both people to learn that they live in a larger domain of relations.

In a sense, analytic relationships can be the precursor to personal relationships. The safer and more restricted analytic relationship can be a training ground for other relationships. While it is possible for individuals within personal relationships to become aware of and to engage in the 'third area' without benefit of an analytic experience, they may have far more difficulty maintaining a sense of his or her own identity while establishing the existence of a 'third area' in which a great deal of mutual process occurs.

Relationships that have not established an area of mutual process usually cannot accept states of radical non-connection – in which genuine empathy for the other person proves to be impossible – without negative judgments about this absence and without writing imaginary disaster scripts for the relationship. The advantage of analytic relationships is that the analyst can carry the awareness of the potential meaning and purpose of such states of mind as total non-relatedness. In effect, the analyst can 'mind the store,' whereas in non-analytic relationships it is more likely that both people may become submerged in despair and abandonment feelings. Even in the analytic relationship, the analyst often requires the help of the analysand when such terribly difficult states such as a total lack of connection are present. Ultimately, success in relationships – analytic or non-analytic – depends upon the courage and capacity of the individuals involved. With adequate courage and capacity, any relationship devoted to experiencing that relationship's depths and mystery can potentially achieve levels of commitment and focus equal to those of the analytic endeavor.

In order to build a strong enough container to engage the personal and mutual madness which is invariably activated within the interactive field, a relationship – whether analytic or non-analytic – should follow the following three steps. The first step requires that partners take each other's perceptions seriously and recognize the truth or fallacy of these perceptions through a serious process of soul-searching. Each person must feel free to articulate specific complaints about actions and attitudes of the other that may be considered injurious or irresponsible; and each person must undertake to listen carefully to the complaints without reacting defensively. This receptivity requires a willingness by both partners to move beyond the usual blaming and scapegoating that can so easily occur and to plumb the depths of one's being in order to discover hitherto unimagined areas of personality or areas that one did not believe were currently active. Unless the goodwill exists to take this initial step, a relationship cannot transform in a creative way. Indeed, not all relationships are workable.

Having achieved awareness of the other's perceptions of oneself, the second step is to realize one's own feelings about the partner and to articulate these perceptions. The mutual exchange of perceptions with one's partner can lead to the awareness that an imaginal dyad can be constructed from the perceptions of each about the other, as if these perceptions were held by an unconscious couple. Whatever one partner believes he or she sees in the other person can, and indeed must, be seriously considered as part of that other person's psyche. Each person must be willing to take ownership of what his or her partner has perceived. This act of inward reflection contributes toward achieving a state of objectivity which allows for a diminished fusion state in the relationship.

The third step requires that both people allow the dyad they have discovered to exist as a quality of the field between them. In other words, they must recognize that they share a field quality defined by the dyad that they have discovered. With this movement toward a state of inner truth, the relationship can become cleansed of narcissistic defensiveness. A 'third thing' of which both people partake and which both people can feel and imagine enables a couple to feel the psychic reality of their relationship. Focusing upon the field itself is a further act of submission. Beyond being able to accept the other's perceptions, now each person can allow himself or herself to be subject to the experience of the field as an enlivened 'third thing.' In this process, one has allowed the metaphorical basis of a dyad to have its own life.

Thus, truly hearing one person's complaints about the other enables the individuals to make an imaginal leap of recognition to see that the conflict between them is a metaphor for an unconscious dyad that each person can experience. Each person can then see that he or she can be *either part* of this dyad. Accordingly, as soon as one partner accuses the other of some deed and, in fact, finds this accusation heard in depth by his or her partner, the way is suddenly opened for the accuser to recognize that he or she is capable of, and may often be guilty of, exactly the behavior being criticized. Far more than a process of projecting and owning one's projections, such recognition is a window into a third, subtle domain. Through this window both members of the couple may glimpse, however briefly, the powerful metaphorical nature of their relationship. Metaphor, Baudalaire said, can move the world. Through grasping the living metaphor of a 'third area' of the relationship, both people become sensitized to its larger significance and to its power to move them along paths that can be new and frightening, but filled with meaning.

This psychic reality of the 'third area' is a container which makes it possible to live through the very difficult states of non-relatedness that plague relationships. Only when the terrifying void of love and compassion characterizing non-relatedness can be understood by both people to be part of a transformative process can a feeling of kinship emerge; and it is exactly this feeling of kinship which will nourish, sustain, and gradually strengthen both the couple and the relationship itself. This transformative process can be accomplished only through faith, education, and imagination. The penetrating power of the imagination required to appreciate the transformative potential of relationship within an interactive field experience is comparable to the spiritual illumination which is essential for the transformative process of alchemy.

The combination of sun and devastated landscape in the twenty-second and final painting of the *Splendor Solis* is fundamental to the alchemical understanding of the transformation of relationships. All relationships, indeed all interactional processes, share the experience of a union state in which new structures of relationship to oneself and to others are forged, followed by the experience of the death of that creation. This *coniunctio–nigredo* sequence, inspired by a fundamental law of nature that new life is not possible without the death of old forms, is the essence of transformation in alchemical thinking.

The death of a union state may take many forms, such as the termination of a job, the betrayal of a marital relationship, the illness or death of a partner, the completion of a creative work, or the inability to finish that work. Whatever the case, the symptoms of the *nigredo* include despair, depression, loss of self-esteem, and anger. Attempts to cope with such symptoms may include manic flights to restore the relationship as it once was, the madness of self-deception and arrogance that denies any shadow motives or meaning, or grandiose assumptions that if the partner would only just change his or her attitude the catastrophic feeling of loss would disappear. Such narcissistic preoccupations not only render union states inadmissible to conscious life but also stand squarely against the transformative potential of the experience of the death of structure inherent within relationships.

As the fulcrum of transformation, the *nigredo* stage assumes many different forms when it emerges in relationships. It may appear, as if out of nowhere, following an intense period of passion and closeness, when suddenly and for no apparent reason, interest in the other wanes. Or the *nigredo* may creep in over time, gradually undermining the sweetness of hope and connection that once existed. In either case, an experience of death will occur in any relationship which, for good or ill, will transform it.

This transformation seriously challenges the individuals involved in a relationship to become aware of their lack of connection. The fear of the *nigredo* often tempts the couple to force the appearance of being connected when in fact, if they dare to look deeply within, each of them will recognize that no connection exists. The two partners live in parallel universes, and they might as well be speaking foreign languages to one another. For those who suffer the *nigredo* without blaming each other for the issues of despair, madness, and non-relatedness that feel so persecutory and abandoning, a new life may then enter the relationship.

The tendency of the media to idealize and caricature relationships or to promote the expectation that success in relationships is a commodity to be learned in workshops or by following simplistic behavioral or belief systems makes it even more difficult for people to accept a fundamental lack of connection without also feeling an overwhelming humiliation for this 'failure.' Yet this 'failure' to be related, indeed the impossibility of relatedness at certain times in a process, is an indispensable part of the mystery and transformation of deep relationships. Whereas scientific approaches generally teach people to look for some 'new solution' to deny their distress and to find ways to re-establish the feeling of connectedness as quickly as possible without suffering through the *nigredo* phase, alchemical approaches generally teach people to work within the context of their reality, especially when an absence of felt connection is the dominant interactive field quality. Moreover, the alchemical way teaches that despair *belongs* to relatedness; the problem lies in becoming despairing about despair. The *nigredo* becomes the central transformative function if the partners in the relationship not only feel their individual sense of loss and despair but also begin to see that the relationship itself, as they have known it, has died – always a tenuous, frightening moment.

Like the landscape in the twenty-second painting of the *Splendor Solis*, the darker states of despair, loss, failure, pain, and suffering are important creative features of life. Whereas the untransformed sun of narcissism only knows inflated or deflated values, the purified sun represents a state in which defensive idealization is transformed into compassion for one's own and another's imperfection. In the light of compassion, guilt, anxiety, and shame cease to be linked to what others may think of one. Instead, seen through compassion, these emotions signal to the ego its failure to recognize and relate to the demands of the inner self.

The capacity to respect and to see the other, whether that be the transcendent self or the mystery of another person, can thus be created. For as the sun meets the earth, a spiritual self is internalized. Because a 'mirror' now rests deep within a person, his or her need for outer 'mirroring' becomes neither an incessant preoccupation nor a need too dangerous to recognize. Such a person is able to state his or her need to be seen by another person in a serious and deep way. Equally, he or she is now capable of feeling such empathy for another person. The capacity for these empathic acts now exists because an inner 'cleansed mirror' – purified of regressive, narcissistic impulses – has been created. Such a person can now mirror another by deeply reflecting an inner self, and mirroring becomes no longer only a matter of 'getting into someone else's shoes,' itself an accomplishment of no small value. Rather, a new and more authentic kind of mirroring emerges, one that reflects from the spiritual vantage point of the self.

Through this *nigredo*, both people in a relationship can begin to create and to experience a far deeper and more meaningful quality of relatedness. Through the death of union, relationship can gradually take on a sacred, symbolic character. In the background of the twenty-second painting of the *Splendor Solis*, the heavenly city (presumably Jerusalem) with a steeple reaching into the sphere of the sun resonates as the earthly counterpart to the descending sun. The heavenly city suggests the presence of an inner attitude which indicates that an emerging 'background object' carries the feeling-tone and image of one's highest aspiration – to become a self in the deepest and most complete way.

As individuals in relationships learn to tolerate the demands of growth, including experiences of humiliation and the death of the former structure of the relationship, cultural forms may be affected. In interaction with social structures, transformed individual consciousness has a multiplying effect which can lead other people to become opened to a transformative path. This multiplying effect of a transformed and reflective life and a deepened capacity for relationship is a central value in alchemical thinking.

Only through the metaphorical transformation of 'lead into gold' can the mystery of relationship be more widely engaged and experienced. Only through the metaphorical transformation of 'lead into gold' can people be helped to appreciate relationship's immeasurable depth, its subtle role in furthering individuation, its embrace of unpredictable and chaotic states of mind, and its foundation in the healing capacity of love.

Bibliography

Adler, Alfred. 1964. *The Individual Psychology of Alfred Adler*, edited by Heinz and Rowena Ansbacher. New York: Harper.

Bateson, Gregory *et al.* 1972. 'Towards a Theory of Schizophrenia.' In *Beyond the Double Bind*, edited by Milton Berger, 5–27. New York: Brunner Mazel.

Bion, Wilfred. 1970. *Attention and Interpretation*. London: Maresfield.

Burkert, Walter. 1987. *Ancient Mystery Cults*. Cambridge, Massachusetts: Harvard University Press.

Burland, Cottie. 1980. *The Aztecs*. New York: Galahad Books.

Cameron, Anne. 1981. *Daughters of Copper Woman*. Vancouver: Press Gang Publishers.

Casteñeda, Carlos. 1971. *A Separate Reality*. New York: Simon and Schuster.

Corbin, Henri. 1969. *Creative Imagination in the Sufism of Ibn Arabi*, translated by Ralph Manheim. Princeton: Princeton University Press.

Couliano, Ioan P. 1987. *Eros and Magic in the Renaissance*. Chicago: University of Chicago Press.

Damrosch, L. 1980. *Symbol and Truth in Blake's Myth*. Princeton: Princeton University Press.

De Rola, Stanislas Klossowski. 1973. *Alchemy: The Secret Art*. London: Thames and Hudson.

Detienne, Marcel. 1989. *Dionysos at Large*. Cambridge, Massachusetts: Harvard University Press.

Edinger, Edward. 1985. *Anatomy of the Psyche*. La Salle, Illinois: Open Court.

Eigen, Michael. 1986. *The Psychotic Core*. New York: Jason Aronson.

Fabricius, Johannes. 1973. 'The Symbol of the Self in the Alchemical "Proiectio".' *Journal of Analytical Psychology* 18, no. 1: 47–58.

—— 1976. *Alchemy*. Copenhagen: Rosenkilde and Bagger.

Ferenczi, Sandor. 1938. '*Thalassa*: A Theory of Genitality.' *The Psychoanalytic Quarterly*.

—— 1955. *Final Contributions to the Problems and Methods of Psycho-analysis*, edited by M. Balint and translated by E. Mosbacher *et al.* London: Hogarth Press and the Institute of Psychoanalysis.

Fordham, Michael. 1969. 'Technique and Countertransference.' *Journal of Analytical Psychology* 14, no. 2: 95–118.

—— 1974. 'Jung's Conception of the Transference.' *Journal of Analytical Psychology* 19, no. 1: 1–21.

von Franz, Maria-Louise. 1966. *Aurora Consurgens*. London: Routledge and Kegan Paul.

—— 1970. *A Psychological Interpretation of the Golden Ass of Apuleius*. Zurich: Spring Publications.

—— 1974. *Number and Time*. Evanston, Illinois: Northwestern University Press.

—— 1975. *C.G. Jung: His Myth in Our Time*. New York: Putnam.

—— 1979. *Alchemical Active Imagination*. Irving, Texas: Spring Publications.

—— 1980. *Alchemy*. Toronto: Inner City Books.

Frazer, Sir James George, trans. 1989. *V, Fasti*, by Ovid. London: William Heinemann Ltd.

Freud, Sigmund. 1958. *The Standard Edition of the Complete Psychological Works of Sigmund Freud*, translated by James Strachey, vol. 12. London: Hogarth Press.

Green, André. 1975. 'The Analyst, Symbolization and Absence in the Analytic Setting.' *International Journal of Psycho-Analysis* 56: 1–22.

—— 1993. *On Private Madness*. Connecticut: International Universities Press.

Grotstein, James. 1981. *Splitting and Projective Identification*. New York: Jason Aronson.

—— 1990. 'Nothingness, Meaninglessness, Chaos, and the "Black Hole" I.' *Contemporary Psychoanalysis* 26, no. 2: 257–90.

Guntrip, H. 1969. *Schizoid Phenomena, Object Relations and the Self*. New York: International Universities Press.

Hillman, James. 1972. *The Myth of Analysis*. New York: Harper.

—— 1980. 'Silver and the White Earth (Part One).' In *Spring*, edited by J. Hillman, 21–31. Irving, Texas: Spring Publications.

—— 1981. 'Silver and the White Earth (Part Two).' In *Spring*, edited by J. Hillman, 21–66. Irving, Texas: Spring Publications.

Holmyard, E.J. 1990. *Alchemy*. New York: Dover.

Hubback, Judith. 1983. 'Depressed Patients and the Coniunctio.' *Journal of Analytical Psychology* 28, no. 4: 313–27.

Huizinga, Johan. 1954. *The Waning of the Middle Ages*. New York: Doubleday.

Irigaray, Luce. 1987. 'Sexual Difference.' In *French Feminist Thought*, edited by Toril Moi, 118–30. London: Basil Blackwell.

Jacobi, Jolande, ed. 1951. *Paracelsus*. Princeton: Princeton University Press.

Jacoby, Mario. 1984. *The Analytic Encounter*. Toronto: Inner City Books.

Jung, C.G. 1953. *Symbols of Transformation: Collected Works*, vol. 5. Princeton: Princeton University Press.

—— 1954. 'The Psychology of the Transference' [1946]. In *The Practice of Psychotherapy, Collected Works*, vol. 16: 165–323. Princeton: Princeton University Press.

—— 1960. *The Structure and Dynamics of the Psyche: Collected Works*, vol. 8. Princeton: Princeton University Press.

—— 1963. *Mysterium Coniunctionis: Collected Works*, vol. 14. Princeton: Princeton University Press.

—— 1967. *Alchemical Studies: Collected Works*, vol. 13. Princeton: Princeton University Press.

—— 1968. *Psychology and Alchemy: Collected Works*, vol. 12. Princeton: Princeton University Press.

—— 1969. *Psychology and Religion: West and East: Collected Works*, vol. 11. Princeton: Princeton University Press.

—— 1973. *Memories, Dreams and Reflections*, edited by Aniele Jaffe. New York: Pantheon.

—— 1988. *Nietzsche's Zarathustra*, edited by James L. Jarret, 2 volumes. Princeton: Princeton University Press.

Kerenyi, C. 1949. 'The Myth of the Divine Child and the Mysteries of Eleusis.' In *Essays on a Science of Mythology*, edited by C.G. Jung and C. Kerenyi, 101–51. New York. Harper and Row.

—— 1976. *Dionysos*. Princeton: Princeton University Press.

Kirk, G.S. and J.E. Raven. 1969. *The Presocratic Philosophers*. Cambridge, England: Cambridge University Press.

Kohut, Heinz. 1971. *An Analysis of the Self*. New York: International Universities Press.

Lacan, J. 1977. *Écrits*, translated by A. Sheridan. New York: Norton.

Lévi-Strauss, Claude. 1966. *The Savage Mind*. London: Weidenfeld and Nicolson.

Lindsay, Jack. 1970. *The Origins of Alchemy in Graeco-Roman Egypt.* Great Britain: Frederick Muller.

Mansfield, Victor and Marvin Spiegelman. 1989. 'Quantum Mechanics and Jungian Psychology.' *Journal of Analytical Psychology* 34, no. 1: 179–202.

McGuire, William and R.F.C. Hull. 1977. *C.G. Jung Speaking.* Princeton: Princeton University Press.

McLean, Adam, ed. 1980. *The Rosary of the Philosophers.* Edinburgh: Magnum Opus Hermetic Sourceworks.

—— 1981. *The Splendor Solis*, translated by Joscelyn Godwin. Edinburgh: Magnum Opus Hermetic Sourceworks.

—— 1991. *A Commentary on the Mutus Liber.* Michigan: Phanes Press.

Mead, G.R.S. 1919. *The Subtle Body*, London: Stuart and Watkins.

Melville, Herman. 1962. *Moby Dick.* New York: Hendricks House.

Monk, Ray. 1990. *Ludwig Wittgenstein: The Duty of Genius.* New York: Penguin Books.

Ogden, Thomas. 1982. *Projective Identification and Psychotherapeutic Technique.* Northvale, New Jersey: Jason Aronson.

—— 1994. *Subjects of Analysis.* Northvale, New Jersey: Jason Aronson.

Otto, W. 1965. *Dionysos: Myth and Cult*, translated by R. Palmer. Bloomington, Indiana: Indiana University Press.

Paglia, Camille. 1990. *Sexual Personae.* New Haven: Yale University Press.

Patai, Raphael. 1994. *The Jewish Alchemists*, Princeton: Princeton University Press.

Racker, Heinrich. 1968. *Transference and Countertransference.* New York: International Universities Press.

Reich, Wilhelm. 1973. *The Function of the Orgasm.* New York: Touchstone Books.

Reed, Henry. 1996a. 'Close Encounters in the Limninal Zone: Experiments in Imaginal Communication. Part I.' *Journal of Analytical Psychology* 41, no. 1: 81–116.

—— 1996b. 'Close Encounters in the Limninal Zone: Experiments in Imaginal Communication. Part II.' *Journal of Analytical Psychology* 41, no. 2: 203–26.

Rosen, Steven. 1995. 'Pouring Old Wine into a New Bottle.' In *The Interactive Field in Analysis*, edited by Murray Stein, 121–41. Wilmette, Illinois: Chiron Publications.

de Rougement, Denis. 1983. *Love in the Western World.* Princeton: Princeton University Press.

Ruland, Martin. 1984. *A Lexicon of Alchemy* [1612], edited by A.E. Waite. York Beach, Maine: Samuel Weiser.

Samuels, Andrew. 1985. 'Symbolic Dimensions of Eros in Transference–countertransference: Some Clinical Uses of Jung's Alchemical Metaphor.' *International Review of Psycho-Analysis* 12: 199–214.

Sass, Louis A. 1992. *Madness and Modernism.* New York: Basic Books.

Schwartz-Salant, Nathan. 1969. 'Entropy, Negentropy and the Psyche.' Diploma Thesis, C.G. Jung Institute, Zurich.

—— 1982. *Narcissism and Character Transformation.* Toronto: Inner City Books.

—— 1984. 'Archetypal Factors Underlying Sexual Acting-out in the Transference/Countertransference Process.' In *Transference and Countertransference*, edited by Nathan Schwartz-Salant and Murray Stein. Wilmette, Illinois: Chiron Publications.

—— 1986. 'On the Subtle Body Concept in Analytical Practice.' In *The Body in Analysis*, edited by Nathan Schwartz-Salant and Murray Stein, 1–31. Wilmette, Illinois: Chiron Publications.

—— 1988. 'Archetypal Foundations of Projective Identification.' *Journal of Analytical Psychology* 33: 39–64.

—— 1989. *The Borderline Personality: Vision and Healing.* Wilmette, Illinois: Chiron Publications.

—— 1990. 'The Abandonment Depression: Developmental and Alchemical Perspectives.' *Journal of Analytical Psychology* 35: 143–60.

—— 1992. 'Anima and Animus in Jung's Alchemical Mirror.' In *Gender and Soul in Psychotherapy*, edited by Nathan Schwartz-Salant and Murray Stein, 1–24. Wilmette, Illinois: Chiron Publications.

—— 1993. 'Jung, Madness and Sexuality: Reflections on Psychotic Transference and Countertransference.' In *Mad Parts of Sane People in Analysis*, edited by Murray Stein, 1–35. Wilmette, Illinois: Chiron Publications.

—— 1995a. 'The Interactive Field as the Analytic Object.' In *The Interactive Field in Analysis*, edited by Murray Stein, 1–36. Wilmette, Illinois: Chiron Publications.

—— ed. 1995b. *Jung on Alchemy*. London: Routledge.

Searles, Harold. 1965. *Collected Papers on Schizophrenia and Related Subjects*. New York: International Universities Press.

Segal, Hanna. 1975. *Introduction to the Work of Melanie Klein*. London: Hogarth Press.

Sheldrake, Rupert. 1991. *The Rebirth of Nature*. New York: Bantam.

Spiegelman, J. Marvin. 1988. 'The Impact of Suffering and Self-Disclosure in the Life of the Analyst.' In *Jungian Analysts: Their Visions and Vulnerabilities*, edited by J. Marvin Spiegelman. Phoenix, Arizona: Falcon Press.

Spiegelman, J. Marvin and Victor Mansfield. 1996. 'On the Physics and Psychology of the Transference as an Interactive Field.' *Journal of Analytical Psychology* 41, no. 2: 179–202.

Stolorow, Robert, Bernard Brandshaft and George Atwood. 1987. *Psychoanalytic Treatment: An Intersubjective Approach*. Hillside, New Jersey: Analytic Press.

Turner, Victor. 1974. *Dramas, Fields and Metaphors*. Ithaca, New York: Cornell University Press.

Vermaseren, Maarten J. 1977. *Cybele and Attis*, translated by A.M.H. Lemmers. London: Thames and Hudson.

Waite, A.E., ed. 1973. *The Hermetic Museum*, volumes 1 and 2 [1678]. London: Robinson and Watkins.

Westfall, Richard S. 1980. *Never at Rest: A Biography of Isaac Newton*. Cambridge, England: Cambridge University Press.

Whyte, Lancelot Law. 1960. *The Unconscious Before Freud*. New York: Basic Books.

Winnicott, Donald W. 1971. *Playing and Reality*. London: Tavistock.

Name index

Subject index

abandonment, feelings of 38, 59, 71, 76, 85, 87, 93–5, 97, 110, 138, 156–7, 163, 174, 176, 181, 192–3, 195–6, 204, 209, 213, 225, 227; *see also* loss; separation
absence states *see* blankness; emptiness
acceptance 225–6; of fear 107, 109; of limitation 108, 111–12, 120; of perception 226; of reality 227
acting out 112, 124, 128–9, 190–91, 202
active: imagination 68, 80, 82, 87, 200; penetration 204–5; reception 205; role 166–7, 200, 204, 209 (*see also* male)
adaptation 100
adolescence, psychology of 33–5; see *also* individuation
adrenalin rush 65
affects *see* emotions
aggression 138, 145; awakening 33
albedo 157–8, 163, 180–82, 184, 200–2, 204, 207
alchemy: and analysis 17–18, 35; and Christianity 147, 148; decline of 10–16; emergence of 7–10; imagery of *see* imagery; mystery of 80, 104, 112, 125–49, 155, 167, 179, 228; paradox of 82; and relationship 228; philosophy of 12, 16, 17, 22–5, 80, 99, 125, 129, 176, 216; symbolism of 7, 10, 22, 24, 33, 63, 78, 82, 102–6, 140; way of 104, 127, 129, 224; wisdom of 126, 142, 150–57, 200; *see also* transformation
alienation 55, 113
analysis 17–18, 25–6, 35; of adolescence 34; and containment 186, 193, 204, 224; *coniunctio-nigredo* sequence 184–8, 193; dangers of 69–72; Jungian 58; of projection 25, 56; and understanding 42, 61, 93, 104, 145, 154,

162, 185, 190, 202, 204, 226; wild 200
analytic: object, interactive field as 19–22, 82, 86–8, 90, 94, 119, 121, 153; *see also* object relations; third area
anger *see* rage
anima/animus 22, 24
anti-worlds 46–9, 51, 53, 81, 83–4, 90, 92, 95–6, 98, 106, 110, 117–20, 122–3, 153, 161–2, 176, 178, 185
anxiety 3, 29, 34, 38, 44, 59, 64–5, 70, 79, 85–7, 96–7, 101, 110–11, 116, 120–1, 129, 141, 156–7, 162, 185–6, 192, 228; reduction 45; *see also* fear
aqua permanens 181
archetypes 5, 18, 21–2, 24, 66–7, 77–8, 84, 93, 96, 114–15, 128, 142, 154, 172, 190–1
Art 77
astral body *see* subtle body
attachment 48, 79, 94
attention: conscious 80; evenly-suspended 19–20, 80, 82, 84–6; fragmented 93, 95, 104, 110, 115
autonomy 73, 129, 190, 218; and relationship 228; *see also* separation
avoidance *see* defences
awareness: analytical 42, 61, 93, 104, 145, 154, 162, 185, 190, 202, 204, 226; blocking 111, 188, 202, 220; bodily 72–3, 80, 94, 158, 206; emotional 80, 202; of interactive field 169, 198; of madness 45–7, 50, 112–13, 127, 188; of opposites 46–8, 50, 57, 64, 89–90, 99, 109–10, 122, 153, 160–1, 175, 179, 223; of splitting 87, 91, 95, 114, 117; and relationship 1, 26, 202, 220, 224; self 14, 117, 157; of soul 16, 18, 26, 50, 100–101; spiritual 209, 212; of transformation 194, 216, 226;

196; of hermaphrodite 126–7, 129,
142–3, 148, 157, 163, 180–81, 186,
196, 201–4, 207–9, 213; of hunt 223;
of incest 208; of King 78, 143–4; of
lion 208–10; of lightening 189; of
luminosity 211; of madness 143; of
matter 100, 102; Mithraic 137; of
opposites 24, 82, 103–7, 126; of pine
tree 134, 135, 136; of redness 158,
163, 181–3, 202, 204, 207; religious
137; of self 175, 223; sexual 134,
138; of silver 204; of stone 108,
157–8, 163, 182, 189, 206–7; of sun
202, 216, 226, 228; of transformation
134, 136, 186, 216; unconscious 33,
136, 173; of vessel 80, 104–5; of
water 133, 157, 161, 163, 194, 198,
204; of wedding 189, 192; of well
202; of whore 185, 187, 189, 190,
191, 200; of wind 133–4; *see also*
metaphor
symptom relief 100

taboo 117, 141, 166, 199
tension 72, 153, 170; of opposites 74,
147
tenth state *see* Rebis
terror *see* fear
thinking process 72
'third area' 5–7, 16–18, 20–2, 26, 36–7,
50, 62–3, 65, 71, 82, 95, 99, 141, 166,
194, 214, 222–6; contradiction of 62;
see also interactive field; subtle body
third: conjunction 207; form 146–7; term
130–1
third thing 127, 129–30, 189, 200, 226;
see also union, of opposites,
tincture, of *prima materia* 145
tragedy 200; *see also* death
trance: logic 47–8; states 4, 71–2
transcendence 16 17, 21, 27, 66, 68, 148,
150, 159, 162, 175, 184, 211, 214, 216,
218, 220; of opposites 67, 205; self
159, 176, 184, 211–12, 214, 228;
splitting 205
transference 4, 6, 21, 22–4, 46, 63, 66, 70,
74, 77, 86, 90, 92, 97, 115, 132, 160,
176, 189, 191, 195, 202, 204; and
coniunctio 195; dynamics 90;
idealized 186, 193; mirror 92;
negative 71, 78, 184, 189; psychotic
37–9, 44–5, 50–51, 81, 83, 87, 92, 111,
115, 118, 179, 185–6; *see also*
countertransference

transformation 2, 3, 5, 6, 114; alchemic
7–8, 11, 14, 24, 28, 63, 80–97, 104,
111, 128, 130–31, 133–4, 142, 144,
147, 150–7, 161–3, 165, 170, 172–3,
175–7, 179, 181, 184, 186, 195–209,
216, 219, 227; awareness of 194, 216,
226; background 117, 172, 228; and
chaos *see* chaos; of consciousness 31,
204; through death 221, 227; fear of
100, 222; failure of 142; and feminine
209; of form 77–9; of initiation
28–32, 35; and madness 36–7, 39, 40,
43, 45, 47, 49, 54–6, 61, 98, 99, 111,
124, 142–3, 157; mystery of 128, 194;
and *nigredo* 227; through opposites
150; and passion 212; path of 157;
physical 11; *prima materia* of 161–3;
qualitative 14; of relationship 93–7,
150–74, 221–8; of self 34–5, 37, 63,
70, 89–93, 99, 181, 184, 219, 222; of
solar forces 203; spiritual 11, 15, 31,
69, 79, 170; of structure 76–9, 89–93,
100, 110–11, 144, 150–51, 159,
205–15, 216, 226–7; of subtle body
26; symbols of 134, 136, 186, 216;
vessel of 8
trauma *see* stress
trust 2, 222
truth 107, 109, 119–20, 124, 209, 226

unconscious 1, 17, 25, 27, 133, 147–8,
190; awareness 168, 221; collective 5,
18, 21, 63; compensatory 147–8;
conscious linkage 22, 24, 74–5, 113,
139, 181, 196, 200, 208, 213–14;
containment of 104; descent into 100,
102; drives 221; dyad 67, 69, 104,
129, 147, 150, 157, 158–9, 161, 163–7,
170, 172–3, 175–6, 185, 190–1, 194,
198, 200, 202–3, 219–22, 226;
experiencing 76, 80, 100, 196, 209,
223; identification 196; imagery 200;
instinct 134, 137, 144, 145, 196;
integration 94, 173, 196;
manifestations 76; *nigredo* 151;
personal 4; power of 221; psychic
72–7, 105, 124; relationship 1, 17, 18,
26, 67, 71, 74, 90; somatic 72–6, 105,
124, 161; symbolism 33, 136, 173;
union 189, 220; withdrawal into
133–4, 136–7, 139, 145, 158, 220, 228
understanding *see* awareness;
consciousness; illumination; meaning
unio mystica 30, 158, 162, 167